Realism and International Relations provides a critical yet sympathetic survey of political realism in international theory. Using six paradigmatic theories – Hans Morgenthau, Kenneth Waltz, the Prisoners' Dilemma, Thucydides, Machiavelli, and Hobbes – the book examines realist accounts of human nature and state motivation, international anarchy, system structure and the balance of power, international institutions, and morality in foreign policy. Donnelly argues that common realist propositions not only fail to stand up to scrutiny but are rejected by many leading realists as well. Rather than a general theory of international relations, realism is best seen as a philosophical orientation or research program that emphasizes – in an insightful yet one-sided way – the constraints imposed by individual and national egoism and international anarchy. Containing chapter-by-chapter guides to further reading and discussion questions for students, this book offers an accessible and lively survey of the dominant theory in International Relations.

JACK DONNELLY is Andrew W. Mellon Professor in the Graduate School of International Studies at the University of Denver. He is the author of *The Concept of Human Rights, Universal Human Rights in Theory and Practice,* and *International Human Rights.*

THEMES IN INTERNATIONAL RELATIONS

This new series of textbooks aims to provide students with authoritative surveys of central topics in the study of International Relations. Intended for upper level undergraduates and graduates, the books will be concise, accessible and comprehensive. Each volume will examine the main theoretical and empirical aspects of the subject concerned, and its relation to wider debates in International Relations, and will also include chapter-by-chapter guides to further reading and discussion questions.

Realism and International Relations

Jack Donnelly

CAMBRIDGE
UNIVERSITY PRESS

CAMBRIDGE UNIVERSITY PRESS
Cambridge, New York, Melbourne, Madrid, Cape Town, Singapore, São Paulo

Cambridge University Press
The Edinburgh Building, Cambridge CB2 2RU, UK

Published in the United States of America by Cambridge University Press, New York

www.cambridge.org
Information on this title: www.cambridge.org/9780521592291

First published 2000
Reprinted 2002

A catalogue record for this publication is available from the British Library

Library of Congress Cataloguing in Publication data

Donnelly, Jack.
Realism and international relations / Jack Donnelly.
    p.   cm.
Includes bibliographical references and index.
ISBN 0 521 59229 1 (hb) – ISBN 0 521 59752 8 (pb)
1. International relations. 2. Realism. I. Title.
JZ1307.D66   2000
327.1′01 – dc21   99-053676

ISBN-13 978-0-521-59229-1 hardback
ISBN-10 0-521-59229-1 hardback

ISBN-13 978-0-521-59752-4 paperback
ISBN-10 0-521-59752-8 paperback

Transferred to digital printing 2006

Contents

Acknowledgments

I began working on this book a decade ago, in the spring of 1989, at the Netherlands Institute of Advanced Study. My long list of debts thus must begin with Peter Baehr, who invited me to participate in his research group, and Dirk van de Kaa, who as Director made the NIAS an incredibly supportive place for scholarly research. Had I been able to remain longer within the comfortable confines of Wassenaar I am sure that the gap between the start and finish of this project would have been much smaller.

Over the years, various incarnations of this work have been commented on, orally or in writing, by numerous friends and colleagues. Michael Doyle, Peter Euben, Daniel Garst, Alan Gilbert, Arthur Gilbert, Peter Haas, Barry Hughes, Micheline Ishay, Bob Jackson, Bob Keohane, Harold Koh, Steve Krasner, Steve Leonard, Andrew Linklater, David Lumsdaine, Terry Nardin, Clifford Orwin, Joel Rosenthal, Eduardo Saxe, Michael Smith, Terry Sullivan, Alex Wendt, and Jim White are the names that appear in my records. I thank you all. To those whom I have forgotten to record, my gratitude is compounded by guilt over my neglect.

I also thank Bassem Hassan and Jacek Lubecki for their fine work as research assistants. Bassem also did much of the work of checking citations. And I owe special debts to four additional people.

Rhoda Howard's careful and skeptical eye, as usual, forced me to greater precision. Beyond the particular contributions of her line-by-line criticisms, her position as a reader outside the debates of international relations theory constantly reminded me to write for the broader audience this book is intended to reach.

Cathy Donnelly read the entire manuscript with unusual care. More often than I might care to admit, she drew attention to bad writing habits and stylistic infelicities, as well as the occasional passage that could only be described as hopelessly obscure. She also regularly and forcefully reminded me that there is more to life than work.

Tim McKeown believed in this project early on and provided much appreciated encouragement as a series of early versions of what have become chapters 2 and 6 were rejected by all the best journals in the field. More immediately, his detailed comments on the next to last draft of chapter 2 helped me to nail down arguments that were not yet sufficiently clear and to avoid some significantly exaggerated claims of my own.

Glenn Snyder's thoughtful observations on the epistemological implications of my line of argument, as well as numerous helpful suggestions for clarifying particular points, greatly improved the final draft. I especially appreciate his help because I know that he disagrees with the substance of a number of my principal arguments.

Finally, I must thank more than a decade's worth of graduate students in Chapel Hill and Denver. If I have succeeded in communicating clearly, it is in significant measure a result of their questions and puzzlement. By refusing to accept easy answers about either the strengths or weaknesses of realism, they have forced me to confront this material with a depth and precision that would have been impossible to achieve on my own.

Introduction

Realism and international relations

The tradition of political realism – *realpolitik*, power politics – has a long history that is typically traced back to the great Greek historian Thucydides in the fifth century BC.[1] Although dominant attitudes towards realism have varied, realist arguments and orientations have been central to the Western theory and practice of international relations. In particular, "modern" international society, whether dated from the era of Machiavelli at the turn of the sixteenth century or that of Hobbes in the mid-seventeenth century, has been closely linked to realist balance of power politics.

The link between realism and international theory is especially strong in the twentieth century. International relations first emerged as an academic discipline before and immediately after World War I, largely in reaction against realist balance of power politics. The discipline was then reshaped immediately before and after World War II by self-identified realists such as E. H. Carr and Hans Morgenthau. Prominent scholar-practitioners, such as George Kennan and Henry Kissinger, have called themselves realists. For most of the post-World War II era realism has been the dominant paradigm in the Anglo-American study of international relations. Even in our post-Cold War era of globalization, realist theories, although much less dominant, still provide a context and motivation for many of the most important theoretical debates in the field.

This book presents a sympathetic but fundamentally critical assessment of the character of realism and its contribution to the study and practice of international relations. My approach is critical yet engaged. I approach realism largely on its own terms yet challenge many of its characteristic arguments and conclusions.

[1] See, for example, Morgenthau (1946: 42), Gilpin (1986: 304), Ferguson and Mansbach (1988: 35, 82), Cusack and Stoll (1990: 1–2, 19), Rosenau and Durfee (1995: 9), Schweller (1997: 927).

Accepting realism's terms of reference does limit criticism to "internal" critique of its coherence and consistency. Some readers may prefer a strategy of "external" critique, which takes on realist assumptions directly. But by circumventing the usually fruitless controversy over first principles and basic assumptions, internal critique can achieve a special power and leverage.

The choice of critical engagement, however, is more than tactical. It also reflects my considered judgment of realism's place in the study of international relations. I accept and value realism as a central and perennial tradition, orientation, or approach. I try to show why realist arguments constantly recur in discussions of international relations. But I also highlight realism's diversity, ambiguity, problems, contradictions, errors, and failures.

To lay my cards on the table at the outset, I see realism as an exaggerated and dangerously one-sided set of insights rather than a successful general theory of international relations. Its enduring contribution lies in the fundamentally negative task of highlighting recurrent political constraints posed by international anarchy and human selfishness. It also has considerable promise as a source of partial, mid-level theories. But realism fails – often spectacularly and tragically – in its aspiration to provide a general explanatory theory of international politics or a prescriptive framework for foreign policy.

I try to give full weight and credit to the insights that have made realism an inescapable feature of the study of international relations. I am more concerned, however, to challenge exaggerated claims for these insights that would constrict international political theory and practice to the realm of power politics. Realists understand, and correctly emphasize, the fact that power has been, and will long remain, a central part of international relations. Most realists, however, systematically slight other no less important dimensions of international politics. Demonstrating this is one of my central concerns.

Outline of the book

Chapter 1 introduces the realist tradition through four complementary paths. I begin with a brief definition that emphasizes anarchy and egoism, and follow with a typology of realist theories. Then, in the central portion of the chapter, I present six realist "paradigms": Thomas Hobbes, Hans Morgenthau, Kenneth Waltz, the Prisoners' Dilemma, Thucydides, and Machiavelli. Finally, I briefly trace the cyclical rise and fall of realism in the academic study of international relations in the twentieth century.

Chapter 2 examines realist accounts of human nature and state motivation. A brief introduction notes that many of our paradigmatic realists emphasize a motivational triad of fear, honor, and interest, as Thucydides puts it, or, in Hobbes' language, competition, diffidence, and glory. I then criticize realist approaches that emphasize human nature, with special attention to Morgenthau. The bulk of the chapter, however, is devoted to a critique of contemporary structural realist efforts to abstract from the attributes of states. I show that realism not only requires substantive motivational assumptions but that the assumptions of contemporary structural realists prove to be very similar to and at least as confused and incoherent as those of earlier realists such as Morgenthau and Reinhold Niebuhr.

Chapter 3 deals with realist accounts of international anarchy, paying special attention to Waltz' *Theory of International Politics*. I argue that Waltz misrepresents anarchy as a formless void and wildly exaggerates its political consequences. Anarchic orders may have considerable elements of "hierarchic" division of political labor, ranging from the differentiation of political functions represented by spheres of influence to considerable elements of international legal obligation. Anarchy implies only the absence of hierarchical government, not an absence of authoritative international governance.

Chapter 4 is a transitional chapter that examines the principal substantive conclusion of structural realism, namely, that states in anarchy "balance" rather than "bandwagon." I argue that balance of power politics depends not on anarchy *per se* but on a fear of predation, which cannot be accounted for independently of the character of those with whom one interacts. I also examine the distinction between system and structure, which has been obscured in much recent realist writing – and which opens up the question of the role of international institutions.

Chapter 5 examines the nature and extent of authoritative order in contemporary international society. I argue that abstracting from international norms and institutions, as structural neorealists encourage us to do, is no more profitable than abstracting from the character of states. After critically examining John Mearsheimer's argument that international institutions have no independent effects on state behavior, I develop two extended examples, dealing with sovereignty and the Prisoners' Dilemma, that illustrate the central role of international institutions in the practice of international relations.

Chapter 6 examines the issue of morality and foreign policy. Although twentieth-century realists characteristically deny a place for morality in international relations – or at least restrict the role of moral concerns to the periphery of foreign policy – their arguments turn out to be remarkably diverse, and even contradictory. Furthermore, a careful examination of Thucydides and Machiavelli reveals that these two paradigmatic realists actually give a considerable place to ethics in international relations. The chapter concludes by arguing that, as with so much else in the realist tradition, a useful cautionary insight is exaggerated into a misleading and dangerous "law" of international relations.

A brief conclusion extends this argument to provide a summary assessment of the contributions and limitations of realist theories of international relations.

Each chapter is followed by discussion questions and suggested readings. The questions revisit some of the central issues raised in the text and often suggest alternative readings or try to push arguments deeper, or in a different direction, than they are pursued in the text. Because they primarily aim to go beyond, rather than merely review, the main points of the chapter, they should be treated as integral parts of the text.

The suggested readings highlight sources dealing with issues raised or left inadequately explored in the text. Although perhaps less integral than the discussion questions, the fact that these are short bibliographic essays, rather than just lists of sources, has allowed me to highlight important topics in the text. I thus encourage all readers to at least glance at these essays, even if they are not at the moment looking for additional reading.

In each bibliographic essay a few especially recommended readings are highlighted in bold type. These are not always the most important sources, but they are both good and relatively easily accessible. Readers will rarely go wrong by starting their further reading with these sources. For convenience, all of the boldfaced readings are collated at the end of the volume in a short list of recommended readings.

Audience and orientation

As the apparatus of discussion questions and suggested readings indicates, this book has been written with advanced undergraduate students in mind. I hope, though, that its audience will be significantly larger – and by that I do not mean just graduate students. I have tried to write for the intelligent reader with an interest, but no formal training, in (the study of) international relations. Although I have no illusions that this is a potential bestseller, or even likely to appear on the shelves of any but large or specialist bookshops, I hope that nonacademic readers who pick it up will find much of interest.[2] I also hope that scholars, no less than their

---

[2] Chapter 1, I believe, should be widely accessible to most readers. Chapters 2, 5, and 6 also speak to issues of broad interest. Chapters 3 and 4 are more "academic," although I hope still accessible. But because each chapter is largely self-contained, if you find yourself getting bogged down in these middle chapters, jump ahead to chapter 5 or even chapter 6.

students, will find large parts of this book valuable. In other words, I have tried to write a book that is widely accessible yet challenging, literate, and complex. And I have tried to avoid stripping the life, excitement, and genuine controversy out of the subject in a spurious and misguided pursuit of "balance."

Some readers may find my extensive use of direct quotations excessive, even annoying. Nonetheless, I am deeply committed to this style of exposition. Allowing realists to speak for themselves provides something of a flavor of the style of their writing. It also allows readers to check my claims immediately. This is especially important in light of the ease with which even a critic who attempts to be scrupulously fair may introduce subtle misinterpretations.

I try to portray realism as a strong and vigorous approach to the theory and practice of international relations. But my criticisms are at least as strong and vigorous. Chapter 1 is largely descriptive. The other chapters, however, are more concerned with evaluating (criticizing) standard realist arguments than describing or defending them.

My orientation, in other words, is undeniably non-realist. Many would call it anti-realist. But, as I suggest at the end of the book, my position is not all that different from that of "realists" such as E. H. Carr and John Herz, as well as Thucydides and even Machiavelli. Furthermore, one can find multiple passages in realists such as Morgenthau and Niebuhr that support such a reading. Therefore, what I have in mind might also be described as a sophisticated, heavily hedged form of realism. Somewhat more precisely, I would say that I have a certain sympathy for and appreciation of a heavily hedged realism as part of a pluralistic discipline of international studies, although my interests and inclinations lie elsewhere.

I would be pleased if realists find my emphasis on their shortcomings extreme but not fundamentally unfair, while anti-realists are impatient with my "excessive concessions" to realism. My goal is to produce a constructive account of the attractions and drawbacks of realism that points the way to transcending the increasingly sterile and formulaic "realism and its critics" discussions that have shaped so much recent writing and teaching in the field. Sound international theory, I will argue, must come to terms with, but refuse to be limited to, realism. Realism should not be ignored. But it should not be allowed to shape the study and practice of international relations, as it has for so much of the past half-century.

1   The realist tradition

One might imagine that defining an old and well-established theory such as realism would be a simple task. A look at the representative sample of recent and prominent definitions in box 1.1, however, reveals considerable diversity[1] – which on further reflection should not be surprising.

Even in traditions with authoritative defining texts, such as Marxism and Christianity, different emphases and antagonistic interpretations are common. We should expect at least as much variety in realism.

Realism[2] is not a theory defined by an explicit set of assumptions and propositions. Rather, as many commentators have noted, it is a general orientation: "a philosophical disposition" (Gilpin 1986: 304); "a set of normative emphases which shape theory" (Ferguson and Mansbach 1988: 79); an "attitude of mind" with "a quite distinctive and recognizable flavour" (Garnett 1984: 110); "a loose framework" (Rosenthal 1991: 7); and "a 'big tent,' with room for a number of different theories" (Elman 1996: 26). Realism is an approach to international relations that has emerged gradually through the work of a series of analysts who have situated themselves within, and thus delimited, a distinctive but still diverse style or tradition of analysis.[3]

---

[1] See Cusack and Stoll (1990: ch. 2) for a review that emphasizes this diversity. More critically, see Goldmann (1988). For further definitions see John, Wright, and Garnett (1972: 96–97), Maghroori and Ramberg (1982: 14–16), Vasquez (1983: 15–19, 26–30), Olson and Onuf (1985: 7), Cox (1986: 211–212), Ferguson and Mansbach (1988: 40–47, 102), Stein (1990: 4–7), Rosenau and Durfee (1995: 11–13), Elman (1996: 19–21), Grieco (1997: 164–168), Labs (1997: 7), Mastanduno (1997: 50).

[2] We should note at the outset that I am concerned here with *political* realism, the tradition of *realpolitik* or power politics. "Realism," however, is also a philosophical doctrine, asserting some kind of correspondence between knowledge claims and an objective external reality. For a good recent overview of the philosophical debate, see Kulp (1997). Katz (1998) offers a defense of philosophical realism that canvasses the leading objections. "Realism" is also the name of a literary school or movement that was of considerable prominence in the nineteenth and early twentieth century (as well as in the mid-twentieth century, in its "socialist" variant). Political realists may or may not be philosophical or literary realists.

[3] On the idea of traditions of international thought, see Nardin and Mapel (1992) and Dunne (1993). More broadly, compare Gunnell (1979).

Box 1.1. *Representative definitions of realism*
(The following passages are direct quotations or very close paraphrases.)

1. The state's interest provides the spring of action.
2. The necessities of policy arise from the unregulated competition of states.
3. Calculation based on these necessities can discover the policies that will best serve a state's interests.
4. Success is the ultimate test of policy, and success is defined as preserving and strengthening the state. (Waltz 1979: 117)

1. Politics is governed by objective laws that have their roots in human nature.
2. The main signpost that helps political realism to find its way through the landscape of international politics is the concept of interest defined in terms of power.
3. Power and interest are variable in content.
4. Universal moral principles cannot be applied to the actions of states.
5. Political realism refuses to identify the moral aspirations of a particular nation with the moral laws that govern the universe.
6. The autonomy of the political sphere. (Morgenthau 1954: 4–10)

1. The international system is anarchic.
2. States inherently possess some offensive military capability, which gives them the wherewithal to hurt and possibly destroy each other.
3. No state can ever be certain another state will not use its offense military capability.
4. The most basic motive driving states is survival.
5. States are instrumentally rational. (Mearsheimer 1994/95: 9–10)

1. The fundamental unit of social and political affairs is the "conflict group."
2. States are motivated primarily by their national interest.
3. Power relations are a fundamental feature of international affairs. (Gilpin 1996: 7–8)

1. The state-centric assumption: states are the most important actors in world politics.
2. The rationality assumption: world politics can be analyzed as if states were unitary rational actors seeking to maximize their expected utility.
3. The power assumption: states seek power and they calculate their interests in terms of power. (Keohane 1986b: 164–165)

1. Realists assume an ineradicable tendency to evil.
2. Realists assume that the important unit of social life is the collectivity and that in international politics the only really important collective actor is the state, which recognizes no authority above it.
3. Realists hold power and its pursuit by individuals and states as ubiquitous and inescapable.

Box 1.1 (*cont.*)

4. Realists assume that the real issues of international politics can be understood by the rational analysis of competing interests defined in terms of power. (Smith 1986: 219–221)

1. The centrality of states.
2. The world is anarchic.
3. States seek to maximize their security or their power.
4. The international system is mostly responsible for state conduct on the international scene.
5. States adopt instrumentally rational policies in their pursuit of power or security.
6. The utility of force. (Frankel 1996: xiv–xviii)

1. The international system is anarchic.
2. Nation-states pursue their own national interests defined primarily in terms of power.
3. Skepticism toward international laws, institutions, and ideals that attempt to transcend or replace nationalism.
4. Primacy of balance of power politics. (Wayman and Diehl 1994: 5)

1. Humans face one another primarily as members of groups.
2. International affairs takes place in a state of anarchy.
3. Power is the fundamental feature of international politics.
4. The nature of international interactions is essentially conflictual.
5. Humankind cannot transcend conflict through the progressive power of reason.
6. Politics are not a function of ethics.
7. Necessity and reason of state trump morality and ethics. (Schweller 1997: 927)

1. History is a sequence of cause and effect, whose course can be understood by intellectual effort, but not directed by "imagination."
2. Theory does not create practice, but practice theory.
3. Politics are not a function of ethics, but ethics of politics. (Carr 1946: 63–64)

1. Groups (states) consider themselves to be ultimate ends.
2. Any measure required for state self-preservation is justified.
3. Law and morality have a subordinate place in international relations. (Schwarzenberger 1951: 13)

Nonetheless, a set of recurrent concerns and conclusions marks these varying works as part of a single tradition. The definitions in box 1.1 share a family resemblance, even though no single set of elements can be found in each. Both realists and their critics agree that the realist "intellectual style is unmistakable" (Garnett 1984: 29; compare Cusack and Stoll 1990: 19; Wayman and Diehl 1994). As an American judge notoriously said of pornography, we may not be able to define it, but we know it when we see it.

This chapter attempts to orient the reader to the realist style, tradition, or approach in four complementary ways: a brief definition; a simple, two-dimensional typology; short summaries of six paradigmatic realist theories; and an overview of the development of realist thought in the twentieth century.

A definition

Realism emphasizes the constraints on politics imposed by human nature and the absence of international government. Together, they make international relations largely a realm of power and interest.

"Human nature has not changed since the days of classical antiquity" (Thompson 1985: 17). And that nature, according to realists, is at its core egoistic, and thus inalterably inclined towards immorality. As Machiavelli puts it, in politics "it must needs be taken for granted that all men are wicked and that they will always give vent to the malignity that is in their minds when opportunity offers" (1970: Book I, ch. 3).

Some realists, such as Reinhold Niebuhr (1944: 19) and Hans Morgenthau (1946: 202), see Machiavelli's claim as largely descriptive. Many, like Machiavelli himself, contend only that there are enough egoists to make any other assumption unduly risky. All, however, emphasize the egoistic passions and self-interest in (international) politics. "It is above all important not to make greater demands upon human nature than its frailty can satisfy" (Treitschke 1916: 590). "It is essential not to have faith in human nature. Such faith is a recent heresy and a very disastrous one" (Butterfield 1949: 47).

Most realists also recognize that "men are motivated by other desires than the urge for power and that power is not the only aspect of international relations" (Spykman 1942: 7). Thus Niebuhr couples his harsh doctrine of original sin with an insistence that "individuals are not consistently egoistic" (1944: 123). He even argues for "an adequate view of human nature, which does justice to both the heights and depths of human life" (1934: 113). Likewise, Morgenthau argues that "to do justice and to receive it is an elemental aspiration of man" (1970: 61). Kenneth

Thompson even contends that "man is at heart a moral being" and emphasizes "the insatiable quest of man for justice" (Thompson 1966: 4, 75; compare Carr 1946: 145).

Nonetheless, realists characteristically give *primary* emphasis to egoistic passions and "the tragic presence of evil in all political action" (Morgenthau 1946: 203). And because these passions are ineradicable, "conflict is inevitable" (Niebuhr 1932: xv). "It is profitless to imagine a hypothetical world in which men no longer organize themselves in groups for purposes of conflict" (Carr 1946: 231). Whatever their other disagreements, realists are unanimous in holding that human nature contains an ineradicable core of egoistic passions; that these passions define the central problem of politics; and that statesmanship is dominated by the need to control this side of human nature.

Realists also stress the political necessities that flow from international anarchy.[4] In the absence of international government, "the law of the jungle still prevails" (Schuman 1941: 9). "The difference between civilization and barbarism is a revelation of what is essentially the same human nature when it works under different conditions" (Butterfield 1949: 31; compare Schuman 1941: 9; Spykman 1942: 141). Within states, human nature usually is tamed by hierarchical political authority and rule. In international relations, anarchy not merely allows but encourages the worst aspects of human nature to be expressed. "That same human nature which in happy conditions is frail, seems to me to be in other conditions capable of becoming hideous" (Butterfield 1949: 44).

The interaction of egoism and anarchy leads to "the overriding role of power in international relations" (Schwarzenberger 1951: 147) and requires "the primacy in all political life of power and security" (Gilpin 1986: 305). "The struggle for power is universal in time and space" (Morgenthau 1948: 17). "The daily presence of force and recurrent reliance on it mark the affairs of nations" (Waltz 1979: 186). "Security" thus means a somewhat less dangerous and less violent world, rather than a safe, just, or peaceful one. Statesmanship involves mitigating and managing, not eliminating, conflict.

The "negative" side of this "positive" emphasis on power and interest is skepticism over moral concerns in international relations. Ethical considerations and objectives, realists typically argue, must be subordinated to

---

[4] Throughout I use "anarchy" as it is ordinarily used in the international relations literature; that is, in the literal sense of absence of rule, lack of government. As we shall see in greater detail in chapter 3, anarchy does *not* imply chaos, absence of order; it is simply the absence of "hierarchical" political order based on formal subordination and authority. Thus Hedley Bull (1977) describes international relations as taking place in an "anarchical society" of states.

"reason of state" (*raison d'état*). Realism "justifies and necessitates political policies which a purely individualistic ethic must always find embarrassing" (Niebuhr 1932: xi). "Realism maintains that universal moral principles cannot be applied to the actions of states" (Morgenthau 1954: 9). "Other criteria, sadder, more limited, more practical must be allowed to prevail" (Kennan 1954: 49).

A typology

As a first approximation, we can distinguish subgroupings of realists, thus defined, along two dimensions: the relative emphasis they give to the core propositions of egoism and anarchy and the stringency of their commitment to a rigorous and exclusively realist analysis.

Structural realists give predominant emphasis to international anarchy. For example, John Herz argues that international anarchy assures the centrality of the struggle for power "even in the absence of aggressivity or similar factors" (Herz 1976: 10; compare Waltz 1979: 62–63). Contemporary structural realists are also often called "neorealists," in an effort to emphasize their "newness" and the differences from most earlier realists arising from their strong structuralism.

Biological realists emphasize a fixed human nature. For example, Morgenthau argues that "social forces are the product of human nature in action"; "the social world [is] but a projection of human nature onto the collective plane"; political problems are "projections of human nature into society" (1948: 4; 1962a: 7, 312). Such realists "see that conflict is in part situationally explained, but . . . believe that even were it not so, pride, lust, and the quest for glory would cause the war of all against all to continue indefinitely. Ultimately, conflict and war are rooted in human nature" (Waltz 1991: 35). "The ultimate sources of social conflicts and injustices are to be found in the ignorance and selfishness of men" (Niebuhr 1932: 23).

Although such theorists are often called "classical" realists, this label tells us nothing about the substance of their orientation. The category "classical" is a residual: those who are not structural (neo)realists. The label biological, by contrast, is substantive and positive, pointing to their emphasis on human nature. And by refusing to define categories in terms of the currently dominant structuralist turn, it maintains neutrality between competing approaches to realism.

It is easy, and dangerous, to overemphasize the differences between biological and structural realism. Structural realists, as we will see in some detail in the next chapter, must make motivational assumptions about states and individuals. For example, Christian saints and Hobbesian egoists will behave very differently in an environment of anarchy. Conversely, most biological realists recognize at least quantitative differences in behavior in anarchic and hierarchic structures. For example, Morgenthau gives considerable attention to the structure-induced patterns of behavior of the balance of power (1954: chs. 11–14, 21).

Nonetheless, the difference in emphasis does distinguish structural realism, especially in its contemporary neorealist forms.[5] Furthermore, principally structural theories are likely to make greater allowances for change and for non-realist "hedges," because anarchy is more susceptible to amelioration than human nature. "The essential nature of man may not be altered, but human behavior in general is sometimes improved, by the establishment of an order of things which has the effect of reducing temptation," and in some instances "a healthy disposition of forces can be attained for long periods which, so to speak, makes human nature better than it really is" (Butterfield 1960: 25; 1949: 33).

This reference to "hedges" leads to the second dimension of variation in realist theories to which I want to draw attention.

Radical realists adopt extreme versions of the three realist premises of anarchy, egoism, and power politics. The Athenian envoys at Melos in Thucydides' *History*, discussed in the following section, advance such a view. One rarely, however, encounters a (consistently) radical realist.

Strong realists adopt realist premises in a way that allows only modest space for politically salient "non-realist" concerns. They also tend to present realism as a positive theory of (international) politics or statesmanship. Morgenthau and Kenneth Waltz are exemplary strong realists.

Hedged realists accept the realist definition of the "problem" of international politics – anarchy and egoism – but show varying degrees of discomfort with the "solution" of power politics.[6] For example, E. H. Carr argues that "we cannot ultimately find a resting place in pure realism" (1946: 89). Herz similarly notes that "the human cause will be lost if the liberal ideal is forgotten, even as surely as it is lost if left to the utopian Political Idealist" (1951: v; compare Niebuhr 1944: 126).

---

[5] A more "scientific" approach (and a related emphasis on explanation rather than prescription) also gives most neorealist writings a very different "feel." This is evident, for example, if we compare Morgenthau's discussion of the balance of power (1954: chs. 2–4, 9–12) with Waltz' (1979: 118–122). Furthermore, neorealist structuralism typically presents hierarchic domestic politics and anarchic international politics as qualitatively different realms that must be studied with logically incompatible theoretical frameworks (Waltz 1979: chs. 5, 6). In sharp contrast, many earlier (principally biological) realists – notably Morgenthau and Niebuhr, not to mention Machiavelli and Thucydides – wrote about both domestic and international politics.

[6] Michael Doyle (1990) uses the label "minimalist" to describe something very much like this position. He then fills out his typology with "fundamentalist" and "structural" realism, to refer to roughly what I call biological and structural realism.

Hedged realism gradually merges into views that are fundamentally something else. At some point, (non-realist) "hedges" become as important as the (realist) "core," making it misleading to label the resulting position or argument "realist." Where that point is, and its implications for realist approaches to international relations, will be a recurrent theme in chapters 4–6.

Six realist paradigms

The preceding sections attempted to distill something like an "essence" of realism. The remainder of this chapter is more faithful to the vision of realism as a less precisely defined tradition or orientation. This section provides brief summaries of six paradigmatic models that have helped to shape that tradition.

The idea of paradigms is especially appropriate for thinking about the development and transmission of traditions. One learns a tradition not by memorizing a set of propositions but by studying and applying classic models. Students are encouraged to think and work "in the style of" the classics, which provide "a series of points that serve to structure debate within the tradition and between it and other approaches" (Cusack and Stoll 1990: 53). This section summarizes six such paradigms, drawn from Golden Age Athens, sixteenth-century Florence, seventeenth-century England, and twentieth-century America. Although others might have been chosen, together these six present a good indication of the range of views that are characteristically labeled realist.

We begin with Thomas Hobbes, who perhaps most closely fits the definition of realism offered above. We then look at Hans Morgenthau and Kenneth Waltz, the leading biological and structural realists of the past half century. Our fourth paradigm is the game theory model of Prisoners' Dilemma, which offers a still different route to characteristic realist conclusions. Finally, we look at Thucydides and Machiavelli, who (along with Hobbes) are generally considered to present the most powerful expressions of realism in the Western tradition of political theory.

Thomas Hobbes

Thomas Hobbes, the seventeenth-century English polymath, is said to have enjoyed telling people that he was born in fear, his mother (allegedly) having given birth prematurely on hearing the news of the invasion by the Spanish Armada. His mature political views were deeply influenced by the violent disruptions of the English Civil War of the 1640s. Chapter 13 of *Leviathan*, published originally in 1651, presents a fine example of a strong realism that gives roughly equal weight to egoism and anarchy. Assuming only that people are naturally equal, that they are driven by competition, diffidence, and glory, and that they interact in the absence of government, Hobbes draws the famous conclusion that the natural condition of man is a state of war.

Hobbes begins with natural equality, which he demonstrates in typically "realist" fashion: even "the weakest has strength enough to kill the strongest, either by secret machination, or by confederacy with others" (par. 1).[7] If some were much more powerful than others, social order might be forcibly imposed. Rough equality of capabilities, however, makes this anarchic world one of inescapable and universal danger – given Hobbes' account of human nature.

"In the nature of man, we find three principall causes of quarrell. First, Competition; Secondly, Diffidence; Thirdly, Glory" (par. 6).

Competition "maketh men invade for Gain" (par. 7). Because we are all equal, each of us expects to have (at least) as much as anyone else (par. 3). In a world of anarchy and scarcity, to acquire anything of use is to tempt others "to come prepared with forces united, to dispossesse, and deprive him, not only of the fruit of his labour, but also of his life, or liberty" (par. 3).

"From equality proceeds diffidence" (par. 3), fear, and "from diffidence warre" (par. 4). In the absence of government "there is no way for any man to secure himselfe, so reasonable, as Anticipation" (par. 4). The best defense is a good offense; "by force, or wiles, to master the persons of all men he can" (par. 4).

As if this were not bad enough, men are also vain, driven by a desire for glory. This leads them to fight over "reputation," "a word, a smile, a different opinion, and any other signe of undervalue" (par. 7).

Whether for safety, reputation, or gain, men will "endeavour to destroy, or subdue one another" (par. 3). Although fighting may not be constant, the threat of force is ever present (par. 8). Any dispute may at any moment degenerate or erupt into violence. "During the time men live without a common Power to keep them all in awe, they are in that condition which is called Warre; and such a warre, as is of every man, against every man" (par. 8).

Such a condition, beyond its insecurity and obvious material shortcomings, precludes pursuing "higher" human aspirations. There can be "no Arts; no Letters; no Society" (par. 9). Furthermore, "the notions of Right and Wrong, Justice and Injustice have there no place" (par. 13).

---

[7] All otherwise unidentified references in this subsection are to chapter 13 of *Leviathan*, by paragraph in the C. B. Macpherson edition (Hobbes 1986).

Hobbes summarizes these sad circumstances with one of the most famous passages in the history of Western political thought: "And the life of man, solitary, poore, nasty, brutish, and short" (par. 9).[8]

Men, of course, are not *only* competitive, fearful, and vain – even if such a simplified model does continue to provide grist for the mills of many feminist comics. Hobbes recognizes "passions that encline men to Peace" (par. 14). He also recognizes that we possess reason, which "suggesteth convenient Articles of Peace, upon which men may be drawn to agreement" (par. 14). We want something better. We can even figure out rules of coexistence and cooperation. But without a government to enforce those rules, we remain condemned to war. Without the restraints of superior power, men cannot control their impulses to take from others, to react with excessive fear, or to demand greater respect than others are willing to give freely.

To imagine a pre-social state of nature is to engage in a thought experiment that strips away social artifice to reveal a fixed, constant core of human nature. Human nature, for Hobbes, cannot be changed. Competition, diffidence, and glory may be controlled by superior power – which taps in another way the core motive of fear. But they cannot be eliminated.

Given our nature, we put our natural freedom to destructive, even self-destructive, use in the absence of government. The task of politics thus is to replace anarchic equality with hierarchical political authority, a "common Power to feare" (par. 11), a superior "power able to over-awe them all" (par. 5). But international relations remains a domain of anarchy, a state of war, in which "Kings and Persons of Soveraigne authority . . . [are] in the state and posture of Gladiators; having their weapons pointing, and their eyes fixed on one another" (par. 12). Barring world government, there is no escape from this state of war.

Hans Morgenthau

Hans Morgenthau, an American refugee from Nazi Germany, was one of the leading realists of the 1950s and 1960s and perhaps "the purest as well as the most self-conscious apostle of realism" of his generation (Parkinson 1977: 163). Most would agree with John Vasquez (1983: 17) that "Morgenthau's work was the single most important vehicle for establishing the dominance of the realist paradigm" in the study of international relations, especially in the United States.

---

[8] In Hobbes' vision, we are so constituted that the only possible good thing we could say about such a life, namely, that it is short, in fact is the "worst of all" (par. 9). We cling desperately even to such a miserable life. As Woody Allen put it more humorously, the food in that restaurant is terrible – and the portions are so small!

A prolific academic and journalistic writer, Morgenthau became best known to students of international relations for his succinct statement of the "principles" of realism in the first chapter of his book *Politics Among Nations*.[9] These principles, presented in sharp, vigorous, accessible prose, summarize a simple yet wide-ranging philosophical, theoretical, and political world-view.

1. "Political realism believes that politics, like society in general, is governed by objective laws that have their roots in human nature" (1954: 4).
2. "The main signpost that helps political realism to find its way through the landscape of international politics is the concept of interest defined in terms of power" (1954: 5).
3. Power and interest are variable in content across space and time (1954: 8–9).
4. "Realism maintains that universal moral principles cannot be applied to the actions of states" (1954: 9).
5. "Political realism refuses to identify the moral aspirations of a particular nation with the moral laws that govern the universe" (1954: 10).
6. "The difference, then, between political realism and other schools of thought is real and it is profound . . . Intellectually, the political realist maintains the autonomy of the political sphere" (1954: 10).

Morgenthau's strong biological realism will make him a central figure in chapter 2. And in chapter 6 we will have occasion to examine his impassioned warnings against a moralistic foreign policy.

Kenneth Waltz

Kenneth Waltz' 1979 book *Theory of International Politics* was for a decade the most influential theoretical work in the academic study of international relations, the central text of contemporary neorealism. Today it remains a touchstone for both realists and their critics. Waltz presents an excellent example of strong structural realism.

"Despite wide variations in the attributes and in the interactions" of states and other international actors, Waltz is impressed by "the striking sameness in the quality of international life through the millennia" (1979: 67, 66). These similarities, he argues, arise from a persistent structure of international anarchy.

Political structures are defined and distinguished first by their ordering principle: political actors ("units") either are or are not arranged in hierarchical relations of authority and subordination. International rela-

---

[9] This chapter first appeared in the second edition of 1954 and has remained essentially unchanged in all later editions.

tions is a domain of anarchic (non-hierarchic) political structures (1979: 88–99). Order is not imposed by higher authority but arises from the interactions of formally equal political actors. The differing constraints, opportunities, and rules of anarchic and hierarchic structures lie at the heart of the conventional distinction between comparative and international politics.

Political structures are also defined by the differentiation of functions among their units. "Hierarchy entails relations of super- and subordination among a system's parts, and that implies their differentiation" (1979: 93). A standard civics text example is the separation of legislative, executive, and judicial powers.

In anarchic orders, however, Waltz argues that each state is a separate, autonomous, and formally equal political unit that must count ultimately on its own resources to realize its interests. In anarchic environments, "each unit's incentive is to put itself in a position to be able to take care of itself since no one else can be counted on to do so" (1979: 107). All important functions thus must be performed by each and every state. There is little international division of political labor, no sharp differentiation of functions among states (1979: 93–97).

The principal differences between states, Waltz argues, "are of capability, not function. States perform or try to perform tasks, most of which are common to all of them; the ends they aspire to are similar" (1979: 96). States differ not so much in what they seek to achieve, but in their capabilities to achieve ends that are largely shared. "National politics consists of differentiated units performing specified functions. International politics consists of like units duplicating one another's activities" (1979: 97).

The third defining feature of a political structure is the distribution of capabilities among its units. If all international orders are anarchic and there is no significant differentiation of functions among states, international political structures can be distinguished from one another simply by the distribution of capabilities among actors. Historically, this means that international political structures are defined by the changing fates of great powers (1979: 72, 94). More abstractly, international orders vary according to the number of great powers. Waltz emphasizes the difference between bipolar systems, dominated by two superpowers, and multipolar systems, where there are three or more great powers (1979: chs. 7–8).

"If there is any distinctively political theory of international politics, balance-of-power theory is it" (1979: 117), because it conceives of states simply as concentrations of power competing in an anarchic environment. Waltz argues that balance of power politics prevails whenever "two or more states coexist" in an anarchic order "with no superior agent to come to the aid of states that may be weakening or to deny to any of them

the use of whatever instruments they think will serve their purposes"
(1979: 118).

The central conclusion of balance of power theory is that states in
anarchy "balance" rather than "bandwagon"[10] (1979: 126). In hierarchic
political orders, Waltz argues, political actors tend to "jump on the bandwagon" of a leading candidate or recent victor, because "losing does not
place their security in jeopardy" (1979: 126). But in anarchy, to jump on
the bandwagon of a rising power is to court becoming prey to that power
not too far down the road. A state must always be concerned with its *relative* power. The power of others – especially great power – is always a
threat, never a lure. Weak states may have no alternative but to guess right
and hope that early alignment with the victor will ensure their survival
and (at least some) other vital interests. Only foolhardy great powers,
though, would accept such a risk. Rather than bandwagon, Waltz argues,
they will "balance" against the growing power of another state.

Structural pressures to balance explain central yet otherwise puzzling
features of international relations. Consider the American–Soviet alliance
in World War II. A common enemy brought together two countries with
intense internal and historical differences that had made them the harsh-
est of rivals for the preceding two decades. After the war, though, they
again became almost rabid rivals – but not, in this version of the story,
because of internal or ideological differences, but because of the distribution of capabilities. Wherever two dominant powers face each other, each
is the only real threat to the security of the other, and they cannot but be
enemies. Each must, whatever its preferences or inclinations, balance its
power against the other.

Waltz' structural realism does not deny the existence, even the importance, of internal differences among states. It does, however, attempt to
"abstract from every attribute of states except their capabilities" (1979:
99), in order to highlight the ways in which the distribution of capabilities
in an anarchic order shapes relations. "One may behave as one likes to.
Patterns of behavior nevertheless emerge, and they derive from the structural constraints of the system" (1979: 92). States "are free to do any fool
thing they care to, but they are likely to be rewarded for behavior that is
responsive to structural pressures and punished for behavior that is not"
(1997: 915). Or, as John Mearsheimer puts it, "in the final analysis, the

---

[10] The metaphor of bandwagoning is from American electoral politics. When a candidate
begins to look like she will win, there is a strong tendency for neutrals, undecided voters,
and even opponents to side with her, in order to share in her victory. In the language of a
simpler era of campaigning, dominated by parades rather than television, they will "jump
on the bandwagon." "Bandwagoners" attempt to increase their gains by siding with the
stronger party.

system forces states to behave according to the dictates of realism, or risk destruction" (1995: 91).

The Prisoners' Dilemma

Contemporary social science has been strongly influenced by the pursuit of rigor and formalization, whether through mathematics, statistics, or formal logic. Game theory, which originated in economics after World War II, is a formalization that has had considerable popularity in the study of international relations over the past two decades.[11] It seeks to model the dynamics of strategic interactions in which an actor's behavior depends in part on the anticipated behavior of others. One particular game – Prisoners' Dilemma – offers a striking realist paradigm.

The game of Prisoners' Dilemma The simplest game theory models involve two rational actors, each of whom has available two strategies, one of which is fundamentally cooperative ("cooperate") and the other of which is essentially competitive ("defect"). The four possible outcomes in such two-by-two games are summarized in figure 1.1. The payoffs to each player are recorded in the cell representing the intersection of their chosen strategies, the first payoff being that for the player at the left ("row"), the second for the player at the top ("column"). A particular game is defined by the relative preferences of each of the players for these four possible outcomes.

There are two common ways to label these payoffs. The most general uses the labels D (defect) and C (cooperate), and simply records the paired choices of row first and then column. In other words, working clockwise from the top left in figure 1.1, CC (both cooperate), CD (row cooperates, column defects), DD (both defect) and DC (row defects, column cooperates). Another common set of labels is R, for reward (from mutual cooperation); T, for temptation (defection in the presence of cooperation); S, for sucker (losing as a result of cooperating when the other defects); and P, for penalty (from mutual defection).

These labels derive from one of the most interesting of the seventy-eight possible two-by-two games: Prisoners' Dilemma (PD), named for a story commonly used to elucidate its logic. Two thieves are apprehended by the police and taken in, separately, for questioning. Each is offered a favorable plea bargain in return for a confession and testimony against the other. But without a confession the authorities can obtain a conviction only on a lesser charge.

---

[11] See, for example, Snyder and Diesing (1977) and Oye (1986).

Figure 1.1. A generalized two-by-two game.

Player 2
("column")

Cooperate   Defect

CC R, R	CD S, T
DC T, S	DD P, P

R = "reward" (CC)
T = "temptation" (DC)
S = "sucker" (CD)
P = "penalty" (DD)

The preference ordering of both players in a PD game is T>R>P>S: temptation (confessing) is preferred to reward (mutual silence), which is preferred to penalty (mutual confessing), which is preferred to the sucker's payoff.[12] Giving in to temptation – defecting (confessing) while one's partner cooperates (remains silent); that is, accepting the plea bargain – provides the greatest gains. But above all else the players in this game want to avoid getting suckered, sitting in prison, for a long time, due to the treachery of one's "partner." If we plug these (ordinal) preferences – temptation is most highly valued (4) and sucker least valued (1) – into the general game outlined in figure 1.1, we obtain figure 1.2.

The dilemma of these prisoners appears when we ask whether their rational strategy is to defect (confess) or to cooperate (remain silent). If they cooperate (CC), each gets their second best outcome (the top left cell, with the "reward" payoffs of 3,3). But cooperating risks getting suckered. Therefore, assuming substantial (but not wild) aversion to risk, each will choose to defect *even though both know that they both could be better off by cooperating*. Mutual defection is the clear solution to the dilemma, the only strategically sensible outcome. But it leaves both players in a suboptimal position.

Instrumental and substantive "rationality" conflict. The instrumentally rational strategy of defection is substantively crazy: it leaves both players

---

[12] Using the more general labels, DC>CC>DD>CD.

Figure 1.2. Prisoners' Dilemma.

T > R > P > S
DC > CC > DD > CD

Player 2
("column")

	Cooperate	Defect
Player 1 *("row")* Cooperate	CC 3, 3	CD 1, 4
Defect	DC 4, 1	DD 2, 2

worse off than they could be if they cooperated. Yet the preferences of these actors in this structure of interaction preclude any other outcome.

The dilemma might be evaded, or made less severe, if the players could make a mutual cooperation pact and establish some mechanism to enforce it, increasing the likelihood of cooperation by reducing the risk of being suckered. Working from the other direction, increasing the payoffs of mutual cooperation (R) or decreasing the costs of mutual defection (P) would augment the incentives to cooperate even in the absence of enforcement. This might occur in a well-established criminal partnership, which saw this particular interaction as only part of a stream of potentially profitable interactions. An even more radical solution would be to alter the preferences of the players; for example, through a code of honor among thieves that made giving in to temptation no longer the preferred outcome. But unless the structure of interaction or the preferences of the actors can be altered, the dilemma is inescapable.

Realism as PD Realism can be seen as a theory that presents Prisoners' Dilemma as the central feature of international relations. The preference ordering T>R>P>S is a good example of realist egoism and amoralism. International anarchy, it is often argued, precludes enforceable agreements to cooperate. Therefore, international relations are often marked by insecurity, competition, and conflict *even where there are strong incentives to cooperate.*

A variant on PD, with special application to international relations, is what John Herz (1951: 4) first called the "security dilemma." Glenn Snyder's recent restatement of the logic is especially clear.

Given the irreducible uncertainty about the intentions of others, security measures taken by one actor are perceived by others as threatening; the others take steps to protect themselves; these steps are then interpreted by the first actor as confirming its initial hypothesis that the others are dangerous; and so on in a spiral of illusory fears and "unnecessary" defenses (1997: 17).

As Robert Jervis puts it in a classic discussion of the concept, the dilemma arises because "many of the means by which a state tries to increase its security decrease the security of others" (1978: 169).

Herbert Butterfield expresses much the same idea in terms of "Hobbesian fear."

If you imagine yourself locked in a room with another person with whom you have often been on the most bitterly hostile terms in the past, and suppose that each of you has a pistol, you may find yourself in a predicament in which both of you would like to throw the pistols out of the window, yet it defeats the intelligence to find a way of doing it (1949: 89–90).

Anarchy can defeat even our best intentions – which realists tend to see as rare enough to begin with.

A PD formulation of realism does not require assuming either a fixed human nature or a world populated exclusively by consistently egoistic amoralists. In the absence of government, the presence of several unscrupulous actors can force even individuals who would prefer to follow the counsels of reason or their "better" impulses to be "nasty" rather than "nice." For example, those who kept their word would fall victim to less scrupulous neighbors. To return to Hobbes' language, even those capable of mastering their desires for gain and glory will, in an environment of anarchy, be reduced by fear to treating everyone else as a potential enemy – or they will perish or be subordinated to the will of others.

As Georg Schwarzenberger puts it, "the law of the lowest level operates in such a society" because even those who would prefer peace and cooperation "cannot avoid contact with the wholesale addicts to the rule of force." "However restrained a State may be in the conduct of its foreign affairs, it must be suspicious of the intentions of other States whose rulers may be more inclined, and in a better position, to use their power for expansionist ends." "Every generation has its potential or actual black sheep which prevents the others from grazing in peace" (1951: 14, xxi, 156, 15).

Prisoners' Dilemma also usefully emphasizes the political distance between desire and achievement. Mutually destructive competition may not be avoidable even when all parties prefer a cooperative outcome.

Without insurance schemes or other mechanisms that allow actors to risk cooperating, and without a procedure to achieve agreement on how to divide the benefits of cooperation, we may remain locked in a cycle, even a descending spiral, of competition.

Thucydides' Athenian envoys

Realism can be found in ancient as well as modern sources. Probably the most famous text in the realist tradition is the Melian Dialogue (V.85–113)[13] in Thucydides' *History* of the Peloponnesian wars between Athens and Sparta at the end of the fifth century BC. The arguments advanced by the Athenian envoys at Melos are so rigorously realist that they provide one of the few examples of a sustained, consistently radical realism.

Athens, seeking to add the neutral island of Melos to its empire, sends envoys to encourage the Melians to surrender (V.84), in order to save the time, expense, and suffering of a siege. Presenting themselves as sensible men of the world, the Athenians forbid the Melians from even talking about the "specious pretenses" (*onomata kala*, fine phrases; literally, beautiful or noble names) of right and wrong (V.89). Instead they restrict discussion to the safety of Melos (V.87) and "the real sentiments of us both," namely, power and interest. "For you know as well as we do that right, as the world goes, is in question only between equals in power, while the strong do what they can and the weak suffer what they must" (V.89). The (weaker) Melians protest but have no choice but to carry on within these terms of reference.

Freedom, the Athenians argue, is the fruit of power (V.97). For Melos to hold out for independence would be to misjudge the situation, with tragic consequences, "the contest not being an equal one, with honor as the prize and shame as the penalty, but a question of self-preservation" (V.101). "Expediency goes with security, while justice and honor cannot be followed without danger" (V.107). And this, the Athenians contend, is simply the way of the world.

Of the gods we believe, and of men we know, that by a necessary law of their nature they rule wherever they can. And it is not as if we were the first to make this law, or to act upon it when made: we found it existing before us, and shall leave it to exist for ever after us; all we do is to make use of it, knowing that you and everybody else, having the same power as we have, would do the same as we do (V.105.2).

---

[13] All otherwise unidentified references in this subsection are to Thucydides' *History* by book, chapter, and, where appropriate, section. Translations are from the revised Crawley translation (Thucydides 1982) except for those identified as "[Smith]," which are by C. F. Smith in the Loeb edition (Thucydides 1919–23).

The Melians nonetheless decide to fight for their independence, what-ever the odds or the costs (V.112). The Athenian siege succeeds. The Melian men are killed, their women and children are sold into slavery, and a colony is sent from Athens to repopulate the city (V.116).

A very similar logic is evident in the very first speech given by an Athenian in Thucydides' *History*, just before the outbreak of the war, at the congress of Sparta's allies held in Lacedaemon. The Athenian envoys, trying to justify their empire, argue that "those who may use might have no need to appeal to right" (I.77.2 [Smith]). Although they claim "fair title" to the empire (I.73.1, 76.2), they admit that what began as "leader-ship [*hegemonia*] over allies who were autonomous and took part in the deliberations of common assemblies" (I.97.1) has become coercive rule (*arche*, empire).

It was not a very remarkable action, or contrary to the common practice of mankind, if we accepted an empire that was offered to us, and refused to give it up under the pressure of three of the strongest motives, fear, honor, and interest. And it was not we who set the example, for it has always been the law that the weaker should be subject to the stronger (I.76.2; compare I.75.3).

They even accuse their enemies of self-serving hypocrisy. "Besides, we believed ourselves to be worthy of our position, and so you thought us till now, when calculations of interest have made you take up the cry of justice" (I.76.2).

Like the other paradigms we have considered, Thucydides' Athenians appeal to law-like regularities that make international politics a domain of power and necessity. They are of special interest because they emphasize the conflict between the demands of justice and those of power.

The careful reader will note that I have talked not about Thucydides' views but rather of the arguments of the Athenian envoys at Melos and Lacedaemon. Although these and other parts of Thucydides' *History* support a realist reading, there are also substantial hedges. In fact, in chapter 6 I will suggest that the hedges are more important than the alleged realist "core." Nonetheless, the Melian Dialogue is an important touchstone in the realist tradition.

Machiavelli

Among realists of an earlier century, perhaps none stands out more promi-nently than Niccolò Machiavelli, the great sixteenth-century Florentine diplomat, historian, theorist, and playwright. Even today, one of the first words likely to come to mind when one mentions realism or political amoralism is "machiavellianism."

Machiavelli regularly expresses a low opinion of human nature, which in one poem he characterizes as "insatiable, arrogant, crafty, and shifting, and above all else malignant, iniquitous, violent, and savage" (1965: 736). "One can say this generally of men: that they are ungrateful, fickle, pretenders and dissemblers, evaders of danger, eager for gain" (P17[3]).[14] "Men never do good unless necessity drives them to it" (DI.2[3]; compare P23[3]). "All do wrong and to the same extent when there is nothing to prevent them doing wrong" (DI.58[4]; compare DI.Preface[3], 40[9], 46[1], DIII.43[1]).

In such a world, power and security must be paramount concerns. "A prince should have no other object, nor any other thought, nor take anything else as his art but the art of war" (P14[1]). Although well-ordered states rest on both "good laws and good arms . . . because there cannot be good laws where there are not good arms, and where there are good arms there must be good laws, I shall leave out the reasoning on laws" (P12[1]). Even in religion, Machiavelli observes that "all the armed prophets conquered and the unarmed were ruined" (P6[4]).

Machiavelli also tends to subordinate all other considerations to political success. "Men judge of actions by the result" (DIII.35[1]). "So let a prince win and maintain his state: the means will always be judged honorable, and will be praised by everyone" (P18[6]; compare P3[12]).

We should also note Machiavelli's love of the dramatic act of political violence. Consider Cesare Borgia's removal of his henchman Remirro de Orca, who had successfully pacified the Romagna, but at the cost of great bloodshed and hatred. Borgia had Remirro "placed one morning in the piazza at Cesena in two pieces, with a piece of wood and a bloody knife beside him. The ferocity of this spectacle left the people at once satisfied and stupefied" (P7[4]). The ancient Roman love of liberty, Machiavelli notes with admiration, was closely associated with "sacrificial acts in which there was much shedding of blood and much ferocity; and in them great numbers of animals were killed. Such spectacles, because terrible, caused men to become like them" (DII.2[6]; compare DIII.49[2,3], P17[5]).

The praise of such exemplary violence reflects more than personal psychological peculiarities or the habits of a more violent age. For Machiavelli, the evil and egoistic passions at the core of human nature often can be repressed only by force, and at times only by ferocious cruelty. In Machiavelli's world, even the good must "know how to enter into evil, when forced by necessity" (P18[5]).

---

[14] Most citations of Machiavelli are incorporated into the text as follows: P = *The Prince*, by chapter and paragraph in the Mansfield translation (Machiavelli 1985); D = *The Discourses [on the First Ten Books of Livy]*, by book, chapter, and paragraph in Crick's revised Walker translation (Machiavelli 1970).

As in the case of Thucydides, below I will emphasize the non-realist elements in Machiavelli's work. There can be no doubt, however, that realism lies at the heart of Machiavelli's political theory.

Realism and the study of international relations

The remainder of this chapter provides a brief sketch of the place of realism in the twentieth-century study of international relations. It also introduces the reader to several additional realists whose work will appear in later chapters.

The first generation

International relations, although long studied by historians and lawyers, emerged as a distinct academic discipline or sub-field only in the early twentieth century, especially in the aftermath of World War I. This first generation of professional students of international relations was dominated by "idealists," whom we can more neutrally call liberal internationalists.[15] Galvanized by the failure of balance of power diplomacy to prevent devastating war, they were committed to using human reason and organizational ingenuity to replace the old order of national interests with a new order of common interests. For example, the explicitly pacifist Carnegie Endowment for International Peace (founded in 1910) played an important role in the development of the discipline in the United States.

The dominance of liberal internationalists, such as Pitmann Potter and James Shotwell in the United States and Norman Angell and Alfred Zimmern in Britain, was so complete that when the international crises of the 1930s discredited "idealism," there was no mainstream alternative to fill the void.[16] The first major figure to attempt to reshape the field was E. H. Carr, who left the British diplomatic service to take up the chair in international relations at Aberystwyth in 1936. Carr immediately

---

[15] For a useful recent review of interwar idealism, which stresses its diversity and continuing contemporary relevance, see Long and Wilson (1995). See also Long (1996) and Lynch (1999).

[16] In 1930, eighteen of the twenty-four American international relations specialists with the rank of full professor specialized in international law or organization (Thompson 1952: 438). Frederick Schuman, whose 1933 *International Politics* is arguably the first academic realist international relations text, was only a junior faculty member at Chicago, where the international relations program was dominated by the eclectic but decidedly non-realist Quincy Wright. Morgenthau spent the early and mid-1930s in Europe studying, practicing, and teaching international and administrative law. Georg Schwarzenberger in 1937 was, of all things, working for Lord Davies' New Commonwealth Institute studying reform of the League of Nations.

redesigned the curriculum, replacing the previous focus on the League of Nations with an emphasis on power and history. And just as World War II was breaking out, he published *The Twenty Years' Crisis, 1919–1939: An Introduction to the Study of International Relations*, which Carr described in the preface to the 1946 edition as having been "written with the deliberate aim of counteracting the glaring and dangerous defect of nearly all thinking, both academic and popular, about international politics in English-speaking countries from 1919 to 1939 – the almost total neglect of the factor of power" (1946: vii).

In 1946 as well, Morgenthau published his first book, *Scientific Man versus Power Politics*. Both Carr and Morgenthau noted their debt to an American Protestant theologian, Reinhold Niebuhr, whose 1932 book *Moral Man and Immoral Society* had a profound impact on the emerging realist movement. Niebuhr argued that "the inability of human beings to transcend their own interests sufficiently to envisage the interests of their fellow men as clearly as they do their own makes force an inevitable part of" politics. "It will never be possible to insure moral antidotes sufficiently potent to destroy the deleterious effects of the poison of power upon character." "Power sacrifices justice to peace within the community and destroys peace between communities" (1932: 6, 21, 16).

The larger the group within which we operate, Niebuhr argued, the less the power of sympathy, and thus the greater the distance between moral ideal and political reality. International relations, involving interactions among the largest social groups, thus stands at the pinnacle of immorality. "A perennial weakness of the moral life in individuals is simply raised to the *n*th degree in national life." The best we can hope for is an ethically paradoxical patriotism that "transmutes individual unselfishness into national egoism." "The nation is at one and the same time a check upon, and a final vent for, the expression of individual egoism." "A combination of unselfishness and vicarious selfishness in the individual thus gives a tremendous force to national egoism, which neither religious nor rational idealism can ever completely check" (1932: 107, 91, 93, 94).

Another central figure in the development of realism's post-World War II dominance was George Kennan, a principal architect of the American policy of containment. Kennan's 1950 Walgreen Lectures at the University of Chicago, published in 1951 (along with two essays from *Foreign Affairs*) as *American Diplomacy*, provided a powerful and accessible critique of moralism and legalism in US foreign policy. In his 1954 book *The Realities of American Foreign Policy*, Kennan continued to lament "the great American capacity for enthusiasm and self-hypnosis," calling on the United States to restrict itself to an international politics of power and security. "In most international differences elements of right and wrong, comparable to those that prevail in personal relations, are – if they exist at all, which is a question – simply not discernable to the outsider." Government in general, and foreign policy in particular, Kennan claimed, "is primarily a sorry chore consisting of the application of restraint by man over man, a chore devolving on civilized society, most unfortunately, as a result of man's irrational nature, his selfishness, his obstinacy, his tendency to violence" (1954: 26, 36, 48).

A number of lesser realists also rose to prominence in the 1940s and 1950s. In the United States, Nicholas Spykman and Frederick Schuman both published successful realist textbooks in the early 1940s. These were followed not only by Morgenthau, but also by a number of less-known realists such as Robert Strausz-Hupé and Stefan T. Possony. Two other notable refugee realists who first made academic names for themselves in the United States in the 1950s were Henry Kissinger, who became Secretary of State in the early 1970s, and John Herz, who, as we noted above, coined the term "security dilemma."

In Britain, Georg Schwarzenberger's *Power Politics*, first published in 1941 and revised in 1951, provided one of the most radical expressions of realism. Schwarzenberger emphasized "the constancy of mutual suspicion and fear." "The overriding role of power in international relations dominates thought and action in this field." Although "rulers and statesmen are well aware of the existence of rules of international morality," the necessities of power rarely allow them to act on these rules. International morality, like international law "is both subservient to power politics and . . . flourishes best where it does not interfere with the international struggle for power" (1951: 157, 147, 220, 224).

By 1960, realism was so dominant that one review of the field concluded that "genuine anti-realists are hard to find" (Fox and Fox 1961: 343). And it is worth noting that realism spanned the political spectrum, from Schuman and Carr on the Marxist left to Strausz-Hupé and Possony on the rabidly anti-communist right. The study of international relations, born in idealism after World War I, had been effectively refounded after World War II on realist premises.

Realism reconsidered

In the late 1950s and 1960s, however, an anti-realist counter-attack developed momentum, focusing on problems in realist accounts of the national interest and balance of power. Criticism was focused especially on Hans Morgenthau, who made claims for realism that can only be described as wildly extravagant.

Morgenthau's argument that states "act, as they must, in view of their interests as they see them" (1962a: 278), reflected not an uninteresting tautology but an extreme, even excessive, theoretical claim. Even a sympathetic critic such as Robert W. Tucker saw Morgenthau's work as riddled with "open contradictions, ambiguity, and vagueness." "If the national interest is analogous in nature to gravity, then what is the reason for the repeated failure of statesmen to see what is self-evident?" (1952: 214, 216). If statesmen act according to the national interest defined in terms of power, then they should not need to be exhorted to do so, and there should be nothing for Morgenthau the policy analyst to criticize.

Morgenthau likewise described the balance of power as a "necessary outgrowth" of international politics, a fact of international political life that "cannot be abolished" (1948: 126; 1951: 155). But Morgenthau also wrote that the "uncertainty of all power calculations not only makes the balance of power incapable of practical application, it leads also to its very negation in practice" (1948: 155). On careful examination, even the meaning of "balance of power" proved obscure. As Inis Claude noted, Morgenthau admitted to using the term in four different senses, and in practice added a fifth (1962: 25–27, 27ff. *passim*).

During the 1960s, realism in the United States was steadily losing its dominance.[17] By the end of the decade, it was in serious decline. And in the 1970s, a significant substantive and theoretical challenge arose within the mainstream of the discipline from a fundamentally non-idealist brand of liberal internationalism that emphasized newly developing processes of international interdependence. Instead of a realist world of autonomous sovereign states, alone and adrift in the sea of international anarchy, the new liberal internationalists of the 1970s presented a world of multiple actors, bound together in a complex web of conflictual and cooperative relations.

Robert O. Keohane and Joseph Nye's *Power and Interdependence* (1977) presented a "complex interdependence" model of international relations characterized by multiple and varied international actors, a profusion of international issues that were not hierarchically ordered or centrally controlled, and the declining utility of force, along with a declining capacity to transform power in one dimension (e.g. military might) into power in another (e.g. economic prosperity).[18] Although this

---

[17] Realism in Britain, however, although no longer hegemonic, remained the most important perspective in the discipline.

[18] A decade later, Keohane and Nye (1987: 728–730) claimed that they saw their work more as a complement to realism than a replacement. At the time, however, most scholars, on both sides of the issue, took *Power and Interdependence*, not unreasonably, as an alternative to and critique of realism.

perspective never predominated – it was largely ignored in mainstream security studies and foreign policy analysis – it firmly established a substantive alternative to realism within the mainstream of the discipline. It also fostered the dramatic rise in the study of international political economy, which substantially expanded the scope of standard topics considered in the field.

The neorealist revival

Realism in its classic postwar form never completely died out. Even today it persists on the margins of the discipline, in the work of relatively isolated but respected figures such as Tucker, and in academic enclaves such as the University of Virginia, where Kenneth Thompson, Morgenthau's former student, research assistant, and collaborator, has self-consciously sought to preserve the tradition. In Britain, Martin Wight and Herbert Butterfield introduced a heavily hedged realism into the still thriving "English School," associated most closely with Hedley Bull. And a growing appreciation for the classics is expressed in the work of some younger American realists, such as Randall Schweller.

Realism's return to academic dominance in the 1980s, however, arose from the work of a new generation of scholars who sought to establish realism on the foundations of positivist social science. The key figure in this "neorealist" revival was Kenneth Waltz, whose work was discussed above. Although this change in intellectual fashion parallels the renewed emphasis on power and conflict in American foreign policy under Ronald Reagan, neorealism was rooted primarily in internal disciplinary developments.

Many of the claims for interdependence were extravagant, almost begging for rebuttal. Waltz in particular developed his theory in opposition to the interdependence perspective, which he argued "both obscures the realities of international politics and asserts a false belief about the conditions that may promote peace" (1970: 222). Furthermore, the ruins of classical postwar realism, which for all its problems did contain important insights, lay waiting for a more coherent social scientific reformulation.

Structural neorealism looked for methodological guidance to microeconomic rational choice analysis, as illustrated in the discussion of Prisoners' Dilemma above. States are seen as unitary actors that rationally calculate their actions in order to improve their material welfare. Structural realists also have tended to adopt the so-called nomological-deductive model of social science. Theory is seen as a deductive system of propositions to explain the occurrence of law-like regularities in a carefully delimited domain of inquiry.

Structural realism, as a result, has had modest, largely academic, aspirations, especially in contrast to the grand historical and prescriptive pronouncements of earlier realists such as Morgenthau. For example, Waltz admits (1979: 121) that his theory does not aspire to determinate predictions of particular actions. And neorealists have generally been reticent to draw policy prescriptions from their theories.

The difference between generations is perhaps best illustrated by their treatments of the national interest. Morgenthau saw the national interest as objective and subject to discovery by realist analysis. Neorealists, however, usually see the national interest (beyond the minimal goal of preserving sovereignty and territorial integrity) as subjective and given – "exogenous" to the theory – rather than a subject of inquiry or analysis. (These conceptions are discussed in more detail in the next chapter.)

The hegemony of neorealism, however, was short-lived. Neorealism's indeterminate generalities soon came to seem intellectually far less sustaining, and much less helpful to the actual work of research, than they initially appeared. Such substantive problems will be a central focus of later chapters. The key blow, though, was the collapse of the Soviet empire.

Neorealism, as Waltz admits (1986: 338), cannot comprehend change. During the Cold War, this theoretical gap seemed acceptable to many. But when the Cold War order collapsed seemingly overnight, even many otherwise sympathetic observers began to look elsewhere – especially because that collapse was intimately tied to ideas of democracy and human rights and processes of technological and economic change, important concerns of liberal internationalism that were excluded by neorealist structuralism.

But realism, although in decline, has not been eclipsed. Although knocked from the commanding heights of the discipline, realism remains one of the most robust campers at a lower elevation, prominently championed by younger figures such as John Mearsheimer, Barry Posen, Randall Schweller, Stephen Van Evera, and Stephen Walt, and in journals such as *International Security* and *Security Studies*. And for all of realism's shortcomings and challengers, no other theory seems poised for an ascent to the top.

Whether one loves it or hates it – or is at once fascinated and repulsed – the student of international relations cannot ignore realism. The following chapters record some of my efforts to come to terms with what I see as a complex mixture of insights, errors, and dangerous exaggerations in the realist tradition.

Discussion questions

- Most readers have at least implicit views on political realism. What are yours? Are you basically sympathetic or hostile to realism (however you might understand that term)? Keep these initial attitudes and understandings in mind as we move through this book.

- Which type or style of realism seems most plausible or attractive (or least implausible or unattractive) to you? Whether you see yourself as a realist, anti-realist, or neither, what seem to be the strongest elements of the realist position? The weakest? Why?

- The chapter often talks of realism as a tradition. What does this description imply? What difference would it make to talk about realism as a theory? A paradigm? An approach?

- Examine the representative definitions in box 1.1. Is there anything that is shared by (almost) every one? Is that what "defines" realism? Or is there instead a family resemblance, a clear kinship despite the lack of any single thread running through all of them? Assuming that realists do somehow share an unmistakable intellectual style, exactly how should that style be characterized?

- What do you think of categorizing realists as "radical," "strong," or "hedged"? Are hedged realists *really* realists? What would be the consequences of treating everything short of radical realism as a more or less close approximation of the "true" realist theory? (What do you think of the idea of "the 'true' realist theory?")

- Is there such a thing as "human nature"? If so, is it fixed and largely given? Or is it better seen as a wide range of potentialities that are expressed in very different ways at different times and places? Are these really two conceptions of the same "thing"?

- Whether you believe in "human nature" or not, is the standard realist account of the basic elements of human motivation plausible? What sort of hedges have to be included before you are willing to answer yes? Consider Hobbes' account, which emphasizes competition, diffidence, and glory. What is lost by abstracting from other motives? What is gained by focusing on these in particular? How would you evaluate the balance between losses and gains?

- What is the place of reason in human nature? How is reason related to the passions? Does passion readily swamp reason? In what circumstances? Is creating a superior power to enforce the conclusions drawn by reason really the key to peace and civil order? How are reason and power thus understood related to values and interests?

- In discussing Prisoners' Dilemma it is suggested in the text that instrumental and substantive rationality conflict; that is, that the (instrumentally) rational pursuit of interests leads to (substantive) results that the actors would never "rationally" choose. How common are such problems of unintended consequences? How important are they? Is it especially important to draw attention to them in situations of anarchy? Why? Are they more frequent? More pressing? Harder to resolve?

- Is it true, as Prisoners' Dilemma suggests, that in certain central and recurrent cases international conflict arises not merely unintentionally but inescapably, despite the fact that the actors do not want to compete? How often? In what types of common international situations? In what issue areas? What might be done to change this situation? That is, are there ways to reduce the frequency or intensity of the dilemma?

- Let us assume, for the sake of argument, that the conflicts and constraints to which realists point are, if not an inescapable element of international relations, at least sufficiently pervasive that any sound international theory must pay them special attention. How do you rate the relative contributions of "human nature" and international anarchy in producing such a world? How do the six paradigms rate their relative importance? Are there other central factors not captured in the categories of structural and biological realism?

- How common is the security dilemma? That is, how often do the defensive endeavors of states appear as offensive threats to other states? What kinds of conditions are likely to exacerbate the dilemma? What conditions may lessen or even eliminate it?

- If human nature is constant, why isn't realism a theory of politics in general, rather than a theory of international relations? What does your answer to this question say about the plausibility of biological realist theories? What does it suggest about the relationship between political structures and the interests of actors? Whatever your own views, try to answer this last question from the perspective of both biological and structural realism.

- If international anarchy is a constant, how do we account for the great diversity of international orders across history? If human nature is constant, how can we account for this diversity? Can realism, at the level of generality we have discussed it so far, get much of a handle on variation or change?

- Why isn't an *international* social contract an option to escape the Hobbesian state of war? Why do realists think it is possible to escape the state of war nationally but impossible internationally? *Is* it really impossible? Is a state of war really escaped nationally? In *all* nation-states? Equally?

- Are there "laws" of (national or international) politics? In what sense of that term? Are these "laws," as Morgenthau claims, rooted in human nature? In anarchy? What difference does it make to talk about "law-like regularities" rather than laws?

- Waltz aspires to explain international relations entirely on the basis of structure, without recourse to appeals to human nature. Is this plausible? Can realists really make do without substantive assumptions about human nature or state motivation? (Think carefully about this last question; it will be a central issue in the next chapter.)

- *Has* it always been the law that the weaker should be subject to the stronger? Assuming that in some sense there is such a law, who made it? Or, to ask the question in a slightly different way, where did it come from? What gives it the force of law? Is there no appeal against it?

- What makes realism more "realistic" than other theories or approaches? Certainly the world described by the Athenian envoys at Melos – or any other realist for that matter – is not the world that we inhabit today. At best it is a dramatic simplification of a much more complex reality. Should we allow realists pre-emptively to disparage alternative accounts as in some important sense "unrealistic"? Even if we grant that realism is profoundly insightful, can it also be characterized as "unrealistic" in an ordinary sense of that term?

Suggestions for further reading

As noted in the Introduction, each chapter is followed by a short bibliographic essay that suggests further reading. The present essay, which is considerably longer than the others, focuses on the six paradigms that provide the heart of this chapter – Hobbes, Morgenthau, Waltz, the Prisoners' Dilemma, Thucydides and Machiavelli – plus some of the more important "secondary" figures.

Hobbes

Hobbes' *Leviathan* is not the most accessible of works, especially if one sits down and tries to read it from cover to cover. Not only is much of the first dozen chapters devoted to issues of method, metaphysics, and epistemology, but also Hobbes' views on topics such as the nature of language, sense perception, and ideas are likely to strike a late twentieth-century reader as odd, if not downright crazy. **Chapter 13**, however, once one gets used to the seventeenth-century prose, is a brilliant brief presentation of a strong realism that gives balanced consideration to structure and motivation. (When I teach this text I often suggest to my students, only half jokingly, that 90 percent of what is of interest about realism can be found in these few short pages.) Chapters 14 and 15, which develop further issues of liberty, justice, and obligation, also repay careful reading, although they are not easy going. Those who want more might consider chapters 16–21, 26, 29–32, 35, 42, 43, 46, 47, and the Review and Conclusion. Among the many editions of *Leviathan*, those of Macpherson (Hobbes 1986) and Tuck (Hobbes 1996) are both excellent and readily available.

The secondary literature on Hobbes gives relatively scant attention to his international theory. One of the few sustained exceptions is the edited collection *Hobbes: War Among Nations* (Airaksinen and Bertman 1989). Alker (1996: ch. 11) provides a thoughtful exploration of the assumption of anarchy in international relations theory centered on the Hobbesian conception. For an interesting, although sometimes dense, discussion of Hobbes as an international theorist, see Donald Hanson's "Thomas Hobbes's 'Highway to Peace'" (1984). Beitz (1979: 27–50) provides a strong argument against conceptualizing international relations as a Hobbesian state of nature (because of the existence of international inequality, interdependence, and mechanisms that create reliable expectations of reciprocal compliance with rules). Readers with a philosophical bent will profit from the discussion of the logic of conflict and cooperation in a Hobbesian state of nature by Kavka (1986: chs. 3, 4).

Morgenthau

Hans Morgenthau was a prolific writer. His best-known work, *Politics Among Nations*, although conceived as a textbook, is literate, challenging, and wide-ranging. The famous first chapter, which presents Morgenthau's six principles of political realism, first appeared in the second edition (1954) and remained essentially unchanged through the sixth, posthumous edition of 1985. This is absolutely essential reading.

Morgenthau's major philosophical work is *Scientific Man Versus Power Politics* (1946), a scathing attack on liberal and rationalist approaches to politics. *In Defense of the National Interest* (1951) provides Morgenthau's most sustained application of his position to questions of foreign policy. In my view, however, Morgenthau's great strength was not as a theorist – quite the contrary, in chapters 2 and 6 I try to show that Morgenthau is an extraordinarily sloppy and inconsistent theorist – but as an essayist. His three-volume collection, *Politics in the Twentieth Century* (1962a; 1962b; 1962c) is a rich mine of lively and often insightful essays on a wide range of subjects. Volume I has several essays well worth reading: on general themes, see, for example, chs. 1, 4–6, 8; on moral issues, see chs. 20, 21, 25, 26. Especially brilliant – although entirely inconsistent with his general theory – is "Love and Power" in volume III. Morgenthau's later collection, *Truth and Power* (1970), is also valuable.

For secondary sources on Morgenthau, perhaps the most useful starting point is Michael J. Smith's *Realist Thought from Weber to Kissinger* (1986: ch. 6). Robert Jervis' essay "Hans Morgenthau, Realism, and the Study of International Politics" (1994) sympathetically but not uncritically situates Morgenthau within the development of the discipline. See also Gellman (1988). *Truth and Tragedy*, a tributary volume edited by Kenneth W. Thompson and Robert J. Meyers (1977) is also valuable. Those interested in social history should enjoy Joel Rosenthal's *Righteous Realists* (1991) which places Morgenthau within a broader movement in postwar American foreign policy. Greg Russell's *Hans J. Morgenthau and the Ethics of American Statecraft* (1990) and A. J. H. Murray's "The Moral Politics of Hans Morgenthau" (1996) are also useful. Perhaps the most penetrating short critique of Morgenthau is Robert Tucker's review of *In Defense of the National Interest* (1952). It is one of those genuinely rare gems, a book review still worth reading almost half a century after it was written.

Waltz

Kenneth Waltz' *Theory of International Politics* (1979) is the central and seminal text of neorealist theory. Chapter 1 lays out Waltz' (sophisticated positivist) methodological position. Chapters 2 and 3 critique respectively "reductionist" theories that seek explanations based on the attributes of actors and earlier systems theory, which Waltz argues fail to distinguish adequately unit and structure. **Chapters 4–6** are the heart of the book, providing an outline of structural theory as Waltz understands it, a detailed account of the differences he sees between anarchic and hierarchic political structures, and Waltz' distinctive version of balance of power theory. Chapters 7–9 apply the perspective to questions of economic relations, military affairs, and the management of international relations. Waltz's essay "Realist Thought and Neo-Realist Theory" (1991) provides a shorter introduction to his perspective. "The Emerging Structure of International Politics" (1993) offers his views on the nature of the post-Cold War international order.

The critical literature on Waltz is immense. Perhaps the best starting point is *Neorealism and Its Critics*, a volume edited by Robert Keohane (1986). The chapters by **Keohane ("Structural Realism and Beyond"), John Ruggie ("Continuity and Transformation in the World Polity"), Robert Cox ("Social Forces, States and World Orders")**, and Richard Ashley provide critiques of increasing severity (and decreasing accessibility). The volume also contains Waltz' entirely unyielding reply to his critics. David Baldwin's *Neorealism and Neoliberalism: The Contemporary Debate* (1993) is another standard collection. Two essays by Alexander Wendt, **"The Agent-Structure Problem in International Relations Theory"** (1987) and **"Anarchy is What States Make of It"** (1992), are essential reading. David Destler's "What's at Stake in the Agent-Structure Debate" (1989) is also useful. Barry Buzan's chapter in *The Logic of Anarchy* (Buzan, Jones, and Little 1993) is one of the most sophisticated sympathetic critiques of Waltz' structuralism. The chapters by Dale Copeland, Randall Schweller, and Charles Glaser in Benjamin Frankel's *Realism: Restatements and Renewal* (1996b) offer powerful critiques of characteristically Waltzian positions from within the realist camp.

Prisoners' Dilemma

Game theory is a highly formal branch of economics that in its fully developed form is largely inaccessible to those without quite a substantial mathematical background. For an example, see Myerson (1991). James Morrow's *Game Theory for Political Scientists* (1994) is somewhat more accessible but still relatively technical. Nicholson (1992: part 2) usefully situates game theory within the general framework of assumptions about rationality in international relations.

The average reader of this book, however, probably should begin with Snyder and Diesing's *Conflict Among Nations* (1977: 37–52), which clearly lays out the general orientation and several basic game models without any mathematics. For a strong argument that game theory provides a general foundation for international theory, see Snidal (1985) reprinted in Oye (1986). For applications that focus more on cooperation than conflict, see Stein (1990).

On the Prisoners' Dilemma (PD) in particular, Robert Axelrod's "The Emergence of Cooperation Among Rational Egoists" (1981) is a good starting point, as is his book-length treatment, *The Evolution of Cooperation* (1984). Joanne Gowa's sympathetic yet critical review of Axelrod's book (1986) is also valuable. On strategies for ameliorating the dilemma, Axelrod and Keohane's **"Achieving Cooperation Under Anarchy"** (1985; reprinted in Oye 1986) is the essential – and very accessible – starting point. See also Jervis (1978: 170–186).

On the security dilemma, which explores a fundamentally PD logic in the context of armed states in anarchy, the classic consideration is that of Jervis (1978). Glaser (1997) provides a good recent overview of the current state of the literature, stressing, in addition to Jervis' emphasis on the offense–defense balance (and the clarity of the distinction between offensive and defensive weaponry), the importance of the degree of greed of the adversaries (a theme that I address in a very different way in chapter 2) and their uncertainty about one another's motives.

Thucydides

I must admit to a love for Thucydides that many of my students (perhaps with some justice) find not merely excessive but obsessive. Were I to be transported to a desert island with but one book, there is no doubt that Thucydides' *History* is the one I would choose. Were I forced to choose but one English translation, it would be Richard Crawley's, which combines accuracy, style, and readability. And that translation is now available in a slightly revised form – with marginal summaries for each chapter (which greatly facilitates skimming some of the more dry historical material), excellent maps, a comprehensive index, and a fine series of appendices – in *The Landmark Thucydides* (Strassler 1996). The only drawback is that it is not available in paperback. The Modern Library edition (Thucydides 1982), however, is available in paperback.

Charles Smith's translation (Thucydides 1919–23), however, is a close second; although a bit less elegant, it strives hard for accuracy and, being in the Loeb Classical Library series, has the great virtue of the Greek on the facing page. Although widely available and frequently cited, Rex Warner's translation in the Penguin Classics series (Thucydides 1972) strikes me as too loose at many crucial passages. I do not recommend it. If one is looking for a more colloquial American translation – the principal complaint about Crawley is its rather formal Victorian style – the recent version by Walter Blanco (Thucydides 1998) is, I think, a better bet. This edition also has a useful selection of critical essays and a bibliographic essay even more wide-ranging than what follows here.

Having settled on a translation, the next question is what to read. A bare minimum would be (by book and "chapter" or paragraph) I.1, 22–24, 66–88, 139–146; II.34–54, 59–65; III.36–50, 52–68, 81–85; V.84–116; VI.1, 8–26; VII.60–87. This covers Thucydides' method and account of the "truest cause" of the war; the speeches at Lacedaemon prior to the outbreak of fighting; Pericles' first speech and his Funeral Oration; Thucydides' account of the Plague; Pericles' last speech and Thucydides' summary judgment of Pericles; the Mytilenian and Plataean debates; the civil war in Corcyra; the Melian Dialogue; the debate over the Sicilian expedition; and the defeat and destruction of the Athenians on Sicily. A second tranche might include I.2–21 (the "Archaeology," the ancient history of Greece); I.89–118 (the *Pentecontaetia*, the fifty years between the Persian and Peloponnesian Wars); IV.3–40 (the events leading to the capture of the Spartans at Pylos); IV.58–64 (Hermocrates' speech at Gela); IV.84–88 (Brasidas at Acanthus); V.1–23 (the fall of Amphipolis and the Peace of Nicias); VI.27–61 (the launching of the Sicilian expedition and early fighting); VI.75–93 (speeches of Hermocrates, Euphemus, and Alcibiades); and VII.29–30 (the destruction of Mycalessus).

The critical literature on Thucydides, even when we exclude that of interest primarily to classicists, is immense. Were I to recommend a single work it probably would be Robert Connor's *Thucydides* (1984), an important scholarly study that is also an accessible introductory companion. Cawkwell (1997) is another scholarly but relatively accessible overview. John Finley's *Thucydides* (1963

[1942]) is older but still useful. Hunter Rawlings' *The Structure of Thucydides' History* (1981)is an impressive general reading with intriguing suggestions about the likely nature of the missing books, placing the Melian Dialogue at the physical center of the work, thus underscoring it as the central and fatal turning point in the war. Cornford's *Thucydides Mythistoricus* (1965 [1907]) is in many ways dated, yet still well worth consulting for its reading of the *History* as a classic tragedy with Athens as the hero. For those interested in Thucydides as history, the essential starting point is Donald Kagan's four-volume history of the era (1969; 1974; 1981; 1987).

Directly related to the central subject of this book, Gregory Crane's *Thucydides and the Ancient Simplicity: The Limits of Political Realism* (1998) is thorough and theoretically sophisticated, although some readers may find it too much a classicist's work despite his active and often effective engagement of political and international theory. See also Geoffrey Woodhead's *Thucydides and the Nature of Power* (1970) and Laurie Johnson's *Thucydides, Hobbes, and the Interpretation of Realism* (1993).

Marc Cogan's *The Human Thing* (1981a) begins with a series of commentaries on the speeches in the *History* and then moves to a powerful general interpretation. *The Speeches of Thucydides* (Stadter 1973) and *Individuals in Thucydides* (Westlake 1968) provide good introductions to these two important elements that give so much of the life to the *History*.

If forced to select a single article to recommend, it probably would be Adam Parry's **"Thucydides' Historical Perspective"** (1972). Useful recent articles by political scientists include Michael Doyle, "Thucydides: A Realist?" (1991) and Doyle's discussion of Thucydides in *Ways of War and Peace* (1997: 49–92); Daniel Garst, "Thucydides and Neorealism" (1989); Mark Kauppi, "Thucydides: Character and Capabilities" (1995/96); Laurie Johnson-Bagby, "The Use and Abuse of Thucydides" (1994); and Robert Gilpin, "The Theory of Hegemonic War" (1988). Among literally dozens of other pieces worthy of note, I would (somewhat arbitrarily) single out Henry Immerwahr, "Pathology of Power and Speeches in Thucydides" (1973); two articles by Clifford Orwin, "The Just and the Advantageous in Thucydides" (1984) and "Stasis and Plague" (1988); Marc Cogan, "Mytilene, Plataea, and Corcyra" (1981b); Arlene Saxonhouse, "Nature and Convention in Thucydides' *History*" (1978); Paul Rahe, "Thucydides' Critique of *Realpolitik*" (1995/96); and the chapter on Thucydides in Peter Euben, *The Tragedy of Political Theory* (1990).

On the Melian Dialogue in particular, see Wasserman (1947), Macleod (1974), Bosworth (1993), Alker (1996: ch. 1), Liebeschuetz (1968), and Andrewes (1960). There are a number of good discussions of the Mytilenian Debate. Orwin (1984) is particularly helpful. Andrewes (1962), Kagan, (1975), Wasserman (1956), Wet (1963), and Winnington-Ingram (1965) are also well worth consulting. On the revolutions in Corcyra, and the broader issue of political corruption and decay, see Macleod (1979), Wilson (1982), Orwin (1988), and Wasserman (1954).

On the empire, Romilly (1966) is a good introduction. See also Bruell (1974), Meiggs (1963), Starr (1988), and Ste.-Croix (1954/55). Among book-length studies, Romilly (1963 [1947]) is the essential starting point, although it is most definitely a classicist's book. Forde (1989) is more immediately accessible to non-classicists. Meiggs (1972) is the standard historical source, but is more a reference work than a narrative.

On questions of honor, glory, ethics, and morality, see the last paragraph of the suggestions for chapter 2 and the last two paragraphs of suggestions for chapter 6.

Machiavelli

Machiavelli is in his own way as rich and rewarding as Thucydides. Although in some ways easier to read, he was a much more prolific author. And he comes to us with a popular reputation that needs to be set aside at the outset, even if in the end one agrees – as I most definitely do not – that the popular vision is not all that far from the truth.

The two principal works are *The Prince*, which is short and eminently readable – and notorious – and *Discourses*, which though less known is unquestionably Machiavelli's most important work. The following (by book and chapter) represent a minimum introduction: Dedication; I.1–29, 32, 34–35, 39, 41–46, 49–53, 55, 57–58; II.1, 2, 10, 13, 21–25, 27, 29; III.1, 3, 6, 9, 19–20, 40–42, 44, 47–49.

Of the many translations of *The Prince* I prefer Harvey Mansfield's (Machiavelli 1985), which takes the fewest liberties with Machiavelli's text. (A second edition was published in 1998.) The De Alvarez (Machiavelli 1989), and Skinner (Machiavelli 1988b) editions are also good. For the *Discourses*, I have used the Walker translation (Machiavelli 1970). The more recent translation of Mansfield and Nathan Tarcov (Machiavelli 1996), however, is probably now the English language text of choice.

For those wanting to read other works by Machiavelli, the best starting point is Allan Gilbert's three-volume collection (Machiavelli 1965), which includes an extensive selection of theoretical, historical, and literary works. Among the more rewarding are the *Florentine Histories* (although Mansfield's edition [Machiavelli 1988a] is to be preferred), *Art of War, Life of Castruccio Castracani,* and *Mandragola*, Machiavelli's brilliant satirical play. A revealing selection of letters has been published separately by Gilbert (Machiavelli 1961).

Those interested in Machiavelli's (most fascinating) life should start with Sebastian de Grazia's *Machiavelli in Hell* (1989), a major work of scholarship that also won the Pulitzer Prize for Biography. De Grazia's book is a true intellectual biography in which Machiavelli's work receives no less careful attention than his life. Felix Gilbert's *Machiavelli and Guicciardini* (1965) situates Machiavelli in sixteenth-century Renaissance thought and history; see also Chabod (1965). On Florence, the central focus of Machiavelli's life and work, a good starting point is Bruckner (1983). On Machiavelli as a Florentine civil servant, see Black (1990).

Those looking for a thoughtful general overview and an introduction to the secondary literature should start with Viroli (1998). Gilmore (1972), Parel (1972), and Fleisher (1972) are good general collections of interpretive essays. Coyle (1995) offers a variety of readings of *The Prince*, almost all from outside political science and international studies.

Strauss (1959) and De Alvarez (1999) present interpretations that in varying ways see Machiavelli as a teacher of evil. Along the same lines, but somewhat more subtle, is Harvey Mansfield's *Machiavelli's Virtue* (1996). The title essay is particularly valuable. See also Masters (1996).

The more common scholarly reading today, however, sees Machiavelli as a republican interested in developing participatory politics and civic virtue – the central themes of the *Discourses*. As Rousseau put it in *The Social Contract* (book III, ch. 6), "Machiavelli was an honorable man and a good citizen; . . . this profound politician has had hitherto only superficial or corrupt readers." The most influential work in this tradition is John Pocock's *The Machiavellian Moment* (1975). Chapters 6 and 7 address Machiavelli directly, although all of parts I and II are slow but worthwhile reading. Bock, Skinner, and Viroli (1990) is a useful edited collection pursuing this general theme. Hans Baron, "Machiavelli: The Republican Citizen and the Author of *The Prince*" (1961) is also valuable. Hanna Pitkin's *Fortune is a Woman* (1984) creatively addresses the central issues of autonomy and political participation through the lenses of gender and psychoanalytic theory. For readings of Machiavelli that place him in a humanist context, see Alker (1992; reprinted in Alker 1996: ch. 4), Kocis (1998), Hulliung (1983), Wood (1972), and Gilbert (1939).

Other major realists

The choice of six paradigms was somewhat arbitrary. Among twentieth-century authors, strong cases can be made that Reinhold Niebuhr, E. H. Carr, George Kennan, and Henry Kissinger are at least as interesting and important as Morgenthau and Waltz.

Reinhold Niebuhr was a major acknowledged influence on both Morgenthau and Carr. A Protestant theologian of considerable note, his most important work, the two-volume *The Nature and Destiny of Man* (1941; 1943), is likely to be of interest only to those with a serious theological or philosophical bent. His political writings, however, pursue the same theme of the tension between the desire for transcendence and the reality of a corrupted human nature (original sin) in a more widely accessible form. ***Moral Man and Immoral Society*** (1932) is a genuine classic. (If one wants selected passages, I would suggest pp. xi–xxv, 1–31, 48–50, 83–97, 106–112, 137–141, 168–180.) *The Children of Light and the Children of Darkness* (1944) examines the strength, weaknesses, and tensions between liberal progressivism and realism. Kegley and Bretall (1956) is a good collection of selected works on both theology and politics. The essay "Augustine's Political Realism," available in both Niebuhr (1953) and Brown (1986), does a nice job of drawing the link between his political and theological work. Chapter 5 of Smith (1986) is a good place to start with secondary sources. Meyer (1988) situates Niebuhr in a broader religious and political context. See also Rosenthal (1991).

E. H. Carr's *The Twenty Years' Crisis* (1946) justly remains in print sixty years after its original publication. The first two chapters provide a brilliant brief overview of realism and the opposition to idealism (or what Carr calls "utopia"). Chapter 4 presents a critique of liberal progressivism that has perhaps never been surpassed. Chapters 5 and 6 further develop Carr's accounts of the power and limits of realism. Chapter 7 is a brilliant brief statement of the realist conception of politics. Howe (1994) and Jones (1996) provide readings very similar to the one I present in chapter 6 and the conclusion. See also Smith (1986: ch. 4), Bull (1969), and Fox (1985) for a further introduction to the secondary literature.

George Kennan combines a fine historian's sense of the importance of contingency and the flow of events with a highly developed realist theoretical perspective. For a deeply grounded critique of idealism in US foreign policy there is no better source than his *American Diplomacy* (1951; 1984). *Realities of American Foreign Policy* (1954) and *The Cloud of Danger* (1977) provide thoughtful critiques of American policy in the 1950s and 1970s respectively. For a strong but generally balanced realist argument against morality in foreign policy, there is perhaps no better short introduction than Kennan's "Morality and Foreign Policy" (1985/86). For an application of his perspective to post-Cold War issues of intervention, see Kennan (1995). Smith (1986: ch. 7) provides an excellent overview of Kennan's realism. Stephanson (1989) is highly critical of the coherence of Kennan's work. Rosenthal (1991) argues for a deep coherence, both within Kennan and within other major American realists of his generation. Mayers (1988) is an intellectual biography that leans more towards Rosenthal's interpretation. Hixson (1989) argues for an evolution in Kennan's views away from conventional realism. For a detailed account of Kennan as a diplomat during the crucial immediate postwar years, see Miscamble (1992). For Kennan's own take on his life, see Kennan (1967; 1972; 1989).

Henry Kissinger began his career as a scholar, made his reputation as the leading diplomat of his era, and has enjoyed an extremely comfortable life the past two decades as a self-proclaimed sage. In his first incarnation, his work on Metternich and the balance of power (1957) still is worth reading. The third edition of his collection of essays *American Foreign Policy* (1977) is perhaps the best introduction to his views as a practicing diplomat. Among his recent work, *Diplomacy* (1994) is characteristically thoughtful, and perhaps somewhat less ponderous and self-serving than Kissinger's norm. For an introductory overview that is relatively untainted by the sharp political passions Kissinger usually engenders among those over forty (myself included) Smith (1986: ch. 8) is excellent.

Three realists from the 1940s are also worth consulting. Nicholas Spykman's *America's Strategy in World Politics* (1942) is interesting both for its strong realism and its geopolitical orientation. Frederick Schuman's *International Politics* (1941) is notable for its Marxist orientation. And Georg Schwarzenberger's *Power Politics* (1941; 1951) is as harsh and uncompromising a realist vision as one is likely to find, but with a sociological orientation that does not completely deny the reality of international society. Few readers will want to read any of these books from cover to cover, but they do provide interesting browsing. In the same category is Heinrich von Treitschke's *Politics* (1916), a strong example of continental reason-of-state thinking.

Michael Joseph Smith makes a case for Max Weber as the foundational figure of twentieth-century realism (1986: ch. 2). The crucial work is the essay "Politics as a Vocation," in Gerth and Mills (1946). See also Raymond Aron, "Max Weber and Power Politics" (1971).

I want also to draw attention to two works that are in my view exemplary in realist analysis. Martin Wight's **Power Politics** (1978) is a penetrating examination of the practice of realist power politics in modern European international society. Although Wight himself was not a realist, except perhaps in the most heavily hedged sense of that term, I know of no better analytical overview of the characteristic practices and institutions of great power politics. Robert Tucker's

The Inequality of Nations (1977) is a powerful argument against global economic redistribution based on a realist understanding of the inescapable place of power and inequality in anarchic international relations.

Finally, I would be remiss if by omission I were to suggest that realism has lost its contemporary vitality. Although no more recent realist has the stature of a Waltz, let alone a Morgenthau, Kennan, or Niebuhr, much fine realist work is still being produced. John Mearsheimer has been especially combative and provocative. See especially Mearsheimer (1990; 1994/95). Randall Schweller (1994; 1996; Schweller and Priess 1997) has made creative efforts to reintroduce some of the insights of "classic" realism and integrate them into a richer structuralism. Three of Waltz' students, Stephen Walt (1987; 1996), Barry Posen (1984; 1996/97), and Stephen Van Evera (1999; 1985) have made major contributions. Frankel (1996a; 1996b) and Brown, Lynn-Jones, and Miller (1995) are excellent collections of recent realist writings drawn from the journals *Security Studies* and *International Security*, which readers interested in the latest developments should consult regularly.

If anarchy and egoism are the central features of realism, it is a largely arbitrary decision whether we begin our more detailed discussion with one or the other. I have chosen to start with realist analyses of human nature and state motivation, in part because structural realists suggest that they are unnecessary. I will argue, however, that motives matter centrally to all realist theories. Furthermore, the standard accounts of biological and structural realists are surprisingly similar and profoundly inadequate.

Fear, honor, and interest

Nearly all of our realist paradigms place fear, honor, and interest at the core of human nature and state motivation. As we saw in chapter 1, Thucydides' Athenian envoys at the Congress of Lacedaemon seek to justify their empire by arguing that "it was not a very remarkable action, or contrary to the common practice of mankind, if we accepted an empire that was offered to us, and refused to give it up under the pressure of three of the strongest motives, fear, honor, and interest" (I.76).[1] Hobbes, in *Leviathan*, uses remarkably similar language. "In the nature of man, we find three principall causes of quarrell. First, Competition; Secondly, Diffidence; Thirdly, Glory" (ch. 13, par. 6).[2] Machiavelli likewise speaks of "the things that lead men to the end that each has before him, that is, glories and riches" and of "the distribution of honors and of property than which man esteems nothing more highly" (P25[2], DI.37[2]; compare DIII.6[4, 5]).[3] And one of Machiavelli's best-known maxims

---

[1] All references to Thucydides' *History* are by book and chapter. Translations are from Thucydides (1982), except those identified as "[Smith]," which are by C. F. Smith in the Loeb Classical Library edition, Thucydides (1919–23).

[2] All references to Hobbes' *Leviathan* are by chapter and paragraph in the C. B. Macpherson edition (Hobbes 1986).

[3] Most citations of Machiavelli are incorporated into the text as follows: P = *The Prince*, by chapter and paragraph in the Mansfield translation (Machiavelli 1985); D = *The Discourses [on the First Ten Books of Livy]*, by book, chapter, and paragraph in Crick's revised Walker translation (Machiavelli 1970).

states that "it is much safer to be feared than loved" (P17[3]; compare DIII.21[2]).

This motivational triad can be found in twentieth-century realists as well. For example, Morgenthau's three basic strategies of the struggle for power – policies of the status quo, imperialism, and prestige (1954: chs. 4–6) – seek, in Hobbes' language, safety, gain, and reputation. Somewhat more narrowly, Waltz argues that states "at a minimum, seek their own preservation and, at a maximum, drive for universal domination" (1979: 118). Preservation suggests acting out of fear. Universal domination is the most extreme expression of a desire for gain. This is very similar to Henry Kissinger's (1957) distinction between revolutionary and status quo states.[4]

Almost all the motives to which realists characteristically appeal can be fit, more or less comfortably, into (at least one of) these three categories. More important for my purposes, however, is the fact that each has decidedly different political implications. Fear is an essentially defensive motive; the central aim is to preserve what one already has. As Hobbes in *Leviathan* observes, diffidence leads to invasion for "Safety." Competition, however, "maketh men invade for Gain"; it is fundamentally acquisitive. The pursuit of glory leads men to invade for "reputation" (ch. 13, par. 7). Although competitive, the goal is status or recognition, not material gain.

This chapter emphasizes the political differences associated with the pursuit of these three motives. It also documents the surprising complexity and diversity among realist accounts of human nature and state motivation. In the concluding section, I begin to draw preliminary conclusions about the character and contribution of realist theories of international relations.

Human nature and biological realism

Because biological realists directly engage issues of human nature, we will begin with them in this chapter. Hans Morgenthau, probably the best-known and most influential biological realist, will be our principal focus.[5]

The national interest defined in terms of power

As we saw in the preceding chapter, the first two of Morgenthau's six "principles" of political realism are the existence of "objective [political]

---

[4] Compare Carr (1946: 53, 103–105, 208); Aron (1966: ch. 3); Wolfers (1962: 125–126).
[5] See pp. 11–12 for an overview of biological realist theories, and pp. 15–16 for Morgenthau's theory in particular.

laws that have their roots in human nature" and the centrality of "the concept of interest defined in terms of power" (1954: 4, 5). Morgenthau sees the national interest as a fact to be discovered rather than a matter of contingent and constructed preferences. And these objective interests prescribe the substance of responsible foreign policy. Thus the second of Morgenthau's four "fundamental rules" of diplomacy is that "*the objectives of foreign policy must be defined in terms of the national interest and must be supported with adequate power*" (1948: 440).

For Morgenthau, there is a "logically required connection between interest and foreign policy" (1962a: 93). "We assume that statesmen think and act in terms of interest defined as power, and the evidence of history bears that assumption out" (Morgenthau 1954: 5). States "cannot help pursuing policies designed to serve their national interests" (Morgenthau 1962b: 121). These sweeping pronouncements, however, represent a combination of uninteresting tautology, vague and unhelpful generalities, and patent absurdity.

It is hardly controversial to claim that states usually pursue their perceived interests. If we emphasize "perceived" and understand "interest" broadly, this may even be true by definition — and thus profoundly unilluminating. Random and intentionally self-destructive behavior is ruled out, but this definition allows such decidedly "unrealistic" practices as identifying one's interests with "the human interest," justice, morality, or religion, as well as acting out of compassion, loyalty, friendship, or a sense of legal obligation. The substantive bite to Morgenthau's theory comes instead from the claim that states ought to, even must, define their interests in terms of power; that is, a particular substantive claim about how they perceive their interests.

Morgenthau's criticisms of American foreign policy,[6] however, imply that at least one great power for over half a century did *not* so define (many of) its interests. In fact, most states seem to pursue the welfare and prosperity of their citizens, or some class of citizens, largely independent of considerations of power. Oligarchies thus are often criticized for sacrificing the *national* interest in favor of the particular interests of a

---

[6] For example, one chapter of *In Defense of the National Interest* (1951) is titled "The Four Intellectual Errors of American Postwar Policy" (moralism, legalism, sentimentalism, and neo-isolationism), and the final three chapters are titled "The Failure of Judgment: in Europe," "The Failure of Judgment: in Asia," and "The Failure of Will." Morgenthau's essays include titles such as "The Decline and Fall of American Foreign Policy," "What is Wrong with Our Foreign Policy" (1962b), "The Subversion of Foreign Policy," and even "The Problem of the National Interest" (1962a). One volume of essays even begins by claiming that "it is the purpose of this book to lay bare the inner weakness of American foreign policy, both in its overall conception and in its responses to the concrete issues of the day" (1962a: 2).

ruling elite. Democracies are often chastised, by realists in particular, for subordinating vital national interests to short-term political or economic advantages, passing fads, and moral goals.[7] States simply do not, even as a rough first approximation, seek (only) power.

Even where states do pursue power, Morgenthau's account is hopelessly vague.

A political policy seeks either to keep power, to increase power, or to demonstrate power . . . A nation whose foreign policy tends toward keeping power and not toward changing the distribution of power in its favor pursues a policy of the status quo. A nation whose foreign policy . . . seeks a favorable change in power status pursues a policy of imperialism. A nation whose foreign policy seeks to demonstrate the power it has, either for the purpose of maintaining or increasing it, pursues a policy of prestige (1985: 52–53).

Unfortunately, Morgenthau offers no theoretical account of when and why a state will chose one strategy over another.

For example, Morgenthau argues that policies of imperialism – what Kissinger calls "revolutionary" policies – arise primarily out of victory in war, defeat in war, and opportunities presented by the weakness of others (1985: 67–69). In other words, success, failure, and opportunity characteristically trigger imperialism. This is not very illuminating. Furthermore, not all victorious powers seek to overthrow the status quo *ante bellum*. The Congress of Vienna – where France was largely restored to its prewar situation, despite having fought against much of the rest of Europe for much of the preceding quarter-century – provides a classic example of victorious great powers declining territorial aggrandizement. Many great powers have been satisfied to coexist with, rather than seek to conquer, weaker neighbors, as the continued existence of Canada indicates.

Morgenthau's theory simply cannot tell us whether a state will seek safety or gain, prefer to attack or to defend, accept or eschew the risks of expansion.[8] This indeterminacy is theoretically fatal because these objec-

---

[7] For example, Morgenthau bemoans "the incompatibility between the rational requirements of a sound foreign policy and the emotional preferences of a democratically controlled public opinion" (1962c: 106) and laments "the corrupting effects that considerations of domestic politics can exert upon the conduct of foreign policy" (1962a: 409). "The conduct of American foreign policy suffers from the handicap that our constitutional system compels us to live continuously in the shadow of past or future elections" (1962b: 8). Likewise, Reinhold Niebuhr speaks of the "natural weakness of democratic government in the field of foreign policy" (1940: 65), because democracies have a more difficult time anticipating the future and making necessary sacrifices.

[8] There is one special case where Morgenthau would seem to have a determinate answer. Defeated and subordinated great powers are strongly inclined to prefer "imperialism," that is, a fundamental alteration in their favor of the terms of relations with a dominating victor.

tives separately may imply radically different policies and together cover an immense range of possible behaviors. Morgenthau's three strategies, rather than explaining state actions, merely provide a typology for categorizing a wide array of divergent, even contradictory, behaviors.

The will to power

Most states are indeed strongly inclined to seek power. Pursuing goals other than the national interest defined in terms of power often is dangerous, even counterproductive. But even Morgenthau's case for these lesser (although still important) claims is undermined by an exaggerated emphasis on a one-sided account of human nature.

The pursuit of power, Morgenthau argues, is an inescapable consequence of the "elemental bio-psychological drives . . . to live, to propagate, and to dominate [that] are common to all men" (1948: 16–17). "All men lust for power" (1962a: 42). "Man's aspiration for power is not an accident of history; it is not a temporary deviation from a normal state of freedom; it is an all-permeating fact which is of the very essence of human existence" (1948: 312).

This appeal to a natural will to power – "the *animus dominandi*, the desire for power" (1946: 192) – puts a particularly stark face on Morgenthau's realism. "It is this ubiquity of the desire for power which, besides and beyond any particular selfishness or other evil purpose, constitutes the ubiquity of evilness in human action" (1946: 194). Even if we could overcome the Hobbesian drives of competition, diffidence, and glory, we would still lust after power.

Beneath all else, and even setting aside the instrumental value of power, Morgenthau sees man – in a dark twist on Aristotle's famous definition of man as a political animal (*zoon politikon*) – as a power-seeking animal. In an equally dark twist on Rousseau's observation that man is born free but everywhere lives in chains, Morgenthau claims that "man lives in chains, but everywhere he wants to be a master" (1962a: 312). "The aspiration for liberty and equality is only the first phase of a struggle for power in which those who are oppressed want first to be equal with their oppressors and, once they have achieved this equality, want to oppress their equals" (1962a: 196).

This line of argument suggests an unusually strong biological realism. "The power of man over man [is] an ineluctable outgrowth of human nature" (1962c: 7). "The social world [is] but a projection of human nature onto the collective plane," simply "man writ large" (1962a: 7). Political problems are "projections of human nature into society" (1962a: 313).

Reinhold Niebuhr likewise emphasizes "the natural egoistic impulse with which all life is endowed" (1934: 198), "the perennial and persistent character of human egoism in any possible society" (1944: 79). For Niebuhr, "the ultimate sources of social conflicts and injustice are to be found in the ignorance and selfishness of men" (1932: 23). He even argues that "the will-to-power of competing national groups is the cause of the international anarchy which the moral sense of mankind has thus far vainly striven to overcome" (1932: 18–19).

Human nature and power politics

Rooting power politics principally in human nature makes realism a theory of politics in general, rather than a theory of international relations. If "the aspiration for power over man . . . is the essence of politics" (Morgenthau 1946: 45), if "politics is rivalry for control over the instruments of power" (Schuman 1941: 7), then we blur the lines between national and international politics.

Some realists accept such a conclusion. For example, Niebuhr's most influential book, *Moral Man and Immoral Society* (1932), stresses the tragic inability of *all* social groups to give the weight to moral concerns that individuals typically do in (some of) their personal relations. Frederick Schuman, drawing the obvious conclusion from his claim that "all politics is a struggle for power" (1941: 261), analyzed the national interest as nothing more than the selfish interests of the dominant groups in a state (1941: 263–264). More recently, Ashley Tellis (1995/96: 89–94) has suggested that realism should be seen as a general theory of politics based on a universal drive for domination.

Morgenthau too argues that "the desire to dominate . . . is a constitutive element of all human associations" (1948: 17). "Domestic and international politics are but two different manifestations of the same phenomenon: the struggle for power . . . The difference between domestic and international politics . . . is one of degree and not of kind" (1985: 52).

Yet Morgenthau's most famous book, *Politics Among Nations*, by its very title suggests a categorical distinction between national and international politics. Most other realists also recognize – and structural realists emphasize – a qualitative difference between anarchic and hierarchic political orders, "between politics conducted in a condition of settled rules and politics conducted in a condition of anarchy" (Waltz 1979: 61). Hobbes' sovereign allows individuals within a polity to escape the war of all against all that continues to dominate relations between states.

Such a categorical distinction between national and international politics is also implied in the characteristic realist attacks on international justice and other foreign policy concerns beyond interest defined in terms of power. Even if one accepts realist amoralism as a regrettable necessity in international relations, it is descriptively inaccurate and prescriptively perverse in national politics. Extremely repressive dictatorships do suggest that the similarities between national and international politics may be as striking as the differences when hierarchic rule rests on little more than superior power. But history presents us with many examples of the sort of relatively humane national politics that realists argue is impossible internationally. For example, politics in the liberal democratic welfare states of Northern Europe over the past several decades has been shaped by an expansive conception of social justice.

Only by focusing on anarchy can we account for both the predominance of power in international relations – assuming, for the moment, that this is indeed true – and the undeniable possibilities for the considerable subordination of power to law, order, and perhaps even justice in domestic politics. International relations may approximate a Hobbesian state of nature. In domestic politics, however, it is the exception rather than the rule, even in highly repressive regimes, for individuals to lead lives that are solitary, poor, nasty, brutish, and short. States, by providing considerable personal security, allow individuals to act on Hobbes' "passions that encline men to peace," as well as other "higher" desires and values. By enforcing rules of cooperation, hierarchic political orders allow even selfish actors to escape the Prisoners' Dilemma. Realism *as a theory of international politics* cannot rely primarily on human nature.

Anarchy, power, and international politics

If power politics is at the heart of international relations, it is largely because of international anarchy. Natural desire may be an additional reason that states seek power. The predominance of egoistic desires in others may dramatically intensify the fearful pursuit of power. Anarchy, however, must be a central part of the explanation for the predominance of power politics in international relations. Thus Morgenthau's strong assumptions about the will to power are unnecessary – and the principle of theoretical parsimony enjoins us never to make controversial assumptions that are unnecessary to reach our conclusions.

Anarchy creates strong tendencies to power politics without the need to make unusually strong assumptions about the corruption of human nature. One need assume only that enough egoists exist to force others to behave (somewhat) like them. If the diffident and competitive are regularly rewarded with greater security and success than the trustful and cooperative, anarchy will push states towards a power politics of self-interested conflict, irrespective of their preferences.

Morgenthau's will to power is also substantively implausible. A natural desire to dominate may be *one* reason that states seek power. For example, Henry Kissinger is reputed to have called power the ultimate aphrodisiac. But power is not desired primarily, let alone exclusively, for itself. Even selfish interests cannot be reduced to power. Wealth, for example, is usually desired for the pleasures, not (merely or even primarily) the power, that it brings.

Power can be used to acquire, or at least improve the prospect of one's access to, many – realists might say most – objects of desire. But to the (considerable) extent that states seek power for instrumental reasons, the ends for which power is sought, not power itself, drive foreign policy. To define the national interest in terms of power largely confuses means with ends.

The failure of the structural dodge

If anarchy is essential to any plausible realist theory of international politics, can it *alone* account for realist power politics? Structural realism can be seen as an attempt to push this possibility as far and as hard as possible, thereby circumventing the theoretical problems posed not just by Morgenthau's particular account but by any substantive theory of human nature. As we focused on Morgenthau in the preceding section, here we will focus on Kenneth Waltz, the leading structural realist of the past two decades.[9]

The structural dodge

The idea of "states in anarchy," abstracting from both the attributes of states and their interactions (Waltz 1979: 80), lies at the heart of contemporary structural (neo)realism. As Waltz puts it, we can say "a small number of big and important things" (1986: 329) about the behavior of (any) states knowing only that they interact in anarchy. This chapter focuses on structuralist efforts to "abstract from every attribute of states except their capabilities" (Waltz 1979: 99), reflected in Waltz' language of "units," characterless political entities.

We know, of course, that states have a great variety of particular interests that motivate their behavior. Structuralists, however, look for deep

[9] See pp. 10–12 for an overview of structural realist theories, and pp. 16–18 for Waltz' theory in particular. The realist conception of structure is outlined on pp. 16–17 and discussed further on pp. 83–85.

patterns, law-like regularities, that arise from the common predicament of international anarchy. To be able to say some important things about international relations without knowing or assuming anything of substance of the motives or interests of states would indeed be a theoretical achievement of considerable practical value.

I argue, however, that this "structural dodge"[10] – the attempt to circumvent the need for a substantive account of state motivation through an appeal to anarchy – cannot succeed. Motives cannot be left out of structural theories. Even the most rigorously structural theory requires a substantive account of state motivation.

Motives matter

Waltz justifies abstracting from state motives or interests through an analogy with microeconomics. "An international-political theory does not imply or require a theory of foreign policy any more than a market theory implies or requires a theory of the firm" (1979: 72). But he is mistaken in thinking that this means no theory at all. "Market theory does not deal with characteristics of firms" (1996: 55), in the sense that characteristics are assumed rather than explained. But as Waltz himself notes, "economists think of the acting unit, the famous 'economic man,' as a single-minded profit maximizer" (1979: 89). In fact, all the predictions of neoclassical economics arise from the fact that it "assumes that men are profit maximizers" (1996: 55).

A structural theory of international politics must likewise make motivational assumptions. International structure alone – which, recall, for Waltz means only the distribution of capabilities in anarchy (1979: 88–99) – predicts nothing. Structural forces may impinge on all actors. But the consequences of structure are *not* independent of the character of the actors. State motives are not "background noise," perturbing influences, or "intervening variables."

As we saw above, Hobbes' war of all against all arises not simply from anarchy but because equal individuals driven by competition, diffidence, and glory interact in anarchy. In the face of any particular anarchic structure, Homeric heroes seeking glory through great deeds, Nietzschean individuals driven by a will to power, and *homo economicus* all may behave differently from each other – and from Hobbesian egoists driven by a fear of violent death. As Herbert Butterfield colorfully puts it, "wars would

---

[10] This terminology is combative but I believe descriptive. Structuralism has been deeply influenced by the desire to evade (dodge) the problems associated with substantive theories of state motivation. And the pejorative overtones of the term are justified if I am correct about the futility of this effort.

hardly be likely to occur if all men were Christian saints, competing with one another in nothing, perhaps, save self-renunciation" (McIntire 1979: 73).

The Prisoners' Dilemma (PD), which is often used to elucidate the logic of realism,[11] arises from particular actor preferences. If unilateral cooperation is preferred to mutual defection, PD becomes "Chicken," a game with a very different strategic logic. If mutual cooperation is preferred to free-riding, the game becomes "Stag Hunt," where rational actors will (in certain circumstances) cooperate rather than compete.[12] And these variations occur despite a constant structure (distribution of capabilities in anarchy).

"Structurally we can describe and understand the pressures states are subject to. We cannot predict how they will react to the pressures without knowledge of their internal dispositions" (Waltz 1979: 71). But without knowing how states are expected to respond to the pressure they face, what use is the theory? To abstract from *all* attributes of states (other than capabilities) leaves a theory no predictive or explanatory power.

Waltz therefore, sensibly but inconsistently, does not. Rather than "take states with whatever traditions, habits, objectives, desires, and forms of government they may have" (1979: 99), he makes substantive motivational assumptions. "The theory is based on assumptions about states" (1996: 54). "The motivation of the actors is assumed" (1979: 91).

There is a profound difference between abstracting from all particulars and assuming certain ones. Assuming that firms seek to maximize profits is to abstract from all *other* motives, not from all motives. Waltz likewise must make particular substantive assumptions about the motives or interests of states. And the substance of those assumptions gives much of the character to his theory.

Survival

It would be a relatively minor matter to allow structural realists simple, clear, and coherent substantive assumptions about state motivation. And Waltz does repeatedly claim to assume a single motive: survival. "I built structural theory on the assumption that survival is the goal of states" (1997: 913). States "are unitary actors with a single motive – the wish to survive" (1996: 54). "The survival motive is taken as the ground of action." "By assumption, economic actors seek to maximize expected

[11] See pp. 19–23.
[12] On these and other two-by-two games relevant to international relations, see Snyder and Diesing (1977: 37–52, 88–101) and Jervis (1978: 170–186).

returns, and states strive to secure their survival." "I assume that states seek to ensure their survival" (1979: 92, 134, 91).[13]

Such an assumption, however, makes war unlikely and inexplicable. If all states value only survival – as they must if survival is the sole motive assumed in the theory – there will be no aggression to impel survival-seekers to fight. This would be, as Randall Schweller puts it, "a world of all cops and no robbers" (1996: 91). At least one state seeking new acquisitions is necessary to generate the realist world of inescapable conflict and fear of violent death. "What triggers security dilemmas under anarchy is the possibility of predatory states existing among the ranks of the units the system comprises. Anarchy and self-preservation alone are not sufficient to explain the war of all against all" (Schweller 1996: 91).

An appeal to uncertainty, which is at the heart of the logic of the security dilemma,[14] does not help. Uncertainty can only lead to conflict when at least one state is known or suspected to pursue acquisitive gain rather than survival – a situation that is ruled out by (abstracted from in) this specification of the model.

It simply is not true that "balance-of-power politics prevails wherever two, and only two, requirements are met: that the order be anarchic and that it be populated by units wishing to survive" (Waltz 1979: 121). Moralists and imperialists, for example, usually wish to survive but will not necessarily balance power. At least two other conditions must be met: (1) survival must be (perceived to be) at stake; and (2) those whose survival is at stake will not risk it for other values or interests.

Waltz seems to be at least vaguely aware of this when he says that the assumption of survival "allows for the fact that some states may persistently seek goals that they value more highly than survival" (1979: 92) – and thus may not pursue balance of power policies. But allowing for the existence of other motives, let alone motives that override survival, effectively abandons the microeconomic model.

The economist's assumption of profit maximization treats other motives as if they did not exist. Assuming profit maximization does *not* allow other interests to be valued more highly *within the theory* (whatever the facts may be in the world). And the rigor of neoclassical economics comes in large measure from this radical simplifying assumption.

---

[13] The assumption of survival as an overriding motive is also common among "classical" realists. For example, Henry Kissinger argues that the statesman's "first goal is survival" and in counseling against the temptations of moralist idealism warns us that we should not "substitute wishful thinking for the requirements of survival" (1977: 46, 204). Nicholas Spykman likewise argues that "the struggle for power," which he sees as the essence of international relations, "is identical with the struggle for survival" (1942: 18). Morgenthau even goes so far as to speak of "the moral principle of national survival" (1954: 9).   [14] See p. 20.

Assuming only survival, though, leads to an obviously inadequate theory. As we have already seen, if all states sought (only) survival, in any strong and direct sense of that term, there would be no aggression, no war, and no conflict. And as Schweller notes, "many large-scale wars were initiated by precisely those states that valued expansion more than their safety" (1996: 106). If a realist theory cannot even get that much right, it is unlikely to be of very much use or interest.

Multiple motivational assumptions

Realism becomes more plausible, at least on its face, if survival is seen as a primary, but not the sole, motive of states. For example, when John Mearsheimer writes that "the most basic motive driving states is survival" (1994/95: 10), that "a state can have no higher goal than survival" (1990: 44), he means only that states will choose survival in cases of conflict with other interests, not that they are for the purposes of theory assumed to pursue only survival. Likewise, Joseph Grieco's claim that states "must have survival as independent agents as their primary interest" is not meant to imply that he abstracts from all other state interests (1988b: 602).

Such a change in the place of survival, however, may lead to very different predictions – especially in a world where survival is not very often at stake. And once the gate is open, a whole range of additional motives rush in.

Realists commonly conflate survival with independence, autonomy, or sovereignty. For example, Waltz argues that states "strive to maintain their autonomy" and "work to maintain a measure of independence and may even strive for autarky" (1979: 204, 104). Mearsheimer adds that "states want to maintain their sovereignty" (1994/95: 10). Stephen Krasner identifies the core interest of states as "territorial and political integrity" (1978: 13, 41). And Andrew Kydd defines "elimination" (failure to survive) as a state being "deprived of sovereignty, and its territory and population made subject to another state (or states)" (1997: 121).

Political units, however, can survive in anarchy without being sovereign or independent, just as individuals can survive when enslaved or imprisoned. This is the choice, for example, that Athens' realist envoys offer the Melians in Thucydides' *History*. Sovereignty and survival are (subtly yet fundamentally) different concepts that today are nearly perfectly correlated but often have not been. Separate political units in tributary systems such as the Chinese or Ottoman empires lacked sovereignty (and "full" independence). In feudal Europe and Japan, separate political units sought to preserve an existence that was not sovereign. Nineteenth and early twentieth-century international law devoted extensive attention to numerous forms of "imperfect" sovereignty.[15]

Realists also postulate more acquisitive motives. Waltz provides an extreme example when he claims to build his theory on the assumption that states "at minimum, seek their own preservation and, at maximum, drive for universal domination" (1979: 118). If this passage does not directly contradict the claim to assume *only* that states seek survival, Waltz must see survival and domination as fundamentally similar motives. This odd possibility is suggested by the use of the language of minimum and maximum, which can be read to imply quantitative variation along a single dimension.

Survival, however, is not a small quantity of domination, nor is domination a surplus of survival. They are qualitatively different ends that often imply conflicting behavior. A drive for domination, for example, is likely to risk survival. Lacking a political equivalent of money, a common measure with which to compare relative values attached to these disparate goods, a quantity of one simply cannot be converted into a quantity of the other. Without additional substantive assumptions we cannot even rank state preferences for survival and domination.

No less problematic is the fact that the area "between" survival and domination cannot be plausibly represented as either a lot of survival or a little domination. It is something else as well – actually, *many* other things. Therefore, this vast range of state goals, which encompasses most of international relations, falls outside a survival-domination model.

It is not surprising, then, that Waltz imputes a variety of additional motives to states, introducing ever growing motivational confusion. "The first concern of states is . . . to maintain their positions in the system" (1979: 126). Preserving one's relative position, however, is neither survival nor domination. It is obviously inconsistent with domination (except for hegemons). And preserving one's position may require risking survival.

"Pride knows no nationality." "Over time, unbalanced power will be checked by the responses of the weaker who will, rightly or not, feel put upon" (Waltz 1993: 66, 79). Pride and feeling put upon are matters of reputation or esteem, not survival, domination, autonomy, or position.

"In the European-centered politics of the three centuries that ended with World War II, five or more great powers sought to coexist peacefully and at times contended for mastery" (Waltz 1979: 144). Peaceful coexistence, however, is neither survival nor independence, and is a very particular kind of "security." In addition, peace is sometimes valued

[15] See pp. 139–143 for further development of some of these examples.

independently. As Waltz observes, states share a "concern for peace and stability" (1979: 175).

The simple pursuit of gain must also be prominent in any plausible set of motivational assumptions. "Countries have always competed for wealth and security" (Waltz 1993: 54). "Internationally, the force of a state is employed for the sake of its own protection and advantage" (1979: 112). "States develop along certain lines and acquire certain characteristics in order to survive and flourish in the system" (1986: 337). Wealth, advantage, and flourishing are neither a small quantity of domination nor a large quantity of survival. They are objectives of a different order.

These varied motives share a "realist" emphasis on self-interest. But predicted behavior may differ dramatically depending on whether states seek to survive, maintain their relative positions in the system, increase their strength, preserve their autonomy, coexist peacefully, improve their welfare, respond to slights, or achieve universal domination. And Waltz, like most other realists, shifts from motive to motive entirely without theoretical justification.

A complex, many-sided, account of state motivation is in itself not a theoretical problem. One might even suggest that any general theory of international politics is likely to prove profoundly inadequate if it does not recognize considerable complexity in state interests and objectives. But Waltz like Morgenthau lacks a theoretical account of which motive will prevail when. Therefore, when faced by multiple and inconsistent "realist" predictions, realism – and above all structural realism – provides no theoretical basis for choosing among them.

It is important to note that this discussion does not confuse "foreign policy" – particular, unit-based, internal explanations or forces – with structural accounts of international politics (Waltz 1996). Using Waltz' own accounts, we have seen that a structural theory of international politics, as developed by the structural theorist most committed to abstracting from the attributes of states, simply cannot get by without substantive motivational assumptions.[16]

Realism as grand theory

Three strategies for addressing this mess seem promising: (1) find some broader coherence in these multiple motivational assumptions about

---

[16] Were I to canvass other realists, the range of motives appealed to would increase even further. I have relied on Waltz to show that a single theorist, who is regularly commended for his rigor and deeply committed to abstracting from unit attributes, gets into – and later I will suggest cannot help but get into – such a motivational muddle.

states; (2) develop a consistent realist theory based on a single motive or coherent set of motives; (3) recognizing multiple and variable motives, develop multiple, not necessarily consistent, "realist" theories.

Attempts to find a deeper coherence generally see realism as a general theory with relatively grand aspirations. Pursuing the development of multiple, even competing, realist models, by contrast, treats realism instead as a philosophical orientation or paradigmatic "research program."[17] In this section I critically examine prominent recent efforts of the first type. At the end of the chapter I begin to address the second.

Both Waltz and Morgenthau, the leading figures of the two dominant strands of twentieth-century American realism, seek a general theory of international politics based on law-like behavioral regularities. Morgenthau pursues "the eternal laws by which man moves in the social world" (1946: 220). Similarly, Waltz stresses "the striking sameness in the quality of international life throughout the millennia" and seeks to explain "why different units behave similarly . . . despite their variations" (1979: 66, 72).[18]

Such a project seems plausible in part because Morgenthau and Waltz treat human nature or state motivation as theoretically unproblematic. For Morgenthau, human nature is constant and readily known. "Human nature, in which the laws of politics have their roots, has not changed since the classical philosophers of China, India, and Greece endeavored to discover [its] laws" (1954: 4). Along the same lines, Morgenthau's student and collaborator Kenneth Thompson argues that "human nature has not changed since the days of classical antiquity" (1985: 17). For Waltz, abstraction from the particulars of state interests depends on anarchy imposing a certain constancy in state behavior, at least in the aggregate. As Mearsheimer puts it, "in the final analysis, the system forces states to behave according to the dictates of realism, or risk destruction" (1995: 91).

In contrast to such suggestions that we can profitably talk about "states" in general, in the abstract, I will argue that state motivation is inescapably variable, not constant. Therefore, realism, especially structural realism, cannot serve as a general theory of international relations.

---

[17] Although strategies that consistently postulate a single motive may seem to point towards general theory, in practice they lead in the other direction.

[18] Waltz is too careful (coy?) to use the definite article in the title of *Theory of International Politics*. He is no less careful, however, not to use the indefinite article – compare, for example, John Rawls' *A Theory of Justice* – suggesting at least an aspiration to provide *the* theory of international politics.

Absolute versus relative gains

A number of recent theorists have suggested that realism is distinguished by its emphasis on "relative gains." For example, Stephen Walt, in his recent survey of international relations theory, identifies the focus on relative gains as one of realism's most important contributions to the discipline (1998: 35).[19] The central claim is that states aim not simply to increase their (absolute) wealth, power, or utility, but to increase the *gap* between their own holdings (of wealth, power, or whatever) and those of other states. "One of the key insights of the realist approach to international relations is that nation-states are consistently sensitive to considerations of relative gain and advantage" (Mastanduno 1991: 78).[20]

The pursuit of relative gains is usually seen to arise from anarchy, and the resulting fear for survival, independence, or security. Waltz, for example, argues that states in anarchy

> are compelled to ask not "Will both of us gain?" but "Who will gain more?" If an expected gain is to be divided, say, in the ratio of two to one, one state may use its disproportionate gain to implement a policy intended to damage or destroy the other. Even the prospect of large absolute gains for both parties does not elicit their cooperation so long as each fears how the other will use its increased capabilities (1979: 105).[21]

But from structure alone we cannot know how intense that fear will be.

Consider a series of similar claims from a well-known article by Mearsheimer (1990: 44–45). "When security is scarce, states become more concerned about relative gains than absolute gains." But when *is* security "scarce"? And *how much* more concerned will they be? "Anarchy forces states to reject agreements that result in asymmetrical payoffs that shift the balance of power against them." Rarely, though, will asymmetrical payoffs shift the balance of power. What can we expect when they *do not* shift the balance? "Since a state can have no higher goal than survival, when push comes to shove, international political considerations will be paramount in the minds of decision-makers." But how often *does* push come to shove? And when it does not, what force do relative gains considerations have? Without answers to such questions – which anarchy cannot provide – we usually will be at a loss to know when to assume that states will seek relative gains.

---

[19] Grieco (1988a) triggered much of the recent discussion. Snidal (1991a; 1991b; 1993) and Powell (1991; 1993a; 1993b) are the standard critiques. I take my arguments here to be largely variations on or extensions of their arguments, without the microeconomic and game theoretical apparatus that is central to their presentation.

[20] Compare Waltz (1979: 80), Waltz (1993: 49), Hoffman (1973: 8–9), Schuman (1941: 41).

[21] Compare Grieco (1988a: 487), Grieco (1988b: 602), Mearsheimer (1990: 12), Mastanduno (1991: 78).

Grieco's argument that "anarchy and the danger of war cause all states always to be motivated in some measure by fear and distrust" (1988a: 498) similarly dodges the crucial issue of what that measure is. A lot of greed often will overpower a little fear. Grieco may be correct that "the coefficient for a state's sensitivity to gaps in payoffs . . . will vary, but it will always be greater than zero" (1988a: 501). If low, however, the impact of this sensitivity may be negligible, especially in the presence of substantial absolute gains.

In much the same vein, Mearsheimer (1994/95: 11) argues that "although the level of fear varies across time and space, it can never be reduced to a trivial level." But it simply is not true that in some relations the level cannot be trivial. Consider, for example, the United States and Canada.[22] And even accepting Mearsheimer's claim, we can expect very different behaviors from states gripped by an overpowering Hobbesian fear of violent death and those under the influence of a just barely greater than trivial fear.

Even setting aside these problems, it turns out that "relative gains" usually are in fact about long-run absolute gains. For example, John Matthews argues that states will be concerned "if a relative gain in a current round of interaction creates advantages that allow additional gains in future rounds" (1996: 114). In the Waltz quote above as well, future damage or destruction – absolute losses – drives current concerns with "relative gains." And Michael Mastanduno, examining American responses to Japanese industrial policy, found that in economic relations with Japan, American "relative gains" concerns "reflected primarily anxiety over US economic welfare," and that "America's growing financial dependence on Japan . . . has the potential to reduce the future real income of the United States" (1991: 75, 77). The real issue, in other words, was future absolute gain (welfare, real income).

Grieco (1997: 175) suggests that Mastanduno's findings support the relative gains hypothesis. But in his discussion, he confuses competition over the distribution of gains with the pursuit of relative gains. Those pursuing absolute gains will also compete over how much gain they acquire. To take the classic market example, buyers and sellers compete over prices, and often refuse to consummate a sale, because the price they are offered is too high or too low. This is competition over the distribution of gains in a pure absolute gains context. They are simply seeking to maximize their returns, irrespective of the impact on their wealth or income relative to each other or anyone else. The fact that states compete over the distribution of gains simply does not establish that they are pursuing relative gains.

[22] This issue is addressed in greater detail at pp. 136–137.

Most examples of alleged relative gains seeking involve states desiring more, absolutely, not just (or even primarily) more than their rivals. States seek "relative gains" principally because of their effects on long-term absolute gains.

Power, balancing, and maximizing

Part of this confusion about the very character of "relative gains" would seem to arise from the relativity of power. Power depends as much on the capabilities of others as on one's own. Armed with a machine gun, I have considerable power against an opponent armed only with a kitchen knife. But facing an armored battalion, the same material capabilities (my machine gun) provide me with little power.

The pursuit of power thus defined does not involve "maximizing" as we usually think of it. The goal is not to have as much as possible of some thing but rather to improve one's standing relative to someone else. This would seem to be what Waltz has in mind when he claims that "the first concern of states is not to maximize power" (1979: 126). To maintain or improve one's relative power position often will require balancing rather than maximizing capabilities.

Nonetheless, capabilities are absolute. And there are good reasons why states may seek absolute increases in their capabilities independent of relative gains considerations. Furthermore, in addition to capabilities, the power calculus of states must also take into account motives.

Waltz' claim that "states balance power rather than maximize it" (Waltz 1979: 127) simply does not follow from anarchy alone. In addition, we must assume that states (1) are fearful rather than competitive, and either (2) fear all other states more or less equally, or (3) value absolute gains only to the extent that they do not even marginally reduce relative position. If *every* objective of states is judged by its contribution to the balance of capabilities, balancing can be expected to be the norm. If *all* power in the hands of others is threatening, then states will balance rather than "bandwagon."[23] But under less extreme assumptions, balancing cannot be assumed.

We know that states do not balance against *all* concentrations of capabilities. At most, they balance against *threatening* capabilities – which is in significant measure a matter of perceived intentions. Not every gap created by differential distributions of absolute gain is perceived as threatening. And these are not isolated or unsystematic exceptions to the rule, but patterns of no less importance than the "law-like regularity" of balancing.

---

[23] On the metaphor of bandwagoning, see p. 18, n. 10.

The logic of balancing sees the victor not as a potential source of shared gain, but as a rising threat likely to turn on her "allies" when the opportunity presents itself. "Balancers" attempt to reduce their risks by siding with the weaker party. They focus not on the chance for (absolute) gain but on the gap in capabilities and the dangerous uses to which a rising power might put its (relative) superiority. But such a logic flows only from particular substantive assumptions about both the balancer and her adversaries. The overwhelming power of fear that leads to balancing arises not simply from anarchy but from very particular assumed motives.

In different circumstances, or under different assumptions, states, as Schweller has clearly shown, regularly and in patterned ways "bandwagon" as well as balance; that is, side with a stronger or rising power, rather than against such a power.[24] "The question of whether balancing is more common than bandwagoning is a misleading one. They are not opposite behaviors. The motivation for bandwagoning is fundamentally different from that of balancing" (Schweller 1994: 106).

In other words, the fact that power is relative does not necessarily lead states to pursue relative gains (balance). Capabilities, which are an element of power, are absolute. Threat, which is at the heart of the logic of balancing, is a matter of the intentions of others. The power of fear arises not only from anarchy but from one's own preferences. And gain often competes with fear.

We cannot know whether states will balance (pursue relative gains) or bandwagon (pursue absolute gains) without knowing their motivations. And there is no good reason why a general theory of international relations should assume one or the other. In fact, to the extent that it does, it excludes a large and important part of international relations from its coverage.

Another way to cut into the problem is to note that most contemporary realists see power as an instrumental value sought not because of a natural desire to dominate but for the goods and opportunities it makes available. And the principal goals that realists typically see power used to realize – e.g. survival, security, prosperity, and autonomy – are more absolute than relative goods. Maximizing absolute gains is therefore a plausible motivational assumption that Powell (1993a; 1993b) has formally demonstrated can lead to characteristic "realist" conclusions.

Realism, therefore, is not in any special way associated with the pursuit of relative gains. Glenn Snyder and Paul Diesing's *Conflict Among Nations* (1977), which is often seen as a paradigm of early neorealist work (Keohane 1986b: 175–177), assumes utility maximization (absolute

---

[24] For a quantitative analysis supporting this conclusion, see Jones (1994).

gains). And Gilpin, despite his claim that "politics is about relative gains" (1975: 35), bases *War and Change in World Politics* (1981) on the assumption of rational utility maximization; that is, absolute gains. Even Waltz, despite his denials (1986: 334), at points assumes maximization – and thus by implication the pursuit of absolute gains. For example, he explicitly argues that survival only *qualifies* the fundamental assumption of maximization (1979: 89, 105). And it is hard to understand his constant comparison with neo-classical microeconomics – e.g. "balance-of-power theory is microtheory precisely in the economist's sense" (1979: 118) – unless a maximizing pursuit of absolute gains is assumed in addition to diffident balancing.

Competition, diffidence, and indeterminate predictions

States are driven *both* by acquisitive competition for absolute gains and by diffident efforts to protect what they already have. As Duncan Snidal notes, "no sophisticated view suggests that states seek only relative gains, just as no sophisticated view argues that states seek only absolute gains" (1991a: 389). But anarchy, like human nature, remains constant while the pursuit of "relative" and absolute gains varies. Structure, therefore, cannot account for these variations. The appeal to relative gains restates, rather than resolves, the problem of *ad hoc* appeals to diverse, even contradictory, motives.

Waltz, as we have seen, oscillates between defensive fear (survival) and offensive gain (universal empire). Grieco likewise argues that the "main goal" of states is to achieve the "greatest gains *and* smallest gap in gains favoring partners" (1990: table 2.3). These are two very different goals, not one; absolute *and* relative gains. What do states do when they conflict? Anarchy provides no answer: as Hobbes so clearly shows, it facilitates both competitive invasion for gain and diffident invasion for safety.

Waltz suggests that his theory yields only "indeterminate predictions" (1979: 124, 122, 71) because it has simplified reality in order to highlight central social forces. Since no theory can explain everything, this is in principle a strong defense. In practice, however, the indeterminacy is rooted in his multiple, inconsistent assumptions.

Waltz plausibly claims that a structural theory requires us "to take firms as firms, and states as states, without paying attention to differences among them" (1979: 72). That would indeed be abstracting from (almost) all attributes. But his disparate motivational assumptions build considerable variation into his states. And as Tellis notes, by not sticking with a single, coherent, determinate account of state motivation, Waltz "succeeds in denuding his systemic approach of what is most distinctive to every structural explanation: the emphasis on structure as the fully efficient cause of all unit actions" (1995/96: 79).

Neoclassical market theory makes even more radical simplifying assumptions than Waltz does but yields determinate predictions because it postulates a single, precise motive: firms are rational profit-maximizers. "The neoclassical theory of the market on which Waltz models his systemic theory of international politics more than adequately explains what any individual firm's behavior would be under a defined market structure with only minimal information about the shape and position of the cost curves facing any particular firm" (Tellis 1995/96: 76). That is why, as Waltz notes, "economists get along quite well with separate theories of firms and markets" (1996: 57). But without a more coherent account of state motivation, Waltz's structural theory of international politics is doomed.

Security, offense, and defense

"Security" might seem to provide an overarching value that integrates relative and absolute gains, or some other broad set of state interests. The same problem, however, reappears: states conceive of their security in both fearful (defensive) and competitive (offensive) ways. This has spawned a growing literature on "defensive" and "offensive" realism,[25] in which questions of motives – that is, how states conceive their vital security interests – are central.[26]

For example, Mastanduno argues that "realists expect nation-states to avoid gaps that favor their partners, but not necessarily to maximize gaps in their own favor. Nation-states are not 'gap maximizers.' They are, in Joseph Grieco's terms, 'defensive positionalists'" (Mastanduno 1991: 79, n. 13). Walt's "balance of threat" theory (1987) powerfully elucidates this logic.

Zakaria, however, argues that "the best solution to the perennial problem of the uncertainty of international life is for a state to increase its control over that environment through the persistent expansion of its political interests abroad" (1998: 20).[27] Mearsheimer likewise argues that "states seek to survive under anarchy by maximizing their power relative

---

[25] Good summaries can be found in Lynn-Jones (1995), Labs (1997: 7–17), and Zakaria (1998: 25–42). These works also provide extensive citations of leading representatives of both positions.

[26] For an unusually perceptive account of the central role of motivational assumptions in Waltzian defensive realism, see Brooks (1997: 449–452).

[27] In much the same vein, although with a more limited purpose, Schweller quotes Raymond Aron: "All great states have jeopardized their survival to gain ulterior objectives" (1997: 929).

to other states" (1990: 12). His states are "short-term power maximizers" (1995: 82); that is, *offensive* positionalists.

This internal debate among realists is often presented as a matter of choosing "the best" or most truly "realist" assumption. For example, Eric Labs asks "Do states seek security by maximizing their relative power or do they seek security by aiming to preserve the status quo?" (1997: 1). The obvious answer is "Both!" And as a plausible general theory of international relations realism needs both assumptions.

A world of defensive positionalists, as we have already noted, would be remarkably peaceful. But without a large number of defensive positionalists or status quo powers,[28] international relations would be very much like a perpetual Hobbesian war of all against all – which it simply is not. And whether one invades for safety or for gain, or chooses not to invade at all, is inescapably (in part) a matter of who one is and with whom one interacts.

Fear may push states towards "a never-ending struggle to improve or preserve their relative power positions" (Gilpin 1975: 35). But we need a theoretical account of when states are likely to seek to improve and when they will seek merely to preserve their position. Anarchy, like human nature, is a constant, and thus cannot explain such variation.

Absolute and relative gains, offensive and defensive realism, are little more than new labels for Kissinger's revolutionary and status quo powers, or Morgenthau's policies of imperialism and the status quo. And the theories of structural realists, like their "classical" predecessors, are silent about when we can expect states to pursue which course.

Rationality

Rationality provides the final strategy to save realism as a general theory of international relations that I will consider here. For example, Kydd claims that "the fundamental assumption behind realism [is] that states can be usefully thought of as unitary rational actors acting strategically under anarchy" (1997: 120). Numerous other realists also appeal to what Robert Keohane calls "the rationality assumption: world politics can be analyzed as if states were unitary rational actors" (1986b: 165).[29]

This rationality, however, is purely instrumental. To say that states

---

[28] It is interesting to note the uses Waltz makes of the notion of status quo powers – that is, states of a particular type – despite his claim to abstract from the attributes of states. See 1979: 186; 1990: 737; 1993: 52–53.

[29] Compare Waltz (1979: 117), Mearsheimer (1994/95: 10), Frankel (1996a: xviii), Kauppi (1995/96: 148), Mastanduno (1997: 50), Labs (1997: 7), Elman and Elman (1997: 924).

rationally pursue utility, whether understood as relative or absolute gains, is just another way of saying, with Morgenthau, that states "act, as they must, in view of their interests as they see them" (1962a: 278). The issue is *how* they see them. Interests become interesting only when they acquire substance – which is provided not by calculating, instrumental reason but by the passions (interests, desires).

As we already noted in discussing Morgenthau, the rationality assumption is consistent with most substantive visions of the national interest. Realism is distinguished from other theories not by the rationality assumption, but by its substantive specifications of the interests of states, leaders, and citizens.[30] Idealists do not assume irrationality but rather offer different substantive accounts of individual and state interests. Altruists and moralists typically act rationally to realize their values. Advocates of world peace through world law usually emphasize its instrumental rationality. Even actions that prove not to contribute to an actor's overall utility often rest on miscalculation or misperception rather than irrationality in any strong sense of that term.

Realism, if it is to serve as a general theory of international relations, desperately needs a substantively plausible and theoretically fruitful account of human nature or state motivation. But neither biological nor structural realism in their leading formulations provides one.

Honor, glory, and heroic realism

Realists might respond that I have at best shown only that leading realists have not yet managed to provide an adequate theory of human nature or a coherent set of assumptions about state motivation. Future realists, however, might succeed where others have failed. In this section I want to suggest that this is unlikely. There is an inescapable multiplicity and variability in the motives of states that is likely to prevent realism from ever providing a useful general theory of international politics.

To develop this argument I turn to two of our other realist paradigms, Thucydides and Machiavelli. Like Morgenthau and Waltz, they place considerable emphasis on competition and diffidence. But unlike their twentieth-century successors, they give no less emphasis to honor and glory.

---

[30] This is an exaggeration. Bureaucratic-politics models, for example, do not assume rationality (at the level of the state). But liberalism, in both its utilitarian and contractarian variants, is deeply committed to instrumental rationality. And social constructivism, rather than postulating irrationality, focuses on the development of and difference between particular substantive rationalities.

The pursuit of glory

Machiavelli calls on us to imitate not merely those who have realized their interests and achieved power and material gain, but those who have been "praised and glorified" (P14[5]). As we noted above, he holds that man "esteems nothing more highly" than honors and property (DI.27[2]; compare P25[2]). And when he notes that in the ancient world "worldly honor" was looked upon as the "highest good" (DIII.2[6]), he is speaking, at least in part, for himself as well.

Machiavelli regularly refers to honor, shame, glory, infamy, or reputation in contexts where most twentieth-century writers would have discussed only safety and gain (and perhaps justice). For example, Piero Soderini's refusal to resort to evil means in the defense of Florence cost him "both his position and his reputation" (DIII.3[3]). Venice's imprudence "caused them the loss of much glory and much prosperity" (Machiavelli 1965: 586). Mercenary armies "led Italy into slavery and disgrace" (P12[6]). Hannibal, when unable to arrange a peace, "did not decline to fight though bound to lose, since . . . if he had to lose, he could at least lose gloriously" (DIII.27[6]; compare DIII.10[4, 6]). Tyrants "fail to see what fame, what glory, security, tranquility, conjoined with peace of mind, they are missing by adopting this course [tyranny], and what infamy, scorn, abhorrence, danger and disquiet they are incurring" (DI.10[2]; compare DI.2[9], P19[3, 6, 7, 11, 12]). And Machiavelli laments the fact that men are so easily "deceived by the false semblance of good and the false semblance of renown" (DI.10[2]).

Cesare Borgia, had illness not stopped him, "would have acquired such force and reputation that he would have stood by himself" (P7[6]). Borgia's reputation, for Machiavelli, is distinct from (although not unconnected with) his power. In fact, Machiavelli often uses "reputation" where we would use power. For example, when he writes that Louis XII "could have maintained his reputation" (P3[11]), Machiavelli means – or at least we would see it as – his political power. Likewise, Machiavelli argues that principalities often arise when the elite "give reputation to one of themselves" as protection against the people, or when the people "give reputation" to one of their own to escape oppression by the elite (P9[2]).

Honor and glory are not always overriding considerations. Fear and interest often take priority (e.g. DI.37[9], P17[4]). But honor is a very strong motivating force. And for Machiavelli honor, glory, and reputation are valued as ends, not means. Reputation may also have instrumental value in the pursuit of power or gain. But that is not why men seek it. Honor cannot be translated into interest (utility, advantage, gain) without qualitatively altering its substance. Honor, like justice, is not simply a highly valued interest. It is indeed highly valued – but not as a (mere) interest.

Honor and glory are also powerful motivating forces in Thucydides' *History*. The Athenians (I.75, 76), Corinthians (I.38, 120), and Spartans (IV.16) stress the honor of leadership, as well as the shame of subordination (IV.86, V.69, 101, VI.80), independent of any material advantages that accrue to alliance leaders and hegemons. Sparta's Brasidas opposes peace because of the honor he gained by success in war (V.16), while Athens' Nicias favors it to preserve his good reputation (V.16). Alcibiades defends his extravagant expenditures by the glory they bring him and the city (VI.16). As Henry Immerwahr puts it, "Thucydides' individuals and states show an almost Homeric sense of pride" (1960: 282).

The size or extremity of an action or event – "the largest army" (II.31), the "greatest surprise" of the war (IV.40 [Smith]), "the most splendid and costly Hellenic force" (VI.31), "the greatest disaster" (III.113) – is a common refrain in Thucydides that rests on the pursuit of glory.[31] Honor and glory are essentially competitive, a matter of distinction, of excelling, demonstrating superiority. They are gained or lost, in more or less discrete parcels, through a largely zero-sum struggle. Great events thus are specially valued for the quantities of honor they make available. "Out of the greatest dangers communities and individuals acquire the greatest glory [*time*, honor]" (I.144).

This line of argument culminates in the claim that the destruction of the Athenian force on Sicily was "the greatest Hellenic achievement of any in this war, or, in my opinion, in Hellenic history; it was at once most glorious to the victors, and most calamitous to the conquered" (VII.87). Although great material gain or loss is also at stake, it is not Thucydides' principal focus. And once their safety is assured, the Syracusans and their allies focus not on material gain but on the glory of their victory (e.g. VII.56, 59, 86).

The pursuit of honor and glory is central even in Pericles' Funeral Oration, which is more often noted for its celebration of Athens' participatory democracy. It is hardly surprising to find that the virtues for which the dead soldiers are praised, and to which the living citizens are called, are concerned with honor and glory. But Pericles also claims that only the love of honor does not grow old, and that honor, not gain, gives the greatest satisfaction (II.44). The final political lesson he draws is that the best men are found where the prize for virtue (*arete*) is greatest (II.46). And in

---

[31] Machiavelli also argues that the things that bring one the most esteem are "great enterprises" and "rare examples" (P21[1]).

calling on the Athenians to become lovers of the city, Pericles encourages them to be inspired by its greatness and reputation. In fact, the power of the city, as demonstrated in the empire, is the proof of his praise. Athens needs no Homer to memorialize it, for it has forced every sea and land to bear witness to its glory (II.43, 41).

Pericles' final speech likewise calls on the Athenians to rise above their current hardships and not tarnish their reputation or fall short of their renown by making concessions to the Peloponnesians (II.61), building to what Adam Parry (1972: 61 n. 18) aptly calls "the great expression of imperial heroism."

Realize that Athens has a mighty name among all mankind because she has never yielded to misfortunes, but more freely than any other city has lavished lives and labors upon war, and that she possesses today a power which is the greatest that ever existed down to our time. The memory of this greatness . . . will be left to posterity forever, how that we of all Hellenes held sway over the greatest number of Hellenes, in the greatest wars held out against our foes whether united or single, and inhabited a city that was the richest in all things and the greatest . . . To be hated and obnoxious for the moment has always been the lot of those who have aspired to rule over others; but he who, aiming at the highest ends, accepts the odium, is well advised. For hatred does not last long, but the splendor of the moment and the after-glory are left in everlasting remembrance (II.64 [Smith]).

For Machiavelli and Thucydides, power politics is about glory as much as fear and gain. Great deeds, beyond any material benefits they may bring, have immense intrinsic value. All three elements of the realist triad – fear, honor, and interest; safety, gain, and reputation – are central motivating forces.

Heroic versus material realism

In sharp contrast, Hobbes, in *Leviathan*, disparagingly refers to the pursuit of reputation as a concern with "trifles" (ch. 13, par. 7). Morgenthau argues that prestige is rarely sought as an end in international relations (1985: 94). And Waltz, like most contemporary realists, treats politics as almost entirely a matter of material interests. These differences are so great that we can distinguish what might be called heroic and material realism, which suggest very different kinds of political behavior.

For example, Waltz claims that "states seek to control what they depend on or to lessen the extent of their dependency. This simple thought explains quite a bit of the behavior of states: their imperial thrusts to widen the scope of their control and their autarchic strivings toward greater self-sufficiency" (1979: 106).

As we saw above, however, the Athenian envoys at Lacedaemon, in addition to fear – first of the Persians, and now of their disaffected "allies" – appeal to the honor of leadership and the material gain of empire. Pericles emphasizes the glory of the empire, rather than any reduction in dependence. And Athens' largest imperial adventure, the ill-fated Sicilian expedition, is driven by desires for glory and gain that Nicias aptly describes as "morbid craving [duseros] for what is out of reach" (VI.13), utterly unconnected with self-sufficiency, and flying in the face of safety.

For Machiavelli as well, glory drives imperial expansion. Venice's non-imperial policy would provide self-sufficiency, but Machiavelli advocates the Roman strategy of imperial expansion, even though it may lead to a shorter life for the state (DI.5.2–5; compare Pocock 1975: 196–199). As Harvey Mansfield notes, for Machiavelli "virtue is shown in conquest, not in domestic self-sufficiency" (1979: 187).

Waltz also argues that "in a self-help system, considerations of security subordinate economic gain to political interest" (1979: 107) and that "considerations of power dominate considerations of ideology" (1991: 31). Honor, however, is unlikely to be so easily subordinated when it is highly valued. There is little shame in subordinating material gain to mortal fear. But honor and glory often require overcoming fear and risking material interests.[32] Thus insults to national honor regularly lead states to policies that have at best an obscure relationship to material security. As we saw above, even Waltz appeals to pride and feeling put upon.

Even the tendency to balance rather than bandwagon, the principal substantive conclusion of Waltz' theory, may be altered when reputation and honor become central considerations. Thus Waltz notes, apparently without appreciating its significance, that Machiavelli did not develop a balance of power theory from his realpolitik views (1979: 117). Was Machiavelli simply careless or obtuse? I think not. A large part of the explanation lies in the fact that balancing is not necessarily rational in the pursuit of glory.

Gilpin presents a different sort of example when he claims that "what interested Thucydides was a particular type of war . . . a war in which the overall structure of an international system is at issue." Thucydides, according to Gilpin, considers the Peloponnesian War "worthy of special attention because of the massive accumulation of power in Hellas and its implications for the structure of the system" (1988: 593). We have seen,

---

[32] "Glory is the means by which we can rise above our fear of death and our love of gain without being asked to rise above our deep-rooted love of our own" (Palmer 1982b: 832).

however, that Thucydides was instead interested in the great accumulation of power primarily for the opportunities it presented for honor and glory. Thucydides' Greeks fought their wars (at least in part) for different reasons than modern materialists would have it. The Peloponnesian War had a very different meaning in that heroic age.

Consider one additional illustration of the differences between heroic and material conceptions of politics, although it is only indirectly relevant to realism. Thucydides and Machiavelli – and the states they describe – contradict the currently popular "democratic peace" thesis that democracies do not fight each other. Athenian democracy, in both its Periclean and post-Periclean forms, was imperialist, not pacific. The empire was made up largely of democratic cities. Both during Brasidas' successful campaigns and following the Athenian defeat in Sicily, Athens fought against democracies. Likewise, Machiavelli prefers republics because of their greater capacity to engage in expansive war, not because they are more peaceful (DI. 6[6–10], II, 1–4).[33] When one of a people's highest ends is to achieve great deeds in battle or the honor of hegemonic leadership, they are unlikely to act like "Kantian," anti-imperialist, bourgeois democrats.

The social construction of state interests

Although I do not want to suggest that we model contemporary international relations on heroic assumptions,[34] the neoclassical economic assumption of independent preferences – the value of a good, service, or opportunity is unrelated to the preferences or holdings of others – may be unduly dismissive of truly relative goods, values, and interests. Even some goods desired entirely for their intrinsic satisfaction have an inescapable relative component. Fred Hirsch's classic examples of such "positional goods" are scenic land, suburban living, and leadership jobs (1976: ch. 3). "One's place in the distribution of income, wealth, and economic power . . . [one's] relative rather than absolute command over economic resources" is crucial to obtaining positional goods (1976: 102).

In politics, dismissing the comparative dimension of interests is often problematic. For example, Robert Jervis speaks in passing of "envy or a mindless desire for status" (1993: 54). Why, though, is a desire for status "mindless" but a desire for wealth "rational?" Envy is neither more

---

[33] For a discussion of the relationship between empire and republic in Rome, see Sullivan (1996: 63–80).

[34] See, however, O'Neill (1999) for an interesting discussion of honor and war and Abrams and Kagan (1998) on honor and other intangible interests in foreign policy.

(instrumentally) irrational nor more (morally) unattractive than the egoistic pursuit of material gain.

Attacks on envy, status, or other truly relative goods involve a prescriptive, substantive theory of individual and state interests. And realists, given their low estimation of human nature, are especially poorly placed to disparage such concerns.[35] Those, such as Machiavelli and Thucydides, who value reputation for itself, or find intrinsic satisfaction in leadership, are not irrational. Even individuals or states that seek to dominate because of its intrinsic pleasures – for example, to satisfy a lust for power – are subject only to *moral* disdain.

Adding reputation, envy, and other truly relative interests would further increase the complexity and indeterminacy of any "realist" account of motivation. But even if we ultimately reject the inclusion of such goods and interests in our contemporary models, for either substantive or methodological reasons, the split between heroic and material realism is of great importance. Like the distinction between offensive and defensive realism, it emphasizes the fact that understandings of fear, honor, and interest, and their relations to one another, vary systematically even within the realist canon.

State interests are not objectively given. The substantive ends that realists see instrumental reason pursuing vary not only accidentally but systematically with culture, history, and circumstance. Human nature as it is expressed in (national and) international politics includes variations that are systematic as well as idiosyncratic. There are inescapable, socially constructed, and thus historically variable, dimensions to human nature and state interests. And without recourse to such constructed values and interests, realist law-like regularities explain little.

Human nature and state motivation: variables, not constants

Gilpin is not exactly wrong when he argues that Thucydides "intended to reveal the underlying and unalterable nature of what is today called international relations" (1988: 591). Thucydides did hope that his work would "be judged useful to those inquirers who desire an exact knowledge of the past as an aid to the interpretation of the future, which in the course of human things must resemble if it does not reflect it" (I.23). But as we have already seen, Thucydides and Machiavelli provide accounts of the central motives of individuals and states that differ systematically from

---

[35] Rhoda Howard has suggested to me an even more radical reading: contemporary realists disparage honor and shame because they rarely experience such feelings and values – in sharp contrast to men and women of earlier times, for whom honor and shame were central to their moral experience.

those of almost all twentieth-century realists. Furthermore, they give no less attention to the variability in human nature and politics.[36]

Realists who stress the constancy of human nature or state motivation tend to imagine that difficult times peel away the veneer of civilization to reveal the "true" nature of man. As one commentator on Thucydides puts it, "in *stasis* [revolution] as in war, human nature is revealed" (Macleod 1979: 52). Difficult circumstances, however, do not simply strip away conventional goodness to uncover a previously obscured natural core. The emaciated body and bloated belly of a severely malnourished child do not reveal the essence of the human physique. Extremity distorts at least as much as it reveals.

Hard times make hard men. As Thucydides notes, "in peace and prosperity states and individuals have better sentiments . . . but war . . . brings most men's characters to a level with their fortunes" (III.82). Difficult times, no less than good times, shape men in their image. War *creates* violent passions as much as it releases them. Both our better and our worse sentiments are in significant measure made, not given.

Machiavelli often expresses an extremely low opinion of human nature. Men are "insatiable, arrogant, crafty and shifting, and above all else malignant, iniquitous, violent, and savage" (Machiavelli 1965: 736). "They are ungrateful, fickle, pretenders and dissemblers, evaders of danger, eager for gain" (P17[3]). "All do wrong and to the same extent when there is nothing to prevent them doing wrong" (DI.58.4). Nonetheless, even he presents a world in which men make contingent, although recurrent, choices to pursue power and interest.

For example, immediately after asserting that "men have, and always have had, the same passions," Machiavelli argues that "men's deeds are sometimes more virtuous in this country than that, and in that than in some other, according to the type of education from which their inhabitants have derived their mode of life" (DIII.43.1). The range of human passions may be fixed. The expression of this "constant" nature, however, varies dramatically with time and place.

Social institutions shape and select human nature. In a poem Machiavelli even suggests that "discipline can make up where nature is lacking" (1965: 737). Machiavelli does emphasize "how easily men are corrupted and *in nature become transformed*" (DI.42.1 [emphasis added]). The pressing need to control the tendency to evil explains much of the exemplary cruelty that Machiavelli advocates, acts that in ancient Rome

---

[36] In fairness to Gilpin it should also be noted that in another essay (1991) he emphasizes the differences between the Cold War and the Peloponnesian War, despite the similarities of hegemonic rivalry.

"because of their unwonted severity and their notoriety, brought men back to the mark every time" (DIII.1.5). But both in becoming corrupted and in returning to virtue, human nature is transformed. And these transformations may last for generations (DIII.43, 46).

Even the evil in men, Machiavelli suggests, may be due to bad institutions and practices.

> Princes ought not to complain of any fault committed by the peoples whom they govern, because such faults are due either to their negligence or to their being themselves sullied by similar defects . . . The Romagna, before Pope Alexander VI . . . exemplified the very worst types of behavior . . . every least occasion was followed by killings and wholesale rapine. It was the wickedness of the princes that gave rise to this, not the wicked nature of man (DIII.29.1).

Any given society may be or become more or less vicious or virtuous. With bad politics, the "malignity" of human nature (DI.3.1) will come to the fore. But good politics, especially if combined with good fortune, may create a society of virtuous and prosperous men.

A model that treats selfish evil as a law-like regularity will only provide accurate predictions in a world of "bad" politics. Even the Athenians at Melos claim only to "make use of" the "law" (*nomos*) of rule of the strong, not that they are compelled to obey it (V.105). And Golden Age Athens, as eulogized in Pericles' Funeral Oration (II.35–46) – a vigorous, democratic city of refined culture and heroic achievements – memorably demonstrates that "higher" potentials may for some time gain the upper hand. A theory that takes into account only "realist" law-like regularities courts analytical and moral disaster. One must know the (variable) substance of the interests of even "realist" actors before their behavior can be predicted.

That substance, however, is equally inaccessible to biological and structural realists. They have no way of determining when individuals or states will act out of fear and when they will act out of interest. And those who try to theorize human nature as a constant are, in the end, forced to treat it as a variable, as we saw in the cases Morgenthau, Waltz, and Grieco.

The character and contribution of realism

The desires of states do regularly run up against the constraints of international anarchy. In anarchic orders, states are exposed more or less directly to the competing desires of other states. This central insight of realism should never be ignored. But before we can say anything of interest about how states are likely to respond to the perennial problems posed by anarchy, we must either know something or make simplifying assumptions about their character, sacrificing theoretical scope for usefully determinate predictions.

States do regularly give very high priority to the pursuit of safety, gain, and reputation. Selfishness and anarchy, especially when they interact, regularly lead states to emphasize security and to seek gain at the expense of others. Policy makers and analysts ignore such patterns only at great risk. But none of these insights, separately or in combination, provides the basis for a general theory of international relations.

I will return to these issues in the conclusion, after we have examined realist accounts of anarchy and morality. Here I outline where my argument is leading, with special reference to the issue of human nature and state motivation, the subject of this chapter.

Multiple realist models

The inescapable multiplicity and variability of state motives fatally undermines efforts to develop realism as a general theory of international politics. And if I am correct that any one of the various motives noted above is too narrow to provide a general theory, we seem to have no option but to see realism as a more or less loosely connected *set* of often inconsistent theoretical models rooted in shared pre-theoretical assumptions.

This still leaves considerable space for realists to play a central role in the study and practice of international relations. For example, once we allow that both balancing and bandwagoning are law-like regularities, we can begin the crucial work of trying to figure out when states can be expected to do which. Schweller has provided one such effort, based on discriminating four different types of states (1994). And in comparing his own work with Stephen Walt's balance of threat theory, Schweller usefully suggests that threatened states are likely to balance but unthreatened states are more likely to bandwagon (1997: 929).

Or consider the question of relative gains. Mastanduno plausibly suggests that "in general, the extent to which state behavior exhibits a concern for relative gains will vary, depending upon whether interaction involves allies or adversaries, and economic or military relationships." He also suggests that dominance reduces sensitivity to relative gains among allies (1991: 79, 81). Even Waltz admits that "when the great-power balance is stable and when the distribution of national capabilities is severely skewed, concern for absolute gains may replace worries about relative ones" (1979: 195), and that "with very secure or very insecure states, the quest for absolute gains may prevail over the quest for relative gains" (1997: 915). Such efforts begin to answer the crucial question of when states are likely to pursue which kinds of interest.

This more modest conception of the character and contribution of realism has recently been described in two complementary ways. Gilpin argues that "realism, like liberalism and Marxism, is essentially a philosophical position; it is not a scientific theory" (1996: 6). A number of other recent realists have described realism as a "paradigm" or "research program,"[37] which provides a "hard core" of pre-theoretical assumptions and a heuristic for developing scientific theories out of those assumptions. In either case, realism is an inspiration for and source of social scientific theories, rather than a theory (or even a set of theories).

Consider Waltz' account of the realist hard core. (1) States' interests provide the springs of action. (2) The necessities of policy arise from unregulated state competition. (3) Calculation based on these necessities can discover policies that best serve a state's interests. (4) Success, defined as preserving and strengthening the state, is the ultimate test of policy (1979). Waltz' own balance of power, Walt's balance of threat, and Schweller's bandwagoning for profit all can be readily derived from this hard core. They are thus all "true," "authentic," and potentially valuable realist theories.

For some purposes we may want to emphasize this shared hard core. For other purposes we may want to emphasize the different secondary assumptions that they make about state motives. But no one is or can be *the* true realist theory. In fact, the predictions of each contradict the predictions of at least one other. And there is nothing wrong with such inconsistency – so long as we consider realism a research program or philosophical orientation.

Thus John Vasquez misses the point when he complains that contemporary realists variously predict bandwagoning and balancing (Vasquez 1997: 905). A single theory that systematically generates contradictory predictions may violate accepted canons of "science." A research program or paradigm, however, need not. Realist theories must be consistent with the hard core of the paradigm, not with each other. In fact, we should *expect* that different secondary assumptions will generate conflicting predictions among different realist theories.

If Vasquez were correct that "as soon as one theoretical variant is discarded, another variant pops up to replace it as the 'true realism' or the 'new realism'" (1997: 906), he would have a legitimate complaint. But if we are serious about treating realism as a research program or philosophical orientation, there can be no single "most authentic" realist theory. There are instead several "true" realist theories that must be consistent with the hard core of the paradigm but need not be consistent with each other.

---

[37] See, for example, Elman (1996: 18), Vasquez (1997), Elman and Elman (1997), Schweller (1997: 927), Wohlforth (1994/95: 95), Waltz (1997: 915).

Realism and its "competitors"

Accepting this understanding of realism means that we must abandon talk of "testing" realism against competitors, with an eye to choosing one over the other, decisively, and in general. Empirical "tests" may show that certain events in the world are (not in)consistent[38] with the hard core of a realist research program. But that does not provide "support" in any strong sense of that term for choosing realism over some competing paradigm. Many events that are explained by one realist theory are also *inconsistent* with at least one other no less authentic realist theory. For example, if balancing and bandwagoning exhaust the possible aligning behaviors of states, as Waltz suggests they do,[39] and if good realist theories predict each, as they do, then any piece of evidence simultaneously confirms and contradicts "realism."

Labs provides an extreme example of the perspective against which I am arguing when he presents offensive (rather than defensive) realism as "the best realist theory available to go forward and do battle with competing approaches to international relations" (1997: 48). Neither, however, will get realists very far in such a battle. As we have seen, both make poor general theories of international relations.

This gladiatorial vision misconceives the nature of "competing" theories of international relations. Offensive and defensive realism are different derivations from the realist hard core. They are not competitors as *the* "true" realist theory. Nor are they contestants in a struggle to provide the best theory of international relations. "Competing" (realist and non-realist) theories are different logics that apply to different parts of international reality.

To take another recent example, Schweller and David Priess argue that

contrary to the popular conception, the "ideal" realist state is not the power-maximizing, malevolent hegemon that attempts to impose its values on others through naked power and eternal crusades. Rather, the ideal is the prudent, benevolent hegemon that understands the limits of coercive power and so promotes legitimacy and emulation of its values while tolerating pluralism and diversity (1997).

In fact, neither is nor can be *the* ideal realist model of the state. Both are plausible and potentially valuable models.

It is understandable that Schweller and Priess should exaggerate in

---

[38] I use this formulation not merely to be cute. There is an important difference between behavior that is "consistent with" realism in the sense that it flows directly from some realist assumption or logic and behavior that is merely not inconsistent with realist assumptions or logic. Although behavior of the first type might be said to confirm or support realism, behavior of the second type does not.

[39] Compare, however, Deudney (1996: 213–216) and Schweller (1998: ch. 3).

response to a common, no less exaggerated, caricature. A better way to make their point would be to suggest that their preferred model is morally more attractive; as policy prescription is likely to lead to "better" outcomes; or is likely to lead to successful prediction or insightful explanation of great-power behavior more often than the alternative model. Nonetheless, some states do act like power-maximizing, malevolent tyrants. It would be especially unfortunate if realist theories, which are so attuned to egoistic self-assertion, did not even try to model the behavior of such states.

Realism and its competitors, and different realist theories as well, are "tuned" to account for different dimensions of international relations. As should be clear from our discussions so far, realist theories are especially well suited to explain certain recurrent forms of international conflict. Liberal internationalist theories, for example, are directed more to explaining certain opportunities for and patterns of cooperation.

Rather than ask which is "better," students of international relations should instead inquire about the profitable uses to which each might be put. Different theories, traditions, or research programs within international relations do different things, rather than vie with one another to do the same thing. Realism, like its "competitors," is a tool that works well for certain purposes, and not well for others.

Traditions and paradigms thrive when and because they tell us something important – but only some important things – about our world. If either we or our world changes, as both are wont to do with distressing regularity, we may change our views of what is insightful. And at any time, "we" are extremely diverse. Therefore, realism, rather than ever decisively "win" or "lose," will continue to wax and wane, become more or less interesting to a greater or lesser number of people.

The problems in realist accounts of human nature and the national interest do not arise from elevating secondary features of international relations to a prime position. But the characteristic realist emphasis on selfishness and fear systematically directs our attention away from other no less important and no less constant aspects of state behavior. It does not and cannot provide an adequate general theory of international relations.

Discussion questions

- What is left out of the realist triad of fear, honor, and interest? Is the mix between "realist" and "non-realist" motives constant? Is the relative weight of fear, honor, and interest constant across time and place?

- Why might someone believe that the national interest could, even should, be defined in terms of power? The obvious alternative is that the national interest is whatever a people or its government say it is. How can realists argue against this? Which account do you find more plausible? Why?

- Are Morgenthau's strategies of the status quo, imperialism, and prestige just more or less direct expressions of fear, honor, and interest? Granting that these are indeed recurrent strategies in international relations, what does this say about structural theories? Such variation cannot be explained by anarchy alone, which would seem to be constant across international orders. Is there some way to account for these different strategies without appealing directly to the interests of states?

- Is there a universal will to power? How might we go about resolving disputes over answers to this question – or any other assertion about human nature?

- What would a theory of international politics look like if it consistently assumed only that states seek survival? Is *any* theory that assumes a single motive likely to be plausible as a *general* theory of international relations?

- Is it true, as structuralists suggest, that the difference between national and international politics is simply that of the same human nature being expressed in radically different structures (anarchy versus hierarchy)? Does structure primarily "filter" motives and interests or does it shape them? To put the question slightly differently, which comes first, interests or structure? (Is there a better way to formulate this question?)

- *Is* it true that a structural theory needs at least an implicit theory of human nature or state motivation? If so, how much theoretical weight must such assumptions bear? Is it possible to develop a structural theory with only modest and relatively uncontroversial assumptions about state motives? What would such a theory look like?

- Even granting that realists typically appeal to multiple motivational assumptions, can we not find a "higher" or "deeper" coherence in these assumptions? In principle? In practice?

- How important are truly relative gains in politics? *Is* it true that most "relative gains" turn out on examination to be long-run absolute gains? Formulating the issue in terms of time-frame creates an apparent parallel with the discussion in the preceding chapter of the relation between passion (short-term interest) and reason. How closely related are these two formulations? What are their relative strengths and weaknesses?

- How important is the fact that realists cannot provide a theoretically plausible account of when states pursue relative gains and when they pursue absolute gains? What are the costs and attractions of depicting realism as a theory that focuses on relative gains, but applies only when states do indeed pursue such gains? In other words, can we see relative gain realism as a powerful *partial* theory of international relations?

- Waltz claims that states balance rather than seek to maximize power. Mearsheimer claims that states are short-term power maximizers. How can we resolve such disputes among leading contemporary realists? What does this dispute tell us about the place of motivational assumptions within realist theories? About the character and coherence of realism understood as a general theory of international politics? What are the implications of saying that either Waltz or Mearsheimer is – must be – wrong? Of saying that both are right in some important cases?

- How is the distinction between offensive and defensive realism related to that between relative and absolute gains? What are the costs and benefits of seeing offensive and defensive realism as two different realist theories that apply in different circumstances?

- *Is* rationality as widely shared a theoretical assumption as is suggested in the text? Is there a particular substantive twist to "realist" rationality? If so, where does it come from? And how (if at all) is this different from making substantive motivational assumptions?

- In the text it is argued that the problem with Waltz' theory is not that it makes radical simplifying assumptions but that his particular assumptions are not fruitful. Do you agree? Why?

- It is further suggested that no single coherent motivational assumption (or theoretically ordered set of assumptions) can make realism a plausible general theory of international relations? Do you agree? Why? Are there different conceptions of a general theory of international relations that might lead you to different responses?

- Let us grant that political actors in ancient Greece and Renaissance Italy were far more concerned with honor and glory than we are. So what? Why should a realist, or any other student of international relations, care? What modifications (if any) would be necessary for a realist to encompass such differences in motivational priorities? Would the necessary changes be different for biological and structural realists?

- Let us grant that interests are socially constructed. If both individual and state interests are shaped by social institutions, what kinds of problems does this raise for structural realism? For biological realism? Can we incorporate this insight in the form of second-order modifications to "pure" (structural or biological) realist theories? Does it create more fundamental problems? What might a social constructivist realism look like?

- What is gained – and what is lost – by seeing realism as the source of multiple theories or models rather than a single general theory of international politics?

- Is the gladiatorial model of theoretical competition really as problematic as Donnelly suggests? Certainly it must have some attractions that explain its wide currency in the discipline. What important insights does a "realism and its competitors" model effectively highlight?

- Is the distinction, drawn in the text, between "consistent with realism" and "(not in)consistent with realism" helpful? Do realists regularly confuse arguments for the second with evidence for the first?

Suggestions for further reading

The problem of human nature – is there any such thing, and if so, what is its substance? – is certainly well beyond our scope in this volume. Bhikhu Parekh's essay "Is There a Human Nature?" (1997) briefly outlines some of the central dimensions and meanings of that question. We cannot, however, entirely ignore the issue because some realists see human nature as the source of their theory. For selections representative of Niebuhr's views, see Davis and Good (1960: 70–91), and, at much greater length, Niebuhr (1941). Morgenthau's most developed account is provided in *Scientific Man Versus Power Politics* (1946).

On the broader issue of human nature and politics, a good starting point is Martin Hollis' *Models of Man* (1977). Stevenson (1974) and Trigg (1988) provide brief summaries of the theories of human nature of major Western philosophers. Chapters 2 and 3 of Waltz' *Man, the State, and War* (1959) provide a classic (critical) examination of attempts to root theories of war and peace in human nature. For more recent examples of such explanations, see Offerman-Zuckerberg (1991: part 4). *Human Nature in Politics* (Pennock and Chapman 1977) is a useful collection of essays by political theorists. Mary Midgley's *Beast and Man: The Roots of Human Nature* (1995) is a fascinating and accessible effort to take seriously the relevance of sociobiology without succumbing to a naive (pseudo-)scientism.

On Morgenthau's notion of the national interest, see *In Defense of the National Interest* (1951) and, more briefly, Morgenthau (1952a). Robert Tucker's **"Professor Morgenthau's Theory of Political 'Realism'"** (1952) provides a devastating brief critique. Good (1960) is much more sympathetic. Friedrich Kratochwil's "On the Notion of 'Interest' in International Relations" (1982) provides a careful conceptual analysis. He shows not only that it is a normative (rather than a descriptive) term but that its meaning shifted dramatically in European international relations in the decades around 1870.

A central issue in recent realist discussions of state motivation has been the claim that states pursue relative gains. Grieco (1988a) triggered much of the debate. Mastanduno (1991: 78–82) and Matthews (1996: 116–121) provide clear and balanced presentations. Duncan Snidal (1991a; 1991b; 1993) and Robert Powell (1991; 1993a; 1993b) are the leading critics.

Those interested in pursuing the heroic conception of politics should begin with Pericles' Funeral Oration and his final speech in Thucydides (II.35–46, 60–64). Homer's *Iliad* is the seminal Greek source. On the social basis of the Homeric world, see Finley (1978). Adkins (1972) provides a good introduction to its political and ethical values. For recent works applying notions of honor and glory to contemporary international politics, see Abrams and Kagan (1998) and O'Neill (1999).

3   Anarchy, hierarchy, and order

Anarchy, the absence of hierarchical relations of authority and rule, largely defines the discipline of international studies. Students of comparative politics study hierarchical political orders, societies that operate under established systems of law and government. Students of international relations study the anarchic interactions of polities that recognize no higher political authority. This stylized picture, like any good carica-ture, highlights essential features of its subject. I will argue, however, that realist accounts of the meaning and implications of anarchy are of severely limited applicability and value.

Anarchy, chaos, and order

The term "anarchy" comes to us from the Greek, meaning, literally, absence of government or rule (*arche*). *Arche* is the term Thucydides uses to refer to the Athenian "empire"; rule of one city over another, in contrast to both the formal equality of alliances and the hegemonic leadership of the first among equals. It is most familiar to us today in common (Greek-derived) definitions of regime types such as monarchy (rule of one) and oligarchy (rule of the few).

In popular discourse, "anarchy" often suggests chaos or violent disorder. But the absence of hierarchical order need not lead to a Hobbesian war of all against all. Individuals and social groups often order and organize themselves in the absence of government. Most realists thus admit the obvious fact that international relations reveals significant elements of order.

Order in international society, however, is established "horizontally" rather than "vertically;" through the interaction of formally equal states rather than being imposed "from above." For example, sovereign states regularly contract with one another (agree to treaties), reciprocally accepting obligations and giving up elements of their "primordial" liberty (sovereignty). Alliances, peace treaties, diplomatic immunity, territorial seas, customs unions, and the United Nations Security Council are but a few familiar institutions of contractual international order. Order (predictability) also emerges out of custom, tacit conventions, and strategic interaction. Power itself can order interactions, both through coercion and through not entirely coercive leadership.

Although international order is not enforced by hierarchic political institutions, considerable decentralized enforcement of international obligations occurs through "self-help": threats, retaliation, negotiation, and similar means mobilized by states on their own behalf.[1] National courts provide substantial elements of decentralized judicial enforcement. "Reputation," the desire to be seen as a trustworthy partner in cooperative endeavors, fosters compliance even by those who place no intrinsic value on their word. And international organizations and regimes, though lacking full governmental authority, may have considerable persuasive, even coercive, capabilities.[2]

Realists tend not to be impressed by the extent of international law and order – which in any case they usually attribute to state power. Instead they (not unreasonably) emphasize the violent and disorderly aspects of international relations. Above all, realists emphasize the fact that states have reserved for themselves the right of war, which embeds violence and thus fundamental disorder at the core of international relations.

The nature and extent of order in international society, however, is an empirical, not a theoretical, matter. The scope and character of international order may change dramatically with time and place. For example, systematic differences in the frequency, occasions, or form of states' recourse to their reserved right of war may make particular eras or systems more or less violent.[3] Although anarchy, like selfishness, is a central part of international relations, it is nowhere near as simple, pervasive, or constraining as realists typically suggest.

Waltz on structure

Although all realists emphasize the constraints imposed by anarchy, contemporary structural neorealists, as we have noted in both of the preceding chapters, place anarchy at the heart of their theories. Waltz, the most forceful and influential advocate of structural realism, will be our principal focus in this chapter.

---

[1] Self-help is a common term of art in the study of international relations. In international anarchy, one cannot rely on the help of government to protect one's interests and rights. Instead, one must rely on "self-help," one's own power and skills, along with whatever assistance one can obtain from friends, allies, or others with concordant interests.

[2] On the extensive range of non-coercive compliance mechanisms in international relations, see Chayes and Chayes (1995: part 2).

[3] See pp. 145–147 for an extended illustration.

The nature of structural theory

Waltz rigidly separates levels and units of analysis. In his first book, *Man, the State, and War,* he distinguished three principal levels at which explanations of international phenomena might lie: the individual, the state, and the international system. Waltz' characterization of these as first, second, and third image theories of international relations – "man, the state, and Waltz" – has become familiar terminology within the discipline.[4]

Third image or system-level theories do not attempt to explain those (substantial) portions of state behavior caused by individuals, small groups, or the interests, character, or internal political processes of states. They seek instead to understand the system-wide forces that shape the behavior of all individuals and groups, whatever their particular character or history.

Waltz further narrows his theory to the *structure* of the system, "the system-wide component that makes it possible to think of the system as a whole" (1979: 79). "The concept of structure is based on the fact that units differently juxtaposed and combined behave differently and in interacting produce different outcomes" (1979: 81). "When offices are juxtaposed and functions are combined in different ways, different behaviors and outcomes result" (1979: 82).

Structure, Waltz insists, must be defined entirely "free of the attributes and the interactions of the units" (1979: 79). It is what remains after these two abstractions, namely, the *arrangement* of the system's parts. In chapter 2 we critically examined structuralist efforts to abstract from the interests or motives of states. This chapter introduces a parallel critique, which will be developed further in chapters 4 and 5, of Waltz' effort to abstract from the interactions of states.

Defining structure

Following Emile Durkheim, Waltz argues that any political structure, at any level of analysis, is defined by three elements: ordering principle, differentiation of functions among the units, and distribution of capabilities across units (1979: 81–82, 88–99).

There are, according to Waltz, two, and only two, political ordering principles: hierarchy and anarchy. Either units are arranged in hierarchical relations of authority and subordination or they are not, in which case the structure is anarchic (1979: 88–89).

---

[4] For a penetrating critique of this classic argument, see Suganami (1996).

Political units are qualitatively differentiated by the functions they discharge, their place in the political division of labor. Functional differentiation, Waltz argues, is largely a consequence of ordering principle. "Hierarchy entails relations of super- and subordination among a system's parts, and that implies their differentiation . . . Anarchy entails relations of coordination[5] among a system's units, and that implies their sameness" (1979: 93).

In hierarchical structures, "political actors are formally differentiated according to the degrees of their authority, and their distinct functions are specified" (1979: 81). For example, legislative and executive functions in the United States are vested in separate institutions (Congress and the President). In Britain, legislative and executive functions are largely fused within a single institution (Parliament). In absolute monarchies, all political authority is vested in a single "unit," the hereditary ruler.

In anarchic orders, Waltz argues, functional differentiation between political units (states) is virtually non-existent. Without a hierarchical division of political labor, all states must perform all, and thus essentially the same, functions. "In anarchic realms, like units coact. In hierarchic realms, unlike units interact" (1979: 104).

The third element of structure, distribution of capabilities (power), concerns quantitative, rather than qualitative, variation among units. For example, the federal judiciary in the United States is a co-equal branch of government, with extensive powers to overrule Congress and the President. Britain's judiciary, although independent of political interference, is largely subordinate to Parliament. This is a structural difference: institutions with similar functions possess different relative capabilities, with system-wide political impact.

Structural theory seeks to explain variations among political systems entirely on the basis of these three factors. It represents an extreme effort to focus on a few deep political forces that have profound effects across wide expanses of time and space. More particularly, Waltzian structuralism draws our attention to the differences between anarchic and hierarchic political orders. Among anarchic (international) orders, it focuses on differences and changes in the distribution of capabilities. If all international orders are anarchic, and if states within an anarchic order are not functionally differentiated, then one international structure differs from another only in the distribution of capabilities among its units (states), as a result of the rise and fall of great powers.

---

[5] The language of coordination emphasizes the fact that international order arises from the interactions of formally equal states. States coordinate their behavior, rather than subordinate their interests or wills to a higher power.

Dichotomy or continuum?

Were the relations between Britain and the states of India during the first half of the nineteenth century hierarchic or anarchic? Between the United States and Central America in the 1920s? Between the Soviet Union and the communist states of Central and Eastern Europe in the 1950s and 1960s? The obvious answer is "both." Such examples, which are easily multiplied, strongly suggest viewing anarchy and hierarchy as end points of a continuum. Some international orders would then be characterized as "mixed," more or less anarchic/hierarchic. Waltz, however, vigorously rejects such a conceptualization and insists instead that anarchy and hierarchy should be seen as a strict dichotomy (1979: 114ff.).

Only in chapter 5 will it become fully clear why I devote such considerable space to what on first sight might appear a secondary theoretical issue. I will argue that unless we recognize the possibility of mixed orders – particularly the possibility of extensive elements of hierarchy within "primarily" anarchic orders – we are likely to obscure the extent and character of international order and underestimate the degree to which international relations rests on more than power.

Anarchy and hierarchy

Waltz claims that "two and only two" ordering principles – anarchy and hierarchy – are needed to cover societies of all sorts. Although acknowledging borderline cases, such as China between the world wars (1979: 116), Waltz judges them to be insufficiently frequent or important to merit the sacrifice in theoretical economy required to introduce additional ordering principles.

In recent decades, under the influence of the principles of sovereign equality and national self-determination, almost all of the globe has been authoritatively allocated to sovereign territorial states. Anarchy and hierarchy thus largely exhaust the range of ordering principles today. But if, like Waltz, we are interested in a general comparative account of political structures, restricting ourselves to anarchy and hierarchy is more problematic.

For example, feudal political order in medieval Europe involved a web of multiple, cross-cutting, and asymmetric obligations and functional differentiations that is hard to conceptualize as either anarchic or hierarchic. The Waltzian dichotomy tells us little about the character or dynamics of feudal politics. In fact, it obscures our understanding by anachronistically misdirecting our attention to categories that simply were not central to feudal society.

China's relations with neighboring states during the Qing dynasty (1644–1911) are no less misleadingly described as (simply either) anarchic or hierarchic. Certainly the Chinese did not see neighbors such as Korea or Assam – let alone the "Western ocean barbarians" from Europe – as formal equals. Quite the contrary, China insisted on tributary relations in which foreign states symbolically expressed their subordination to the Emperor of Heaven. But relations were not simply hierarchical either. Tributaries enjoyed substantial, at times near total, local political autonomy. Hierarchical subordination often was more cultural and metaphysical than political.

The modern Europe-centered international system also is full of what in Waltz' terms can only be seen as "anomalous" cases. For example, the growing powers of the European Union (EU) make it increasingly difficult to describe relations among its member states as simply either anarchic or hierarchic. Members of the EU are both sovereign, and thus engage in anarchic relations with one another (and with states outside the EU), and subordinate to regional institutions such as the European Commission and the European Court of Justice.

Realists are likely to have little interest in most such cases. That, however, is a comment on their own concerns, not on the actual interests and actions of states. In fact, how one selects, defines, and arranges ordering principles is largely a matter of one's interests.

More than two principles are required for broad, comprehensive historical comparisons. Thinking about alternative forms of order is likely to benefit from additional ordering principles as well. Some relatively narrow and specialized contemporary analytical or practical purposes also require additional ordering principles. For example, the Netanyahu government in Israel was at one point interested in the viability of a third kind of order, represented by a Palestinian Authority that was not, and would not become, a (fully) sovereign state.

Realists can plausibly argue that these "exceptions" are of such limited global political significance that there usually is little cost to dispensing with additional ordering principles – especially at the high level of abstraction that Waltz pitches his theory. Others, however, may be no less reasonably interested in, concerned with, or impressed by these many and varied "exceptions."

Deciding how many ordering principles to recognize is largely a matter of the particular purposes one has in mind. It is not imposed by an objective reality "out there." There are theoretical costs and advantages to selecting categories that either highlight similarity and constancy or highlight diversity and change. But there is no theoretically or substantively neutral way of weighing the balance between costs and benefits. And that

balance is likely to shift not only with time and place but with the changing purposes of analysts.

Because there is no neutral solution, though, I am willing, for the sake
of argument, to set aside discussions of a third ordering principle. I will
focus instead on Waltz' claim that anarchy and hierarchy should be
viewed as a rigid dichotomy; or, viewed from the other direction, on the
issue of mixed hierarchic–anarchic orders.

Mixed political orders

Waltz' preference for an anarchy–hierarchy dichotomy reflects his understandable desire to keep structure and process analytically separate. For
example, he properly complains that "students are inclined to see a less-
ening of anarchy when alliances form" (1979: 114), rather than a non-
structural realignment of capabilities held by (distributed among) states.
But Waltz goes overboard in trying to avoid this analytical confusion.

Consider classic protectorates such as Egypt during and after World
War I, or territories such as Andorra and Puerto Rico today. They rest on
a particular arrangement of units; that is, structure, not process. They are
sovereign internally but subordinate externally. For the purposes of
domestic politics, they are hierarchical polities. But in international relations, they are subordinated to a "protecting" power. Rather than an
alliance-like rearrangement of fundamentally like parts, there is a formal
hierarchical arrangement of separate political entities with different rights
and powers.

Spheres of influence present even clearer, if informal, examples of
mixed structures. The German Democratic Republic (East Germany)
enjoyed the rights and powers of a sovereign state, both internally and
externally, only within hierarchically imposed limits laid down by its
forced membership in the communist bloc.[6] East Germany faced most
other states in an anarchic order, but was largely – although not entirely –
hierarchically subordinate to the Soviet Union. And its "special relationship" with the Soviet Union was not temporary, contingent, or accidental.
It was a more or less permanent arrangement that lasted as long as the
country itself and was based on a relatively clear and well-recognized
differentiation of political powers and functions.

For many purposes, it may be useful to emphasize that spheres of (hierarchical) influence are embedded within a larger anarchic structure. But

---

[6] For a more extended discussion of East German sovereignty, see Wendt and Friedheim
(1995). On Cold War era spheres of influence more broadly, see Triska (1986). Bull
(1977: ch. 9) and Wight (1978: ch. 3) provide broad theoretical discussions of the place
of the practice in modern international society.

for other purposes – including many of the purposes of the East German government and the foreign governments that dealt with it – hierarchical subordination was most salient. The subsystem of the Soviet bloc included substantial elements of hierarchy, however anarchic the Cold War global order may have been. Soviet satellites in Central and Eastern Europe were (partially) subject states. There is no compelling theoretical reason to obscure this by insisting on an anarchy–hierarchy dichotomy.

Waltz does make a valuable point when he goes on to note that "the appearance of anarchic sectors within hierarchies does not alter and should not obscure the ordering principle of the larger system" (1979: 115). But the language of sectors clearly indicates a mixture of types. And we will badly misjudge structural pressures and relations within such "anarchic sectors" if we simply treat the entire order as hierarchic. Even more important for our purposes, "hierarchic sectors" may significantly alter the structural dynamics of orders that are "fundamentally" anarchic.

Waltz' reluctance to describe international relations "as being flecked with particles of government and alloyed with elements of community" (1979: 114) also arises from a characteristically "realist" concern that such descriptions are likely to understate the impact of anarchy or overstate the significance of such flecks of hierarchy/government. But by insisting on a rigid dichotomy, Waltz risks overstating the significance of anarchy. He also mistakenly presents this empirical issue as a matter of conceptual logic.

Many paired ideal types, including anarchy and hierarchy, can be represented as either dichotomous or continuous. Although tall and short are usually seen as end points on a continuum, for some purposes we may want to sort people dichotomously, above and below a certain height. The distinction between great powers and lesser powers is a dichotomous cut at a variable (power) that is in some important sense continuous. Neither construction is "natural"; both are largely a matter of purpose or design.

Even where one concept is defined as the absence of the other, as in Waltz' definition of anarchy, we often are free to choose between dichotomous and continuous representations. A dichotomy is likely to be preferable only if (1) the dividing line is sharp and clear; (2) the area "in between" is small; and (3) few important cases fall in that grey area.

For example, treating day and night as a dichotomy is typically useful because twilight and dawn are relatively short periods of transition between the two "pure" cases during which few important activities in the lives of most people typically occur. But when does Christmas morning (and thus many North American children's access to their presents) really start? When is it *really* dark, and thus time to come in from play? In such cases, the dividing line is entirely conventional. (Don't wake us before 7 o'clock. Come in when the street lights go on.) Were such cases more common or more important to those with power we probably would not speak so easily of a day–night dichotomy.

In much the same way I will suggest that the area between the pure ideal types of anarchy and hierarchy is both substantially larger and far more important than Waltz suggests. By presenting anarchy as a featureless void, Waltz' dichotomy obscures the frequency and significance of hierarchical elements in international relations, and hides from our attention many important and interesting aspects of contemporary international political order.

Anarchy, authority, and power

"National politics is the realm of authority, of administration, and of law. International politics is the realm of power, of struggle, and of accommodation" (1979: 113). If this were true we might have the sharp division and lack of important intermediate cases that would justify a dichotomous representation of anarchy and hierarchy. But anarchy is no more a realm of pure power (entirely independent of authority) than hierarchy is simply a realm of authority (entirely independent of power). And making such a "simplifying" assumption often obscures far more than it illuminates.

Force, order, and authority

Waltz' formal definitions of anarchy and hierarchy are couched in terms of authority.

The parts of domestic political systems stand in relations of super- and subordination. Some are entitled to command; others are required to obey. The parts of international-political systems stand in relations of coordination. Formally, each is the equal of all the others. None is entitled to command; none is required to obey (1979: 88).

Political order or rule, *arche*, is for Waltz a matter of legitimate authority. "The difference between national and international politics lies not in the use of force but in the different modes of organization for doing something about it. A government, ruling by some standard of legitimacy, arrogates to itself the right to use force" (1979: 103). In much the same vein, Nicholas Spykman describes international society as "a society without central authority to preserve law and order" and characterizes international relations as "a contest for power in which the players are not subordinate to any superior authority" (1942: 7, 9).

Such a conception draws on Max Weber's familiar definition of the state as the social institution with a monopoly on the legitimate use of force.[7] Within a state, one agency, the government, has a monopoly on legitimate force, at least in the sense that it is authorized to define permitted and prohibited uses of force. Citizens and subjects within a state are largely denied the right to use force against one another.[8]

In anarchic orders, however, each state (unit) has a right to use force more or less when and how it sees fit. Any limits are matters of capability, not right. For Waltz, the special role of force in international relations thus arises not from a predilection of individuals or states to use force – this would be a first or second image (unit level) explanation, relying on the nature of human beings or the character of states – but from the authority of states to use force against one another. States are coordinate with, not subordinate to, one another.

Waltz goes on to argue that in anarchy "authority" is largely reducible to power. "Whatever elements of authority emerge internationally are barely once removed from the capability [power] that provides the foundation for the appearance of those elements. Authority quickly reduces to a particular expression of capability" (1979: 88). Might makes right. Conversely, Waltz sees authority in hierarchic orders as more distanced from power, and typically even a source of power.

Machiavelli, however, emphasizes the fact that Rome, the greatest state of all time, was founded through an act of fratricide (1970, I.9, 18[6–7]). No less a conservative than Edmund Burke reminded us that almost all governments, no matter how legitimate they may be today, can trace their origin to illegitimate acts of force (1955 [1790]: 25, 192). As John Herz puts it, "people, in the long run, will recognize that authority, any authority, which possesses the power of protection" (1976: 101). And at any given time, it is a simple matter – often depressingly easy – to find governments whose authority is "barely once removed from" the coercive power of a dominant elite.

Consider, for example, Guatemala, El Salvador, Zaire, Ethiopia, and Cambodia in the 1970s and early 1980s, or Burma, Somalia, and Haiti in the early 1990s. The authority of these governments rested almost entirely on their control of the means of coercion. Conversely, the European Union (EU) today has considerable authority independent of

---

[7] For a discussion of Weber as a significant realist theorist in his own right, see Smith (1986: ch. 2).

[8] There are, of course, exceptions, most notably self-defense. And there is more historical variability than Waltz acknowledges. For example, some hierarchical societies, including ancient Rome and contemporary Somalia and Sudan, have left enforcement of penalties against murder to the family of the victim.

its (meager) coercive capabilities. In fact, authority is clearly *more* important in relations between EU members today than it was, for example, between rulers and ruled in Guatemala in the early 1980s, when the government was killing hundreds, even thousands, of its citizens every month; or between the Khmer Rouge and the millions of Cambodians butchered in the Killing Fields.

"Wars among states cannot settle questions of authority and right; they can only determine the allocation of gains and losses among contenders and settle for a time the question of who is the stronger" (Waltz 1979: 112). Perhaps. But military coups, which for extended periods have been the principal mechanism by which governments have changed in many countries, often can be described in the same terms.

It simply is not the case, as Waltz would have it, that "nationally, relations of authority are established. Internationally, only relations of strength result" (1979: 112). There may be a greater reliance on relations of authority in most national political orders, most of the time, than in most anarchic orders. But the difference is a matter of degree rather than kind, and subject to considerable contingent empirical variation.

Anarchy and authority

Waltz' attempt to link anarchy to power and hierarchy to authority is especially problematic given his conception of structural theory. Structure, as Waltz reasonably defines it, is about the arrangement of the parts. Power and authority, however, are concerned with how that arrangement is produced or maintained, not its shape.

In defining both anarchy and hierarchy, Waltz uses the language "entitled to command" and "required to obey" (1979: 88). But title to rule can come from either power (e.g. conquest or military coup) or from "legitimate authority" (e.g. election or hereditary right).[9] Conversely, one can be "required" to obey by either superior force or superior authority; by the highwayman or the policeman.

Anarchy is no more a realm of pure power than hierarchy is a realm of pure authority. And it makes perfect sense to speak of mixed political orders that are more or less anarchic or hierarchic. In fact, unless we do so, we needlessly obscure important features of international relations. Just as order can exist in anarchical societies, so can authority, administration, and law.

---

[9] In those cases in which might really does make right, the very distinction between force and authority dissolves.

Even if we grant that counter-examples such as the EU are more exceptions that prove the rule than cases that fundamentally blur the anarchy–hierarchy dichotomy, this is a contingent empirical fact. There is no *structural theoretical* reason why most national governments could not derive their authority from the control of force. Conversely, there is no *structural theoretical* reason why most states could not stand under, for example, the suzerain or imperial authority of some other state, as was the case, for example, during much of the Roman and Ottoman empires.

Legitimate authority typically plays a greater role in most national societies than in most international societies. But domestic politics is, in addition to a realm of authority, administration, and law, a realm of power, struggle, and accommodation. The differences between international (anarchic) and national (hierarchic) political orders are largely matters of quantity, not quality – making the variable continuous, rather than dichotomous. And the relationship between power and authority, in both anarchic and hierarchic orders, is an empirical, not a theoretical, matter. Waltz' insistence to the contrary is not merely mistaken, it obscures important similarities between national and international systems of political order.

Government and centralization

Government has been largely absent in our discussion so far. That may seem odd because although international society may have substantial elements of law, order, and authority, it clearly lacks hierarchical government. But government is a particular kind of institution for delivering law, order, authority, and their many benefits. And other institutions can provide similar services and benefits, as the diversity of contemporary international and regional organizations indicates. To define anarchy simply in terms of government would misdirect our attention to the institutional form, government, rather than the functions of governance, authority, law, and order.

Waltz also appeals to centralization in distinguishing anarchic and hierarchic orders. "Domestic systems are centralized and hierarchic . . . International systems are decentralized and anarchic" (1979: 88).

What counts as "centralized," however, is clearly a matter of context and degree. Regional centralization in Europe is on the rise, and high compared with Asia and Africa. But compared to, say, France, it is low. To insist that all order be described simply as either centralized or decentralized would be absurd.

Furthermore, the distinction between (relatively) centralized and (relatively) decentralized orders is not identical with that between authority-based and power-based orders. Political decentralization can be highly dependent on law and legitimate political authority, as in federal or confederal polities. Conversely, force is a standard – and characteristically realist – mechanism for establishing centralized, hierarchical political order.

In the past half-century, force has operated as a source of centralization primarily within already established states. Tibet is the only prominent example of centralized political authority having been more or less successfully imposed through conquest. But in preceding eras it was a very common mechanism by which centralized states grew at the expense of their neighbors and spread imperial power to distant lands.

A realist rebuttal

Realists might reply that even if the difference is nowhere near as sharp and qualitative as Waltz claims, it is real. Power does tend to have a greater role in anarchical societies. Authority does tend to have a greater role in hierarchical societies. And these tendencies can be explained in large measure by the presence or absence of government.

Fair enough. But this does not support an anarchy–hierarchy dichotomy. And too many realists go on to describe elements of authority and hierarchy in international society as anomalous when in fact they are perfectly ordinary (even if less frequent).[10] The result is to obscure both important differences between anarchic orders and important similarities between anarchic and hierarchic orders.

This bias is built into the very language of anarchy. Rather than adopt the relatively neutral language of horizontal order, realists choose the emotionally charged language of anarchy. Anarchy is also a purely negative formulation – absence of hierarchy – in contrast to the more positive description of hierarchical order. And by defining anarchy largely as a residual category, it is easy to misrepresent anarchic orders as undifferentiated (because by definition they lack the differentiating characteristic by which hierarchy is defined).

Sovereignty and obligation

In addition to power, authority, and government, realists often appeal to sovereignty and obligation to distinguish hierarchic and anarchic orders.

---

[10] This distinction is important. Twins, for example, are an infrequent, but quite ordinary, occurrence. They are not an anomaly in the sense of being an oddity outside the usual order of things. Geniuses likewise are uncommon but quite ordinary. To suggest that they are oddities requiring special explanation by reference to processes outside ordinary nature or nurture would be highly misleading.

These too, however, clearly suggest a continuum rather than a dichotomy, and thus greater similarities between national and international politics than structural realists typically allow. They also suggest that Waltz is mistaken in claiming that there is no significant functional differentiation in anarchic orders.

Sovereignty

John Herz claims that realism arises from "a recognition of the inevitabilities of power politics in an age of sovereign states" (1976: 79), implicitly equating anarchy with a system of sovereign states. Henry Kissinger argues that realism is called for because states "must survive in a world of sovereign nations and competing wills" (1977: 204). Waltz likewise writes that "hierarchic elements within international structures limit and restrain the exercise of sovereignty but only in ways strongly conditioned by the anarchy of the larger system" (1979: 116).

Expressed in the language of sovereignty, anarchy and hierarchy mutually constitute one another. The internal hierarchical sovereignty of states can be seen as creating anarchic external sovereignty relations. Those who are the highest authority nationally recognize no higher international authority. Conversely, the "anarchic" decentralization of authority implied in the recognition of other states as sovereign equals can be see as creating national sovereigns. In this sense, perhaps, we can profitably talk of a dichotomy; one either is or is not sovereign.

When we look more closely at Waltz, though, it becomes clear that he really does not have any strong sense of sovereignty in mind. "To call states 'like units' is to say that each state is like all other states in being an autonomous political unit. It is another way of saying that states are sovereign" (1979: 95). This is simply false. Sovereignty is a *particular kind* of political autonomy. One can be politically autonomous but not sovereign, as feudal and suzerain-state systems indicate.[11]

In any case, sovereignty is a juridical relationship rather than a logically necessary accompaniment to anarchy (or hierarchy). Anarchic (and hierarchic) orders can exist and have existed without sovereignty. Restricting ourselves simply to the West, the ancient Greeks did not possess the concept. Sovereignty was almost completely absent from the theory and practice of the Middle Ages. Only in the late sixteenth and the seventeenth centuries did sovereignty become an important ordering principle of European national politics. Not until well into the eighteenth

---

[11] On feudal and early modern alternatives to the states system, see Spruyt (1994). On suzerain-state systems, see Wight (1977: 23–24, 75–80).

century was sovereignty a central part of European international politics.

Linking sovereignty to a general structural theory of international politics thus makes little sense. In fact, because it is a matter of legal institutions, sovereignty cannot be a feature of structure as defined by Waltz. We will return to this point in chapter 5.

Even the language of autonomy, and the related idea of independence, is problematic. If we mean simply juridical independence, we adopt a very "unrealistic" legal formalism. But if we mean practical autonomy, the capacity to make decisions free from the control of others, we are right back to a continuum, running from great powers down to victims of imperial wars that have not been fully eliminated or incorporated into the metropolitan power.

Obligation

The power of the preceding arguments is suggested by the fact that Waltz, despite his claims to the contrary, actually rejects an anarchy–hierarchy dichotomy at several points. For example, he writes that "structures may be changed . . . by changing the distribution of capabilities across units. Structures may also be changed by imposing requirements where previously people had to decide for themselves" (1979: 108). In other words, obligations alter structures. But obligations, and thus elements of hierarchy, clearly exist in anarchic orders.

Hierarchic orders are defined and distinguished from one another by patterns of obligations between units (individuals, groups, and institutions). Creating patterns of obligations among states likewise alters anarchic international structures by establishing limited domains of authority and subordination. If I am obliged to you, you have authority over me, and my will is (legitimately) subordinated to yours. But because such international obligations do not transform the order into a hierarchy, they must create a mixed order. And to the extent that authority and thus obligation are a sign of hierarchy, anarchic orders can in principle at least be not merely flecked with but full of hierarchy.

These differences, it must be emphasized, are structural. "A structure is defined by the arrangement of its parts. Only changes of arrangement are structural changes" (Waltz 1979: 80). Obligations change the arrangement of the parts, creating, for example, right-holders and duty-bearers, superior and inferior, free and obliged.

We are led even more directly to the same conclusion by Waltz' argument that "within an international order, risks may be avoided or lessened by moving from a situation of coordinate action to one of super- and subordination, that is, by erecting agencies with effective authority and extending a system of rules" (1979: 111). This is a direct admission that it *is* possible to create effective authority and systems of rules that *partially* replace ("anarchic") coordination with ("hierarchic") subordination.

Important differences exist not only between anarchic and hierarchic orders but within both anarchic and hierarchic orders. Such differences can be comprehended only by seeing anarchy and hierarchy as a continuum. And, as we will see in chapter 5, this opens up a range of possibilities and practices that realists typically ignore or denigrate.

Realists are likely to respond that features such as international society, governance in the absence of government, and international organizations and regimes are of relatively minor importance. But even if true, this is a contingent empirical fact. Elements of "hierarchic" authority, rules, and obligations should not be excluded from consideration before the fact by a misguided conception of anarchy and hierarchy as a strict dichotomy.

Functional differentiation

One important implication of treating anarchy and hierarchy as a continuum is that functional differentiation must be (re)introduced into our analysis of anarchic structures. It simply is not true that "anarchy entails relations of coordination among a system's units, and that implies their sameness" (Waltz 1979: 93).

In the complete absence of hierarchy, all states may be forced to perform all important political functions for themselves. Given realist motivational assumptions, states will face strong pressures both to limit the range of their functions and to become very much like one another. Hobbes, in *Leviathan*, captures this nicely when he lists the "incommodities" of his imagined state of nature: "no place for Industry . . . no Culture of the Earth; no Navigation . . ." (ch. 13, par. 9)[12] Both the sameness of the units and the limited range of possible activities arise in significant measure from the inability to reap the benefits of specialization and a division of labor.

But obligations, authority, and systems of rules can introduce a division of political labor between states in anarchic orders. As Waltz notes, in hierarchic orders "broad agreement prevails on the tasks that various parts of a government are to undertake and on the extent of the power they legitimately wield" (1979: 81). Much the same is true in many inter-

---

[12] All references to Hobbes' *Leviathan* are by chapter and paragraph in the C. B. Macpherson edition (Hobbes 1986).

national orders, if we substitute "states (and other international actors)" for "parts of a government."

We have already seen many examples. Supranational organizations such as the EU provide unusually clear examples of functional differentiation through the creation of obligations and subordination. Spheres of influence also involve functional differentiation and division of political labor. Different tasks and powers are allocated to regional hegemons and subordinate powers. And formal protectorates involve a hierarchical subordination and division of political labor remarkably similar to that of federal states.

Great powers

Another good example is the institution of "great powers," which allocates special rights and responsibilities to leading states. For example, Bull argues that although the great powers in contemporary international society "cannot formalise and make explicit the full extent of their special position," largely because of the power of the idea of sovereign equality (1977: 228), they nonetheless play a special role in creating and maintaining international order.

Great powers contribute to international order in two main ways: by managing their relations with one another; and by exploiting their preponderance in such a way as to impart a degree of central direction to the affairs of international society as a whole. More particularly, . . . by (i) preserving the general balance of power, (ii) seeking to avoid or control crises in their relations with one another, and (iii) seeking to limit or contain wars among one another. They exploit their preponderance in relation to the rest of international society by (iv) unilaterally exploiting their local preponderance, (v) agreeing to respect one another's spheres of influence, and (vi) joint action, as is implied by the idea of great power concert or condominium (Bull 1977: 207).

Along similar lines, Martin Wight notes that great powers are defined less by "the quantity or ingredients of power" and more by their "relationship to the states-system as a whole" (1978: 50). Schwarzenberger devotes an entire chapter to "the international oligarchy," those powers that "have arrogated to themselves the function of exercising supreme control over affairs within international society" (1951: 113). These are qualitative distinctions, even if they are rooted in the quantity of power possessed.

Waltz himself devotes the final chapter of *Theory of International Politics* to "The Management of International Affairs." The language of management is a language of "hierarchic" administration rather than "anarchic" struggle. And the managerial role of great powers clearly implies a differentiation of political functions among states. Great powers have not only an unusually large stake in the system but also "act for its sake" (1979: 195).

Realists might reply that this functional differentiation is largely a result of power. Even if true, we should not confuse the source of differentiation with its existence. And not all roles of states are so directly rooted in the distribution of capabilities.

During every period of the Westphalian era, states of various sizes defined their place and role within the system, and were accorded status and recognition by other states, not simply according to their positions of power, even relative to other adjacent units, but also, and often mainly, on the basis of their specific functions within the system (Schroeder 1994: 124).

In fact, Schroeder argues, adopting different roles (which may be related but are not reducible to security) has been a standard survival strategy, illustrated by Britain as the holder of the continental balance, Russia as a guardian of monarchical order, the Low Countries as a neutral buffer and conduit, Denmark and Sweden as neutral guardians of Baltic access, the Ottoman Empire as a buffer, and the multiple roles of the Habsburg monarchy (1994: 125–129). When we further add relationships and interactions, we begin to have the theoretical arsenal to develop the sort of mid-level realist theories and models of the sort I suggested were needed at the end of chapter 2.

Even preponderant power does not always express itself in the same kinds of functional differentiations. For example, formal colonialism and informal spheres of influence divide political functions differently among superior and subordinate units. And among empires, there were striking differences between the Athenian, Roman, Chinese, Ottoman, and British empires – as well as between the British Empire of the eighteenth and early nineteenth centuries and that of the early twentieth century (Koebner 1961; Koebner and Schmidt 1965).

Structure and functional differentiation

Appeals to the imperatives of a structural theory, and the abstractions it requires, cannot rescue Waltz. In defining hierarchic structures we do *not* abstract from *all* attributes and interactions of the units. Hierarchic orders cannot even be described unless some attributes of the units are included. Hierarchies are defined by differences of rights and responsibilities among units and by relations of super- and subordination, both of which introduce qualitative distinctions between units.

For example, the US Congress has particular constitutional (structural) rights, liberties, and duties, and stands in complex relations of superiority, subordination, and equality with the other branches of the federal government and the state governments. To abstract from these political powers and relations would be to misrepresent the structure of American government. To take them into account is not to confuse unit and structure or structure and process. Rather, it is to recognize that the identity of the units has a structural dimension from which a structural theory must *not* abstract.

A structural theory tries to set aside not all qualities and interactions, but only those that are secondary, contingent, historical, or "accidental." In anarchic orders, we are likely to be able to set aside more attributes and interactions of units with minimal analytical distortion. But in so far as there are hierarchical dimensions to a particular international order, we must include certain attributes of the units in our account of its structure.

In a Hobbesian state of nature, totally lacking hierarchy and thus functional differentiation, it may make sense to abstract from all attributes (other than their capabilities). It is probably a useful simplification to say that the only structural relation in which Hobbesian actors stand to one another is war, a complete absence of authority and obligation. But actual international systems are never so simple and undifferentiated. Even Hobbes, in *Leviathan*, recognizes this when he notes, immediately after the metaphor of states as gladiators quoted in chapter 1, that because states "uphold . . . the Industry of their Subjects; there does not follow from it [the state of war], that misery, which accompanies the liberty of particular men" (ch. 13, par. 12). And the fear of violent death clearly does not have the same force and implications in even the most anarchical society of states that it has in Hobbes' state of nature.

If only because there are major differences of power among states, a structural theory cannot ignore all attributes and relations. Rather, it must take into account those that are structural; at minimum, those that involve differentiations of functions. And to the extent that the identities and interactions of units rest on or reflect functional differentiations, a structural theory must *not* abstract from them – in either national or international orders.

Waltz admits that states "differ vastly in their capabilities," and even allows that "out of such differences something of a division of labor develops." But he immediately goes on to argue that this international division of labor "is slight in comparison with the highly articulated division of labor within them" (1979: 105). Slight, however, does not mean none. It is a term of quantitative, not qualitative, distinction; more or less, not either/or. And even if it is true that there is little functional differentiation in contemporary international relations, this does not justify denying, before the fact, as a matter of definition, the existence or possible significance of functional differentiation.

Not only is there functional differentiation in international society, but both the amount and type can and do change with time and place. For example, there is much more of a political division of labor among the states of the EU than among those of, for example, ASEAN. And the nature of that division of labor changed significantly between the Treaty of Rome, which established the European Economic Community, and the Maastricht Treaty, that made it the European Union. Whatever the practical political importance of such differentiation, it is a serious error to confuse arguments of importance with conceptual claims about the inherent and unchanging character of anarchic orders.

The shadow of Hobbes

As we saw in chapter 2, Waltz, despite his claim to abstract from all attributes of the units, draws heavily on a Hobbesian fear of violent death, provoked by the aggressive pursuit of gain (and glory). Here I want to argue that Waltz' denigration of authority, law, obligation, and other elements of hierarchy in international relations is also rooted in a Hobbesian vision that goes well beyond anarchy. And it is these additional assumptions, rather than anarchy *per se*, that give his theory its realist character.

Anarchy and equality

Hobbes, as we have seen, assumes not only anarchy and actors driven by competition, diffidence, and glory, but also actors who are physically and mentally equal. Inequality can be a powerful source of authority, obligation, and hierarchic order, as we have seen with spheres of influence and great powers. And power inequalities are a central reality of international relations. Therefore, it would be a peculiar kind of realism that emphasized the legal formalism of sovereignty over the realities of power. The Hobbesian assumption of equality is thus on its face a most unpromising starting point for international theory.

Only in relations among great powers can we assume rough equality of power. To the (considerable) extent that realists build their theories on assumed equality, they represent not general theories of international politics but rather theories of great power politics. Waltz more or less readily admits this. "Structures are defined not by all of the actors that flourish within them but by the major ones" (1979: 93). "Viewed as the politics of the powerful, international politics can be studied in terms of the logic of small-number systems" (1979: 131).

Most of international relations, however, takes place between states that are not roughly equal in power. As Waltz admits, "international politics is mostly about inequalities" (1979: 94). Nonetheless, his theory assumes equality by insisting on a rigid account of pure anarchy defined in oddly formal legalistic terms. The theory thus is not designed to deal with the vast bulk of international relations.

Realists may respond that they capture "the most important" parts. But this is not an objective scientific judgment. For the billions of people who do not live in great powers, power inequalities are at the heart of what is important to them in international relations.

"Power politics" involves both a logic of equality and a logic of subordination. For the strong, power is simultaneously a source of equality with their equals and a source of superiority over their inferiors. But for the weak, power – the power of others – is largely a source of inequality and subordination. The strong do what they can. The weak suffer what they must, including hierarchic subordination.

Robert Tucker expresses this well when he notes that "the international system has always been in essence oligarchical (unequal) largely because it has been anarchical," that is, because "the utility of a right to self-help is of necessity dependent upon the power at the disposal of those exercising this right." Such power-based inequalities, Tucker argues, are "rooted in the very nature of the international system." "The primordial institution of self-help . . . along with the 'natural' inequalities of states, guarantees that the international system will remain highly oligarchical" (1977: 4, 168, 169).

But Hobbes' logic of anarchy – and Waltz' as well, at least in its formal presentation – is a logic of equality alone. And the assumption of equality is essential to producing "Hobbesian" results, because inequality, especially preponderant power, can be a powerful source of authority, obligation, and hierarchic order.

The Hobbesian sovereign

Because all are equal in the state of nature, Hobbes argues in *Leviathan*, "every man has a Right to every thing" and "every one is governed by his own Reason" (ch. 14, par. 4). This state of pure liberty, however, is exactly equivalent to no one having a right to anything: my "right" obliges no one else to do or refrain from anything. There can be no obligation in this state of nature because obligation is a condition of inequality, of differential rights and duties. In such a state of nature, lacking both obligation and superior power, "every man will and may lawfully rely on his own strength and art, for caution against all other men" (ch. 17, par. 2).

The only way to escape such a state of war, according to Hobbes, is to create

a reall Unitie of them all, in one and the same Person, made by Covenant of every man with every man, in such a manner, as if every man should say to every man, *I Authorise and give up my right of Governing my selfe, to this Man, or to this Assembly of men, on this condition, that thou give up thy Right to him, and Authorise all his Actions in like manner* (ch. 17, par. 12).

Government, for Hobbes, requires a social contract in which each man agrees "*to lay down this right to all things*" (ch. 14, par. 5). And they must give up all their rights, in their entirety, irrevocably authorizing all the actions of their sovereign superior.[13]

For Hobbes, an absolute sovereign is a matter of logic. Any reserved natural rights would leave individuals in a (limited) state of war. And if they all did not give up all their rights, they would lose their equality – an impossible assumption given Hobbes' account of human motivation. For Hobbes the very existence of government requires that everyone be completely, and thus equally, subordinated to the sovereign, who is not party to or bound by the social contract. We face a simple, dichotomous choice: complete liberty or complete subordination; anarchic war of all against all or hierarchic absolute sovereignty; no authority or absolute authority. The striking similarity to Waltz' dichotomous account of ordering principles is, I would suggest, no coincidence.

We know from considerable experience, however, that separation of powers (divided sovereignty) and reserved rights for citizens need not lead to a war of all against all. Limited government is still government, not anarchy. Conversely, and most importantly for our purposes, order and obligation can be provided in the absence of government. The Hobbesian dichotomy of pure liberty or pure subordination, in other words, "abstracts from" most of *both* national and international politics. Only by moderating Hobbes' extreme assumptions – that is, by treating anarchy and hierarchy as a continuum – do these ideal types begin to have much application to everyday national and international politics.

Structure and human nature

Yet Hobbes, however wrong he may be about the need for absolute sovereignty, at least constructs his visions of anarchy and hierarchy out of the same assumptions about the units. The kinds of individuals that produce a Hobbesian state of nature need something very much like a Hobbesian

---

[13] The only exception Hobbes makes is when one's life is threatened by the sovereign, in which case fear relieves one of one's obligation (ch. 14, par. 8; ch. 21, par. 15–17).

sovereign to subordinate them. As Reinhold Niebuhr notes, "consistently egoistic individuals would require a tyrannical government for the preservation of social order" (1944: 123).

Waltz (sensibly) modifies Hobbes' assumptions in his account of hierarchic orders. But he retains Hobbesian assumptions in his account of anarchic orders. Waltz, unlike Hobbes, does *not* construct anarchy and hierarchy as opposites. The opposite of complete lack of subordination (anarchy) is complete subordination – which is Hobbes', but not Waltz', conception of hierarchy/sovereignty.

Waltz' hierarchical polity is made not for Hobbesian individuals who require government primarily to repress their craving egotism but for more "Lockean" individuals; that is, tolerant, somewhat restrained citizens with fairly modest aspirations. In moving from anarchy to hierarchy Waltz changes not only the structure but also the character of the actors.

But people who can make and live in a highly institutionalized liberal democracy will not necessarily produce an international war of all against all. Even if before society they were Hobbesian egoists, once tamed internally into Lockean liberals they may act liberally in their international relations as well, especially in relations with other liberal societies. Anarchy does make peaceful interaction more difficult even for Lockean states, which are likely to be pulled towards acting in a more Hobbesian fashion. The absence of government, however, does not assure that they will (re)turn into radically different creatures in their international relations.

By retaining Hobbesian motivational assumptions in his account of anarchy, Waltz retains all the flaws and exaggerations of Hobbes, with immensely important theoretical implications. Like Hobbes, Waltz grossly overstates the problems of anarchy and underestimates the possibilities for international social orders that rest on anything more than fear in the face of overwhelming power. Whether that bias seriously distorts our understanding of contemporary international society is the question we must address in the next two chapters.

Discussion questions

- How is order established in anarchy? How much order is there in international relations? To what extent is the resulting order due to the uninstitutionalized interactions of states? To what extent does it involve international institutions?

- What is the relationship between anarchy and sovereignty? Does international anarchy create sovereign states? If so, where does anarchy come from? Or do sovereign states create international anarchy? If so, does a theory of international politics not require a theory of the state?

- What does it mean to say that anarchy is "more important" than order in international relations? What is the implicit standard of importance? Are there other plausible standards of "what's important" in international relations? How can we adjudicate between competing claims of importance?

- For what purposes is the realist emphasis on anarchy helpful? For what purposes is it unhelpful, or even positively misleading?

- Is there any relation between abstracting from the attributes of states and abstracting from their interactions? Why is Waltz so committed to both?

- It is suggested in the text that the problem with realist accounts of order is that they improperly treat an empirical question as a theoretical one. Do you agree? Why? (This general issue of distinguishing theoretical and empirical questions will arise at crucial points in the argument in later chapters as well. Keep it – and your initial reflections on it – in mind as we proceed.)

- Waltz's Durkheimian conception of structure is not only common in the discipline but has an undeniable attraction. What, though, are other possible conceptions of structure? What are the comparative strengths and weaknesses of these varying accounts?

- If order emerges out of the interaction of separate units, and if all anarchic orders differ only in the distribution of capabilities, what makes all collections of units in anarchy interact in the same way? Is anarchy *per se* really so powerful?

- Return to Morgenthau's strategies of the status quo, imperialism, and prestige, discussed in chapter 2. Are these not systematic differences in the patterns in which states interact? If so, they would seem to be inaccessible to a structural theory. How much of a problem is that? In chapter 2 it was suggested that these differences arose directly from differences in state motives. Might they also be seen as emerging from "structural" elements not encompassed in Waltz' conception of structure?

- What are the (theoretical and practical) strengths of treating anarchy and hierarchy as a strict dichotomy? What are the weaknesses? How would *you* assess the balance between strengths and weaknesses? What does your answer tell you about your underlying conception of the nature of theory? About your implicit vision of the nature of international relations?

- Waltz is committed, largely on grounds of theoretical economy, to excluding all ordering principles other than anarchy and hierarchy. In principle, what are the costs and benefits of this strategy? In practice? Would your answer to this last question vary depending on time and place? On the purposes you bring to the analysis?

- Is there really a serious theoretical problem with ignoring (abstracting from) "anomalous" cases such as feudal societies or the European Union? What are the advantages and drawbacks of setting aside such cases?

- Donnelly suggests that Waltz' conception of anarchy and hierarchy as a dichotomy falsely generalizes across history on the basis of a contingent feature of contemporary international politics. Do you agree? Why? (Once more, keep the broader issue – the alleged problem of over-generalizing from the present – in mind as we proceed. It will recur repeatedly.)

- What are the strengths and weaknesses of viewing anarchy and hierarchy as a continuum?

- Still another suggestion in the text – which also will recur as we proceed – is that realists confuse their particular interests with what is most important in the field. What do you make of this claim? Is it true, as is further implied in the text, that basic theoretical decisions often rest on intuitive or aesthetic judgments about what seems interesting or important?

- How are force, order, and authority related? Is this a question that has a theoretical answer? Or does the answer vary dramatically with time and place? Both?

- Is the language of "anarchy" really substantively biased? Does it make any real difference if we were to replace characteristic realist talk of anarchy with discussions of horizontal order? Is the difference theoretical? Practical? Both?

- Can there be anarchic orders without sovereignty? Can there be hierarchic orders without sovereignty? If the answer to these questions is yes, what does this say about characteristic realist appeals to sovereignty? How much do such appeals undercut the claim that realism analyzes largely timeless law-like regularities?

- Clearly not all states perform the same functions. Why, then, does Waltz go out of his way to insist that a theory of international politics should abstract from functional differentiation? What would happen to a structural theory that included functional differentiation? Would we still be able to talk about law-like regularities? The *same* regularities that Waltz does? At the same level of generality?

- What is the relationship between anarchy and equality? *Is* equality an essential assumption of Waltz' theory? Why is Waltz so deeply committed to denying, as a theoretical assumption, the obvious fact of gross inequality and subordination in international relations? Are these questions about equality just variants on the earlier questions about functional differentiation?

- Donnelly suggests that Hobbes is much more consistent in his motivational assumptions than Waltz. How might Waltz reply? Would an adequate response require making any significant changes in Waltz' theory?

Suggestions for further reading

Waltz' principal discussions of anarchy are in *Theory of International Politics* (1979), pp. 88–89, 100–116. This is required reading for anyone interested in the topic. Schmidt (1998) provides an excellent book-length historical survey of treatments of anarchy and the related notion of sovereignty within the discipline of international studies over the past century, focusing in particular on pre-World War II authors and controversies.

Helen Milner's **"The Assumption of Anarchy in International Relations Theory: A Critique"** (1991) develops an argument very similar to mine. Her discussion of the impact of interdependence on Waltz' vision of anarchy (1991: 81–85) is especially insightful. Alexander Wendt's **"Anarchy is What States Make of It"** (1992) provides a classic account of the variability of anarchic orders. Alker (1996: ch. 11) and Onuf and Klink (1989) develop similar themes in rather different ways. Ashley (1988) offers an even more radical, postmodern reading. Lake (1996) and Powell (1994) provide more "mainstream" explorations of the problematic dimensions of Waltz' conception of anarchy. Speer (1986: ch. 4) discusses anarchy in the context of a broader argument advocating world government.

Ian Clark's *The Hierarchy of States* (1989) offers a powerful, historically grounded alternative to the Waltzian dichotomy of anarchy and hierarchy. He emphasizes stratification among states and the varying forms that stratification may take in theory and have taken in international practice since 1815. Alexander Wendt and Daniel Friedheim in "Hierarchy Under Anarchy" (1995) make a similar point, exploring the example of East Germany. James Hsiung's *Anarchy and Order* (1997) looks at the contribution of international law in providing order in anarchy. Hedley Bull's *The Anarchical Society* (1977) is the classic argument for the existence of a society of states in a strong sense of that term.

4   System, structure, and balance of power

The structuralist project, as we have seen in the preceding chapters, rests on maximum abstraction. The theoretical strategy is to make the fewest assumptions possible and use the smallest imaginable number of explanatory variables. Structural realists self-consciously sacrifice richness and depth for a simple, rigorous theory that holds widely across time and place.

In chapter 2, however, we saw that allegedly structural explanations typically rely on the interaction of structure and "unit level" (state) preferences. In chapter 3 we saw that anarchy alone has far fewer implications for state behavior than realists often suggest. This chapter extends this line of argument by examining the balance of power, which Waltz presents as a purely structural theory of international politics. I will argue that, once again, allegedly structural explanations either fail or prove not to be structural.

So far we have discussed the distribution of capabilities, the third element of structure, only in the context of the distinction between great powers, whose capabilities make them more or less equal players in international relations, and lesser powers, which appear in structural theories largely as objects acted upon by the powerful. Waltz, however, draws one of his principal substantive conclusions in *Theory of International Politics* on the basis of the distribution of capabilities: bipolar structures are more stable than multipolar structures. Waltz also addresses the balance of power more generally in his well-known argument that states in anarchy "balance" rather than "bandwagon." These claims will occupy us in the first two sections of this chapter. The final two sections introduce a broader critique that emphasizes the difference between system and structure, opening the way for a discussion of international institutions (in chapter 5).

Stability and polarity

Waltz defines an international system as stable if (1) it remains anarchic and (2) "no consequential variation takes place in the number of principal parties that constitute the system" (1979: 162). By this definition, though, multipolarity would seem to be more stable than bipolarity. As Waltz himself notes, the European "multipolar system lasted three centuries," whereas the Cold War bipolar system at the time Waltz wrote had lasted only three decades (1979: 162), and in the end lasted less than half a century. Nonetheless, as Dale Copeland notes, "since the introduction of Kenneth Waltz' neorealist theory in 1979, it has been widely accepted that bipolar systems are more stable than multipolar systems" (1996: 29).

The virtues of bipolarity

Copeland continues by adding that bipolar superpowers "are less likely to fall into a major war" (1996: 29). And on closer examination, "the virtues of bipolarity" (1979: 168) to which Waltz draws attention prove to be concerned not with stability as he formally defines it but with peace among the great powers. When Waltz argues that "two great powers can deal with each other better than more can" (1979: 193), he means that they are better able to avoid general, systemic, or hegemonic war. In much the same vein, John Mearsheimer defines stability as "absence of wars and major crises" (1994/95: 6).

Bipolarity fosters peace, according to Waltz, because of "the simplicity of relations in a bipolar world" (1979: 174). "In the great-power politics of multipolar worlds, who is a danger to whom, and who can be expected to deal with threats and problems, are matters of uncertainty." "Dangers are diffused, responsibilities unclear, and definitions of vital interests easily obscured" (1979: 170, 171) – all of which increase the danger of intentional or accidental war. In bipolarity, by contrast, "who is a danger to whom is never in doubt" (1979: 170). And because the threat each poses to the other is so clear, the superpowers "promptly respond to unsettling events" (1979: 171). Bipolar superpowers are less likely to stumble into war because their close focus on one another induces an iterative process of relatively rapid mutual adjustment.

The other great virtue of bipolarity is that little except fighting the other superpower matters deeply. In a bipolar world, "allies add relatively little to the superpowers' capabilities" (1979: 171). Therefore, particular gains or reversals have little effect on the overall balance. "Each can lose heavily only in war with the other; in power and in wealth, both gain more by the peaceful development of internal resources than by wooing and winning – or by fighting and subduing – other states" (1979: 172).[1] General war

---

[1] Even at this early stage it is worth noting that this simply does not follow from the mere existence of bipolarity. Such a conclusion requires additional assumptions about growth rates, the size of the gap between the superpowers and second tier powers, and the costs and potential gains from war.

almost always appears foolhardy: bipolar superpowers have too much to win by peace, too much to lose by war, and little hope of gain in fighting one another.[2]

Superpowers still compete with one another and are driven apart by their mutual fears and suspicions. But "their concern for peace and stability draws them together" (1979: 175), or at least away from the brink of war. Their joint interest in maintaining their superior position over all others restrains the pursuit of competitive interests that might lead to war. Because they have both the most to lose and the least to gain in a general war – they are already at the top of the international order – Waltz sees bipolar superpowers having a structurally induced interest in system-wide peace and stability that many multipolar great powers do not have.

In addition, the very existence of multiple potential adversaries in multipolar orders creates dangers and difficulties that do not exist in bipolarity. There is always the chance of being ganged up on, which greatly increases the level of fear and hostility. In a bipolar world tension certainly is high, in part because it is so tightly focused on a single adversary. But "because no appeal can be made to third parties, pressure to moderate behavior is heavy" (1979: 174).

Other theorists have further developed the case against multipolarity. For example, Thomas Christensen and Jack Snyder (1990) have elegantly elaborated two logics characteristic of multipolar orders that lead to war: "chain-ganging" and "buck-passing."[3] Multipolar states may be chain-ganged into war by their alliance partners. Many analysts interpret the outbreak of World War I in these terms: Austria attacked Serbia, which dragged Russia into the war in defense of Serbia, which then dragged in Germany in defense of Austria, which led France .... World War II is often presented as a classic example of buck-passing, with France, Britain, and the Soviet Union each hoping that the other(s) would somehow restrain Hitler.[4] Bipolar superpowers, by contrast, have

---

[2] The parallel drawback is that bipolar superpowers have interests across the whole geographical extent of the system. Because "there are no peripheries" (1979: 171), superpowers are likely to overreact and engage in more minor conflicts in places of modest or minor strategic significance. Waltz, however, argues that this is by far the lesser of two evils.

[3] The metaphors are from colloquial American English. A chain-gang is a prison work crew, in which the prisoners/workers are shackled to one another. To "pass the buck" is to try to evade responsibility by attributing it to someone else. President Harry Truman is famous and generally admired for a sign on his desk that read "The buck stops here."

[4] Buck-passing takes place "internally" when states scrimp on their military spending in the hope that others will bear the costs of deterring aggression. See Posen (1984: ch. 2).

no one to pass the buck to and are unlikely to value any ally highly enough to be chain-ganged into a major war.[5]

The remainder of this section presents three lines of criticism of the Waltzian argument for the relative stability or peacefulness of bipolarity.

The Cold War peace

Over the past decade, realists have been repeatedly attacked for failing to predict the end of the Cold War. Beyond noting that their critics did not predict it either, structural realists have responded that they never intended to explain or predict change. As Waltz put it, a decade before the fall of the Berlin Wall, his theory "explains continuities . . . recurrences and repetitions, not change" (1979: 69).

The end of the Cold War has made many people more aware of the limitations of this focus on continuity. But structural realists do have a point when they complain of being attacked not for what they have done but for what they have not tried to do. The long Cold War peace[6] provides a fairer test of the power of structural realism, both in general and for its claims about bipolar stability. Surprisingly, though, both Waltz and John Mearsheimer have advanced remarkably similar accounts that prove to be, in the end, not structural.

Mearsheimer argues that "the distribution and character of military power are the root causes of war and peace" (1990: 6). This reference to the character of military power signals that his explanation of the Cold War peace will not be structural in Waltz' sense of the term. Waltz' states differ only in the *quantity* of capabilities they possess. The character of military power simply is not a feature of structure as defined by Waltz.

In the particular case of the Cold War, Mearsheimer identifies three key factors that led to peace: "the bipolarity of the distribution of power on the Continent, the rough equality in military power between those two polar states, and the appearance of nuclear weapons, which vastly expanded the violence of war, making deterrence far more robust" (1990: 11). The first two factors are indeed structural; they deal with the distri-

---

[5] The countervailing drawback of bipolarity would seem to be proxy wars. But as these are peripheral to the overall balance of power and do not lead to direct fighting between the forces of the superpowers, the order remains stable and *relatively* peaceful (compared to the devastation of a general war).

[6] The moral basis of this characterization, which treats "minor" war in places like Korea, Vietnam, Angola, Cambodia, and El Salvador as if it were peace, is beyond the scope of my inquiry here. This is, however, a particularly striking consequence of Waltz' view that "the theory, like the story, of international politics is written in terms of the great powers of an era" (1979: 72).

bution of capabilities.[7] But the third, nuclear weapons, is not. Its effects are produced through the character of the weapons and the quality of their effects rather than through anarchy or the distribution of capabilities.

In remarkably similar, and characteristically sparse, language, Waltz claims that "the longest peace yet known rested on two pillars: bipolarity and nuclear weapons" (1993: 44). In other words, half the story of the long Cold War peace, even in Waltz' telling, rests on a non-structural feature. For all Waltz' talk about the virtues of bipolarity, the "virtues" of nuclear weapons are at least as important to his story of the maintenance of peace between the United States and the Soviet Union during the Cold War.

Waltz is unusually forceful and direct in asserting the peace-inducing effects of nuclear weapons.[8] "Nuclear weapons dissuade states from going to war more surely than conventional weapons do." "Nuclear weapons have drastically reduced the probability of [war] being fought by the states that have them." "The absolute quality of nuclear weapons sharply sets a nuclear world off from a conventional one" (1990: 743, 744, 732). These effects, however, are entirely independent of the distribution of capabilities; they hold equally for bipolar and multipolar orders. If we take Waltz on nuclear weapons seriously, we can account for the Cold War peace entirely independently of bipolarity.

Structure simply does not account even for the "big picture" in a relatively easy case concerning the subject matter (war and peace) to which structural realism is best suited. The outcome is "consistent" with the theory, in the sense that state behavior was not significantly different from Waltz' structural prediction. But the cause of that outcome was not structure/bipolarity. The distribution of capabilities, even in Waltz' own telling of the story, is not the key to Cold War peace or stability. Because the maximal abstraction of the structuralist project is justified only by its alleged ability to get the big picture right, this failure is of profound theoretical significance.

The logic of bipolarity

A second line of critique takes on the logic of Waltz' argument. This debate goes back at least to 1964, when Waltz first presented his argument

---

[7] We should note, however, that Waltz does not include differences between the great powers in his account of the distribution of capabilities, characteristically simplifying to the extreme by considering only differences between great and lesser powers.

[8] He is sufficiently convinced of these effects that he suggests standard fears of nuclear proliferation are largely groundless. For a lively debate over these views, see Sagan and Waltz (1995).

for bipolarity (1964) and Karl Deutsch and J. David Singer presented an equally classic account of the virtues of multipolarity (1964).[9] Dale Copeland has given this debate a creative new twist, challenging the static nature of Waltzian structural realism.

"In Waltz's formulation, with polarity as the key structural variable, there is nothing to vary *within* either a bipolar or a multipolar system to explain why any system should move from peace to war" (Copeland 1996: 46–47). As we saw above, Waltz denies that his theory can explain a change of polarity; it accounts only for outcomes within a particular order. But with both polarity and anarchy held constant, and functional differentiation ruled out of the picture, "there is nothing to vary to explain changes in the probability of major war" (Copeland 1996: 72). The structural probability of war in bipolar orders therefore must be constant across time, and the same in every bipolar order.

Although odd and unsettling, this is not necessarily fatal if we read Waltz to be arguing that bipolarity eliminates or moderates standard causes of war in multipolar orders (without introducing other causes that counter-balance them). Here is where Copeland's appeal to time and change has substantial power.

Copeland models the range of possibilities by imagining great powers, numbering either two or five, that start out roughly equal. One power then rises to a leading position. The leading power then declines while one other power rises. This cycle highlights three types of situations, which I will call balance (the starting point of equality), divergence (the rise of a single power), and convergence (the simultaneous rise of a second power and decline of the leading power) (1996: figs. 1, 2).

Copeland argues that the starting point of relative equality – balance – has a low probability of war in both bipolar and multipolar orders. "Only if a state is clearly superior to any other individual state in military power can it even contemplate waging a war for hegemony" (1996: 50). Conversely, the probability of preventive war is high in both bipolar and multipolar orders during the phase of convergence. "Assuming states are rational actors seeking primarily their own security, the dominant and declining military great power is most likely to begin a major war" (1996: 48).

The difference between the two orders appears in the phase I have called divergence. In multipolarity, a rising power has little incentive to attack, both because it faces multiple adversaries and because if it does desire to launch a hegemonic war its position will be stronger later (Copeland 1996: 48). Furthermore, "a declining but only equal great power in multipolarity has reason to think that a rising state, as long as it does not grow too preponderant in the system, will also be restrained in its ambitions by the presence of so many great powers; hence a preventive war for security is less imperative" (1996: 50).

In bipolarity, however, Copeland argues that the probability of war is high during the phase of divergence. Because there is only one adversary and the two powers are still almost equal, "in bipolarity a successful bid for hegemony is much easier to achieve" (1996: 50), for both rising and declining superpowers. In addition, neither side has to worry about third parties either taking advantage or altering the balance, because by definition they lack the capabilities to matter much (1996: 50–51).

A further subtle difference occurs during the phase of convergence. Copeland argues that a declining multipolar power has the greatest incentive to attack early in the phase of convergence. As the two powers approach balance, the risk declines. In bipolarity, however, the incentive to attack does not decline as balance is approached. In bipolarity, but not in multipolarity, a declining but only equal great power is likely to risk war.

How does this logic stand up to history? Copeland argues that in the three most prominent examples of pre-nuclear bipolar orders – Sparta and Athens in the fifth century BC, Carthage and Rome in the third century BC, and France and the Habsburgs in the early sixteenth century – war broke out as expected when a previously dominant power was declining and being challenged by a newly rising power even though it felt itself only roughly equal (1996: 60–71). Copeland also suggests that a similar logic brought us perilously close to a war in the Cuban Missile Crisis in 1962 (1996: 71–86). Thus he titles his article "Neorealism and the Myth of Bipolar Stability."

This is not the place to attempt to adjudicate between competing realist theories of the impact of the distribution of capabilities on the balance of power. Copeland, however, must bow to Waltz neither in the power of his logic nor in the historical support that he can muster for it.[10] We thus have a case of inconsistent structural realist theories of the sort that we discussed at the end of chapter 2. Waltz and Copeland present models that are both undeniably realist – they are derived from a common "hard core" of assumptions – yet yield divergent, even contradictory, conclusions because they make different secondary assumptions about the distribution of capabilities or apply them to different circumstances. For my

---

[10] Copeland also suggests that the historical record is kinder to multipolarity than Waltz' abstract logic. He argues that at most one European war can be attributed to chain-ganging, and that even the case of World War I is problematic (1996: 42–43).

purposes that is sufficient: from anarchy and the distribution of capabilities alone, even realists cannot agree on what follows.

The Sicilian expedition

As well as adding a dynamic aspect to capabilities, in contrast to Waltz' static understanding, Copeland makes significantly different motivational assumptions. In discussing the virtues of bipolarity, Waltz assumes something very much like "defensive positionalism":[11] his superpowers will not risk much to push for hegemony, each being willing to settle for something very much like the status quo. Copeland's superpowers, however, are willing to consider a drive for domination. Without that assumption, it is hard to imagine them being willing to risk war when merely equal. At the very least, we have to assume that they see preserving their position as a matter of maintaining strict equality with the other superpower, rather than just qualitative superiority over the lesser powers that still lie below them.

We thus return to the inescapable presence of substantive motivational assumptions. From polarity alone we can predict nothing about the behavior of states in anarchy. Bipolar superpowers need not be conservative. There is no logical reason why a state should be more satisfied to be one of two internationally dominant powers than one of three or four.[12] The conservatism (or aggressiveness) of great powers cannot be explained by the distribution of capabilities independent of substantive motivational assumptions.

Some characteristically realist motivational assumptions suggest that superpowers will act as status quo powers. But other, no less characteristically realist assumptions yield superpowers that seek imperial domination. And Thucydides' account of Athens provides a striking historical illustration of the imperial aspirations of a bipolar superpower.

Following Thucydides' interpretation we typically talk of the Peloponnesian War, in the singular. But it can also be seen as two wars, broken by a long interval of peace. And even if we treat it as a single war, it had two very different phases, separated by seven years in which Athens and Sparta did not fight one another. Furthermore, during the course of "the war." Athens' orientation and behavior changed dramatically despite a constant bipolar structure.

---

[11] See pp. 63–64.

[12] The simplicity of relations may still make bipolar orders more peaceful. I am here only criticizing the argument that bipolar superpowers are more conservative. Exactly the same arguments Waltz makes about having the most to lose and the greatest interest in system stability apply equally to multipolar great powers.

In Thucydides' telling in the *History*, Athens began the war with Pericles' largely defensive strategy: pay attention to the navy, attempt no new conquests, and expose the city to no hazards (II.65).[13, 14] As early as the sixth year of the war, however, Athens was pursuing a more expansive policy. In the seventh year, when Sparta, following its defeat at Pylos, offered peace, Athens refused, at the urging of its new leader Cleon (IV.21).[15] But in reaching for more, Athens overreached. Following a series of reverses at the hands of the Spartan general Brasidas, the Athenians were eventually forced to settle for what is usually known as the Peace of Nicias (IV.78–V.24).

The desire for more, however, proved overwhelming. The final three books of the *History* recount the momentous Athenian decision to invade Sicily, their defeat at Syracuse, and a series of military reversals and internal struggles that eventually led to Athens' defeat.[16] We will return to the Sicilian expedition in chapter 6. Here it is important that we understand that Athens chooses expansion over the status quo, in sharp contrast to Waltz' assumptions about bipolar superpowers.[17]

Nicias forcefully advocates a Waltzian satisfaction with the status quo (VI.9–14). But Alcibiades appeals to a most un-Waltzian imperative to expand.

Men do not rest content with parrying the attacks of a superior, but often strike the first blow to prevent the attack being made. And we cannot fix the exact point at which our empire shall stop; we have reached a position in which we must not be content with retaining but must scheme to extend it, for, if we cease to rule others, we are in danger of being ruled ourselves (VI.18).

In arguing against "the do-nothing policy which Nicias advocates," Alcibiades also appeals to Athens' active character. "My conviction is that a city not inactive by nature could not choose a quicker way to ruin itself than by suddenly adopting such a policy" (VI.18).

[13] All otherwise unidentified references are to Thucydides' *History* by book and chapter. Translations are from the revised Crawley translation (Thucydides 1982).

[14] For an alternative reading, however, see Wet (1969) and, with special reference to the Sicilian expedition, Fliess (1966: 111–113). On Pericles' strategy, see also Cawkwell (1997: chs. 3, 4).

[15] For contrasting readings of Cleon's character, see Lang (1972) and Woodhead (1960). See also Westlake (1968: ch. 5) and the essay "Thucydides and Kleon" by A. W. Gomme (1962). On the Pylos debate in particular, see Flower (1992).

[16] Thucydides' *History* breaks off abruptly in 411, seven years before Athens' final defeat. The standard understanding is that Thucydides died before he could finish retelling the tragedy. But the tragic end was known to Thucydides' readers. For an imaginative reconstruction of what the "missing" books might have looked like, see Rawlings (1981). On politics in Athens in the aftermath of the war, see Strauss (1986).

[17] We should also note that the Sicilian expedition, seen as the start of a new war, contradicts Copeland's logic as well. The two powers at that time were roughly in balance.

Alcibiades' argument, and the decision of the assembly to follow it, reflects a side of the Athenian character that Thucydides emphasizes as early as Book I. The Corinthians at the Congress at Lacedaemon draw attention to "the great contrast between the two national characters" of Athens and Sparta.

The Athenians are addicted to innovation, and their designs are characterized by swiftness alike in conception and execution . . . they are adventurous beyond their power, and daring beyond their judgment . . . They are swift to follow up a success, and slow to recoil from a reverse . . . they alone are enabled to call a thing hoped for a thing got, by the speed with which they act upon their resolutions . . . To describe their character in a word, one might truly say that they were born into the world to take no rest themselves and to give none to others (I. 70).

Polarity simply does not determine whether a great power is a status quo or a revolutionary (imperialist) power. If we are to believe Thucydides, national character is key. Sparta's conservative character, not bipolarity, made it a status quo power. In any case, Golden Age Athens is a decisive counter-example to the Waltzian logic of the virtues of bipolarity based on the structurally induced conservatism of the superpowers.

It will not do for a realist to reply that this incessant activity – *polyprag-mosyne* in the Greek (see Ehrenberg 1947; Adkins 1976) – was the cause of Athens' fall. The question is whether structure allows, even forces, us to assume that bipolar superpowers are status quo powers. Waltz is not prescribing but laying out assumptions for a predictive or explanatory theory. In one of the crucial historical examples of bipolar orders, the Waltzian assumption gets things decisively wrong.

Power, threat, and balancing

Waltz' other major substantive conclusion concerning the balance of power deals with the general phenomenon of balancing. "The expectation is not that a balance, once achieved, will be maintained, but that a balance, once disrupted, will be restored in one way or another. Balances of power recurrently form" (1979: 128). Because this conclusion flows from anarchy rather than from the distribution of capabilities, it allegedly holds for all international orders.

Balancing and bandwagoning

In chapter 1 we introduced the Waltzian distinction between balancing and bandwagoning. Anarchy and hierarchy, Waltz argues, are distinguished by the responses they engender to another actor's growing power. In hierarchic orders, political actors tend to "bandwagon," to give their support to the side that appears likely to win, in order to increase their chance of gaining in the spoils of victory. Because the risks of survival tend to be relatively low, even the diffident can focus most of their efforts on the pursuit of absolute gain.[18] In anarchic orders, however, a rising power – especially one that may be seeking universal domination – appears not as a source of patronage (gain) but as a potential enemy that is likely to turn eventually even on its "friends."

Although in chapter 2 we saw that from anarchy alone we cannot predict balancing, this still leaves open Waltz' claim about the tendency of balances to form. And that conclusion would seem to be strongly confirmed by the regularity with which anti-hegemonic coalitions both form (against powers such as Napoleonic France or Nazi Germany) and then break up once the common enemy has been neutralized or subordinated. But the general argument about balancing is misformulated, even if we set aside the issue of motivational assumptions.

The incentives to bandwagon flow not from hierarchy *per se* but from the anticipated behavior of the winner. Consider, for example, a struggle for leadership in a highly fractious military dictatorship. If winners can at a later date easily demote, arrest, exile, or even kill potential rivals, bandwagoning may not be the preferred strategy. Rival claimants to a throne will also rationally select strategies based on the expected behavior of the anticipated victor. If she is likely to follow Machiavelli's advice of extinguishing the competing ruling line (P3[3]), balancing is the only rational strategy.

Conversely, bandwagoning is not structurally determined when survival is not at stake. For example, it is common and often quite rational for a candidate for political office to continue to contest an election vigorously even when far behind in the polls. In fact, when survival is not at stake, alignment in hierarchical orders would seem to be quite indeterminate.

Furthermore, as we saw in chapter 2, states in anarchy often bandwagon rather than balance. This is most evident in spheres of influence. But even in relations among great and middle powers, whether bandwagoning is a rational strategy depends on the relative risks and benefits of following and opposing a leader – which change from issue to issue and from leader to leader. And lesser powers may ally with a superpower to pursue gain rather than out of fear of the other superpower or the threatening power of a neighbor.[19]

---

[18] On absolute and relative gains, see pp. 58–60.

[19] There also seems to be important variation across time. For example, Barry Strauss (1991) argues that bandwagoning was less common during the era of the Peloponnesian War than during the Cold War.

Balancing is driven not by anarchy but by fear of predation.[20] In some hierarchic orders, survival or long-run prosperity is sufficiently precarious that balancing regularly occurs. The risks in some anarchic orders may be sufficiently low to allow bandwagoning. And such factors, which depend on the character of the actors as well as their capabilities, are non-structural in Waltz' sense of that term. From anarchy or hierarchy alone, we cannot confidently predict either balancing or bandwagoning.

Polarity and balancing

Even if structure does not determine alignment (balancing or bandwagoning), Waltz' more limited argument that in anarchy "balances of power recurrently form" (1979: 128) does seem to have found powerful expression in post-Cold War structural realist arguments against unipolarity or global primacy (e.g. Mastanduno 1997). Concentrating overwhelming capabilities in the hands of a single state starkly poses the danger of imperial domination, allowing us to predict with considerable confidence that potential great powers will balance against an emerging hegemon.

A "benevolent" hegemon may lessen the perceived threat to competitive states by sharing the material gains of primacy. Diffident states may be reassured by, for example, institutionalized commitments, cooperative diplomacy, non-aggressive defense policies, or transparent decision making processes. Even vain states may be partially assuaged by procedures that incorporate them into the rituals of leadership. But fear of the hegemon, especially in the long run, is structurally induced. Thus balancing rather than bandwagoning is to be expected, at least from potential great powers. And the more aggressive the perceived intentions of the hegemon, the more powerful the incentives to balance.

A similar logic applies to the superpowers in a bipolar world. Failure to compete risks transforming bipolarity into unipolarity. Because the threat of imperial domination is clear and immediate, we can expect each side to pursue a balancing strategy. The logic of defensive positionalism, which I argued in chapter 2 does not provide an adequate general theory of state motivation, may indeed be an attractive way to model superpower preferences in a bipolar world.

As we move into multipolar situations, however, structural pressures to balance are regularly swamped by factors such as perceptions and internally generated preferences. Even if states continue to balance, structure

[20] Waltz' account of the impact of nuclear weapons underscores the dominance of fear over polarity. Nuclear weapons exert a stabilizing influence regardless of polarity because they put survival at risk.

alone cannot tell us against whom. As Glenn Snyder notes, "in a multipolar system, who allies with whom is structurally indeterminate . . . each state is logically eligible to be either friend or enemy of any other state . . . there is almost always a degree of uncertainty about who is friend and who is foe" (1997: 18–19).[21] Unless a potential hegemon crystallizes a system-wide threat, it is not even clear how we should define balancing and bandwagoning in a multipolar system. Without knowledge of the motives of allies we cannot say with any confidence whether an alliance in a multipolar world reflects diffident balancing against a common threat or competitive bandwagoning to pursue joint gains against a third party.

It is not surprising then that when we look to history we find that balancing proves not to be all that much more law-like or regular than failures to balance. Paul Schroeder has gone so far as to argue that "it is precisely the broad outcomes and general patterns of international history which neo-realist theory does not explain, or even recognize" (1994: 130), even in the case of responses to potential hegemons, where the balancing logic should be most evident.

For example, British and Austrian reactions to France during the period 1660–1713, Schroeder argues, simply cannot be explained by a logic of balancing. Quite the contrary. James II, who ruled Britain from 1685 to 1688, was dependent on France. Britain "balanced" against France only after a violent change of government, generated for largely internal political reasons, that required invasion of Britain by a Dutch army. And Austria during this period was looking primarily to the Ottoman threat from the southeast, not to France. Even more clearly, the rise of Germany, the United States, and Japan in the half-century prior to World War I had very little to do with balancing against Britain (1994: 135–137, 145–146).

The historical record simply does not support Waltz' claim that "balance-of-power theory applies in all situations where two or more units coexist in a self-help system" (1979: 57). As Schroeder puts it, neorealism gets "the patterns, and the broad outcomes of international history wrong, and predicts things of major theoretical and historical importance which on closer examination turn out not to be so" (1994: 147).

Power and threat

Stephen Walt (1987) plausibly suggests that we can refine and rescue Waltz' underlying insight by seeing states as balancing against external

---

[21] Waltz more or less admits this when, in a passage quoted earlier in this chapter, he notes that in multipolar structures "who is a danger to whom, and who can be expected to deal with threats and problems, are matters of uncertainty" (1979: 170).

threats, not external power (capabilities). Threats, however, cannot be specified without recourse to the character and intentions of states. Therefore, balance of threat theory is not a strictly structural theory. Without knowing who holds particular capabilities and their intentions – as well as who we are and what we value – we cannot say whether there is a threat to balance. For example, the same capabilities in the hands of Britain, Poland, Mexico, Russia, China, Israel, Iraq, and North Korea may pose very different threats to the United States.

Waltz' balance of power logic applies to potential great powers in uni-polar structures because of the near certainty of the hegemon's capabilities being perceived as threatening. When there are only two great powers we can perhaps profitably assume that each will perceive the other as a threat, and thus balance – although Golden Age Athens raises questions about even this. In a multipolar world, however, the existence of at least two potential threats dramatically attenuates the link between external capabilities and threat. And as the fear of imperial domination recedes, it becomes increasingly unfruitful to assume balancing. Waltz' balancing logic thus is primarily a logic of *bipolar* orders, not of international relations in general.[22]

The logic of balancing rests on an active fear for survival. Anarchy alone, however, does not generate Hobbes' overwhelming fear of violent death, as we saw in chapter 2. This is the central insight behind Walt's move to balance of threat theory. But this move largely abandons Waltzian structuralism – which, in my view, is a good thing. For most international orders, the elegant simplicity of Waltzian structuralism is barren.

A theory that applies only to (anti-)hegemony and bipolarity provides a thoroughly inadequate basis for a theory (let alone *the* theory) of international politics. The distribution of capabilities in anarchy explains little about the behavior of other types of states or the consequences of other anarchic structures. In particular, structure alone has little to say about multipolar politics, which has characterized modern Western international relations for most of its history. And, as we saw in the cases of the Cold War peace and Golden Age Athens, even in bipolar orders structure proves a surprisingly weak explanatory variable.

System, structure, and interaction

Even accepting all my arguments so far, it would be premature, however, to abandon system-level or third image realist theories. For example, in

---

[22] A similar conclusion is suggested by the fact that the salience of "relative gains" concerns declines as we move away from bipolarity. See Snidal (1991a).

discussing the Cold War peace, Mearsheimer (correctly) notes that all three factors to which he appeals "are aspects of the European states system . . . and not of the states themselves" (1990: 12). This recalls Waltz' criticism of "reductionist" or "inside-out" (first or second image) theories, which explain outcomes by reference to the attributes of the actors (1979: chs. 2–4). Such explanations frequently are mistaken, because state behavior often reflects external constraints rather than internal preferences.

Waltz counterposes reductionist and *systemic* theories (1979: ch. 4), plausibly arguing that "a systems theory of international politics deals with the forces that are in play at the international, and not at the national, level" (1979: 71). In practice, however, Waltz seems to believe that this means *structural* theory. For example, in talking about the differences between bipolar and multipolar structures, he regularly uses the language of systems: e.g. "the multipolar system," "the bipolar system," "bipolar and multipolar systems" (1979: 162–163, 163ff. *passim*). But system and structure are not the same.

The logic would seem to be roughly the following. If "a system is composed of a structure and of interacting units" (1979: 79), and if reductionist theories are theories about the units, then are systemic theories not structural theories? No, for at least two reasons.

First, as we have already seen with nuclear weapons, there are features "in play at the international, and not at the national, level" that are not structure. Mearsheimer plausibly contends that the character of military power is a system-level, not a unit-level, variable. But it is not a matter of distribution of capabilities, let alone ordering principle or functional differentiation.

Second, in addition to units and structures, a system includes the interactions of units. These interactions take place *between* units, and thus are not "unit-level" phenomena. Waltz implicitly acknowledges this when he insists that a structural theory abstracts from both the attributes of units and their interactions. The interactions of units are *not* reducible to their attributes; if they were, there would be nothing to abstract from once we had abstracted from attributes. And if neither structure nor unit, they must be systemic but not structural.

By reducing system to structure, Waltz ends up with a theory that says too few important things to be of much interest or use – as suggested by Waltz' own reliance on non-structural features to explain something as basic (for a realist) as the Cold War peace. To rescue realism without (re)turning to reductionism we must reconceptualize structure in broader terms or move from a structural to a systemic realism.

Barry Buzan and Glenn Synder provide prominent recent examples of such a move. Buzan, in *The Logic of Anarchy*, distinguishes between what he calls "structural realism," with a broader understanding of structure, and "neorealism," or Waltz' narrower kind of structuralism (1993). Alternatively, we might restore non-structural (in Waltz' sense of the term) systemic variables to our theory. This is Snyder's strategy in his recent book *Alliance Politics* (1997).

In the following section I have chosen to examine Snyder's work for two principal reasons. First, *Alliance Politics* is a more recent and somewhat less known book. Second, Snyder explicitly sees his work as based in and extending Waltz' (1997: 16). By making only modest additions to Waltz' arsenal – and additions that are entirely at the system level – Snyder's work ought to be relatively attractive to those drawn to Waltz' economy and rigor.

As I will suggest in the next chapter, I prefer to go considerably further than either Snyder or Buzan. Nonetheless, their modifications of Waltzian structuralism yield a more plausible and more powerful realism. They also open important channels for constructive communication between realists and non-realists.

Process variables and systemic theory

Snyder begins with a Waltzian conception of international structure (anarchy and polarity, but no functional differentiation), which he distinguishes from unit attributes no less sharply than does Waltz.[23] But he adds three new classes of variables, which he calls relationships, interactions, and structural modifiers. These additions, Snyder argues, respond to the justifiable charge that Waltz is guilty of "excessive parsimony, in the sense that the explanatory gain from some further elaboration would exceed the costs in reduced generality" (1996: 167). By introducing "process variables" into neorealist theory, Waltz' "indeterminate predictions" become quite a bit more determinate.

Relationships

Relationships, Snyder argues, provide "the situational context for behavior," "the conduit through which structural effects are transmitted to behavior" (1997: 20). "If, as Waltz says, system structures only 'shape and

---

[23] Snyder further distinguishes unit attributes into the following: preferences, the importance of which we have seen in chapter 2 above; perceptions, the importance of which we have seen in this chapter in the distinction between threats and capabilities; and (internal) politics, which addresses "second image" internal structural differences between regime types (1997: fig. 1.1).

shove,' relationship patterns give a more decided push" (1997: 32). Snyder identifies four key relations: alignment, interests, capability, and interdependence.

Alignment "marks the lines of amity and enmity in the system." These "expectations in the minds of statesmen about whether they will be supported, opposed, or ignored by other states in future interactions" (1997: 21), are "akin to structure" because they shape "how resources and capabilities are aggregated in the system" (1997: 22).

Among alignments, alliances play a special role in international relations.

> Since commitments have some force, and since states, once allied, become somewhat dependent on each other, alliances in a multipolar system might be said to have quasi-structural effects. They identify friends and foes more clearly, and they aggregate power among friends. Thus they concentrate power in the system and focus insecurities and dependencies between particular states and groups of states. These effects are not greatly dissimilar to those that follow directly from structure in a bipolar system (Snyder 1997: 22).

And alliances, as Snyder emphasizes – in contrast to Waltz' stress on their ephemeral nature – although ultimately provisional, are often very durable.[24]

Conflicting and common interests are the second relational element in Snyder's scheme. Snyder illustrates the importance of this dimension when he notes that conflicting interests may prevent states from balancing, even in response to a common threat (1997: 22–23). This is very similar to my earlier point about the weak relationship between capabilities and perceived threat.

Although common or conflicting interests are often closely linked with alignment, Snyder emphasizes the fact that alliances can just as easily *create* common (or conflicting) interests as reflect or arise from them (1997: 24–25). For example, states that ally primarily to overcome the general insecurity of anarchy may create opponents as a result of their alliance. Within alliances, prior conflicts may be reduced and new common interests created.

Snyder's third relationship is "capability." He rightly notes that by "capabilities" Waltz really means "resources," which exist independently of the use to which they are put. If we instead define structural polarity in terms of resources, "capabilities" refers to the relational aspects of applying these resources.

The classic example in recent realist literature is the offense–defense

---

[24] Snyder also notes that among allies the concern for relative gains is likely to be moderated (1997: 22). Alignment thus may be crucial in determining whether a state acts out of fear (when dealing with adversaries) or out of a desire for gain (when dealing with allies).

balance.[25] Snyder illustrates the point with the work of Thomas Christensen and Jack Snyder (1990) on the periods before World War I and World War II, both of which were multipolar. Prior to World War I, allies were chain-ganged into war because offense was seen to have the advantage; they needed to act quickly to protect vulnerable allies. But prior to World War II, when states believed that defense had the advantage, buck-passing seemed safe because allies were seen to be much less vulnerable.

Once we look at capabilities in this relational sense, rather than as mere resources, it also becomes possible to take into account features such as geography, which have been of great and obvious importance in international relations (and to earlier generations of realists). We can also account for the impact of nuclear weapons, which are not just undifferentiated power resources but resources of a special kind, with limited but extremely important deterrent uses. Nuclear weapons are a resource that provides certain capabilities, but not others, as a result of their particular character. Snyder suggests that this is an illustration of the broader point that material resources have asset-specific characteristics that are obscured in Waltz' abstract notion of "capabilities" that vary only by quantity (1997: 29).

Snyder's final relationship variable is interdependence. In the special context of political-military allies, a state's interdependence "is a function of the degree of threat it faces from its adversary, the extent to which the ally can contribute to deterrence and defense against the threat, and the availability and cost of alternative means of meeting a threat" (1997: 31). More broadly, how a state responds to a threat is partly a function of the options that it has available, which may be constrained as much by its allies as by its adversaries.

In order to predict or explain the behavior of states, we usually need to know how they stand in relation to one another. States rarely fear all external concentrations of power. And even when they do fear everyone else, the intensity and character of their fears is likely to change with their relationships.

To put the point somewhat crudely, it is crazy to commit oneself to a theory, such as Waltz', that predicts that a state will respond in the same way to an ally with which it shares many common interests and an enemy with which it has numerous competing interests; or that great power A will not provoke systematically different responses from great power B, a distant island state with low dependence on allies, and great power C, a

---

[25] See Glaser and Kaufmann (1998), Van Evera (1998), and Quester (1977) for good theoretical and historical discussions.

neighboring state that is highly dependent on great power D for defense against attack. Such a theory may be simple and elegant. It is not very useful.

Interactions

Snyder argues that interaction is

differentiated from relationships by the fact that it is action – policy choice or the implementation of choice – rather than the expectations, values, and power relations that shape action and choice. Interaction is the process by which alignments, interests, capabilities, and dependence are translated into outcomes (1997: 33).

Snyder develops a schema of interactions in security relationships between allied and adversarial states in three "game arenas": preparedness, diplomacy, and military action. The adversary and alliance games are further divided into conflictive and cooperative variants. The resulting framework is summarized in figure 4.1

Figure 4.1. Interaction arenas.(*Source:* Snyder 1997, figure 1–2)

		Preparedness	Diplomacy	Action
Adversary Game	Conflict	arms race	threats of force	war
	Cooperation	arms control	concessions	war limitation or termination
Alliance Game	Conflict	burden-sharing/ joint planning	promises of support	chain-ganging
	Cooperation	free-riding	threats of defection	buck-passing

These interactions are abstract theoretical patterns of behavior, "lawlike regularities," to use Waltz' language. To take the preparedness column of figure 4.1, Snyder suggests that among adversaries arms races are a characteristic mode of competition, while arms control is a characteristic mode of cooperation. Among allies, cooperation characteristically takes the form of burden-sharing or joint planning, while conflict is expressed in "free-riding" or buck-passing.

Where Waltz consigns interactions, and even relationships, to the unit level, Snyder, much more plausibly, restores them to the system level. Waltz' theoretical strategy is to define structure narrowly and then relegate everything that is not structure to the unit level, which he then ruthlessly excludes from his theory. The result, as many critics have noted, is that the unit level becomes a vast, incoherent dumping-ground of explanatory variables, many of which, including Snyder's relationships and interactions, simply cannot be plausibly described as attributes of the units.

It is more consistent with our ordinary language and intuitions to specify what counts as an attribute of the units, then define everything else as system in Waltz' sense of "forces that are in play at the international, and not at the national, level." Alignment, for example, is clearly a force in play at the international, not the national (unit), level. Arms races take place between, not within, nations, as do threats and commitments. This is in effect the theoretical strategy that Snyder has adopted.

Anarchy and the distribution of capabilities remain at the heart of Snyder's theory. If my arguments in chapter 3 are correct, we must also add back in some elements of functional differentiation. Relatively deterministic predictions thus become possible. We can say, for example, not just that states will balance but that certain alignments are more likely than others, and that certain types of alliance dynamics can be expected. Snyder devotes most of *Alliance Politics* to developing and testing such mid-level realist theories of alliances. However one evaluates the success of his particular effort, it presents an extremely attractive model for the development of realist theory.

Structural modifiers

The part of Snyder's model that I am most interested in, however, is the part to which he, with his principal interest in alliances, gives least attention. In a separately published version of chapter 1 of *Alliance Politics*, Snyder identifies a class of systemic factors that he calls "structural modifiers" (Snyder 1996: 168–171). He defines these as

system-wide influences that are structural in their inherent nature but not potent enough internationally to warrant that description. They modify the effects of the more basic structural elements on the interaction process, but they are not interaction itself. They are roughly analogous to macroeconomic influences, like interest rates or government regulation, on microeconomic relations between firms; they affect the behavior of all actors more or less evenly, but they are different in kind from factors like the number of actors (firms) and the distribution of power among them – variables which clearly determine the structure of the system (market) (1996: 169).

Snyder emphasizes military technology and norms and institutions.

I would quarrel with Snyder's calling "system-wide influences that are structural in their inherent nature" (only) structural *modifiers*. If they are inherently structural, why not identify them as part of the structure?[26] But the semantics are less important than the substantive implications of introducing such features into neorealist theory.

As Snyder notes, norms and institutions are clearly structural in domestic society.

They create the hierarchy of power and differentiation of function that are the hallmarks of a well-ordered domestic polity, but that are present only rudimentarily in international society. In principle, they are also structural internationally, because they exert roughly similar influence on all actors, and since with further development they would begin to produce the same sort and size of effects that they do domestically (1996: 169).

This suggests to me at least some extremely interesting possibilities. Snyder, however, does not pursue them, apparently because he shares Waltz' view that there is little functional differentiation in international relations and considerable danger in trying to work with mixed (anarchic–hierarchic) structural forms.

In chapter 2, however, we saw that a dichotomous understanding of anarchy and hierarchy is highly problematic. It is an empirical question whether or not we should use "pure" models in any particular case. And Snyder's decision to separate norms and institutions from structure likewise rests on empirical, rather than strictly methodological or theoretical, considerations.

Norms and institutions are *in principle* structural at the international, no less than the national, level. Snyder claims (1996: 169) that in practice they are not as powerful an influence on state behavior as anarchy and the distribution of capabilities. But where they are – which is an empirical, not a theoretical, question – he seems committed to considering them along with anarchy and the distribution of capabilities. Therefore, we must now address directly the place of international institutions.

Discussion questions

- Waltz explicitly defines stability in terms of change in the number of great powers. In practice, however, he more often talks about the incidence of war among the great powers. What are the strengths and weaknesses of each conception?

- What is the factual evidence on the stability or peacefulness of bipolar orders? How many examples of prominent bipolar orders can you think of? How long did each remain bipolar? In how many did the superpowers fight each other? How often? With what intensity and effects (both human and structural)? How

[26] In private correspondence Snyder has indicated that he now believes that they should be described as (a generally weak) part of structure.

much war was there that did not involve the superpowers directly fighting each other? How does this empirical record compare with, for example, the European multipolar order from 1648 to 1945? In other words, how much does our answer to the broad theoretical question depend on the time-frames and examples chosen? To be even more pointed, to what extent is Waltz' allegedly structural theoretical argument just a (largely unjustified over-) generalization from the Cold War?

- Granting that the Cold War era was substantially more peaceful than the half-century of multipolarity that preceded it, how much of that was due to structure (polarity)? What role did nuclear weapons play? What about other factors? If the United States had been an expansionist rather than a status quo power, would that have made a difference?

- Generalizing from this last question, how do polarity and the interests of states interact in determining the likelihood of war in any particular international order? Does it even make sense to talk about the probability of war without taking into account the aims of states? What about the institutions within which they interact?

- We now have a decade of post-Cold War experience with a multipolar order. Were the 1990s more or less peaceful than an average decade during the Cold War? (What was an average decade? What are the standards or methods for making such a determination?) Has there been a change in the *character* of international violence? How much (if any) of this can be attributed to the end of bipolarity?

- What do you make of Copeland's argument that Waltz' analysis of the impact of polarity is fatally flawed by his failure to take into account time and the direction of change? Does Copeland's argument, as is suggested in the text, really establish that from anarchy and polarity alone we can predict nothing? This seems to suggest that in some way Copeland undermines the structuralist project. Can we not see his work instead as a refinement? How different is such a refined structuralism from that outlined by Waltz? Should we accept the implicit suggestion in the text that the structuralist project should be seen precisely as that, namely, a project rather than a theory?

- Consider still another way to read Waltz' argument on bipolarity: as prescription rather than description; that is, his argument prescribes how bipolar powers might take advantage of the possibilities of bipolarity to reduce the likelihood of great power war, rather than describe how they are structurally impelled to do so. What implications does such a reading have for the character of (structural) realism? Can we more broadly apply this argument that realists misleadingly present prescriptions as description or causal analysis?

- Does the Sicilian expedition really illustrate the importance of the substantive motives of states? Are there other, more realist, ways to read the sorts of changes in Athens highlighted in the text? In particular, can we see them as more rooted in the structure of anarchy than in the character of the state? Might we not even say that Athens' character is transformed by its extended exposure to the perils of anarchy? But if we say that, do we not then need a *theory* of state interests?

- Consider still another reading: Athens always had both defensive and offensive interests and potentials, but as the war progressed anarchy brought the offensive to the fore? What implications would such a reading have for our understanding of structural realism? Clearly it requires forging some link between internal and external politics. But can such a link be forged in a fundamentally structuralist way?

- Waltz argues that the tendency to balance flows from anarchy. In the text it is suggested that it rests instead on the anticipated behavior of victors, and in particular a fear of predation. Which explanation seems stronger to you? Is there some way to combine these two accounts?

- What are the theoretical attractions and drawbacks of moving from balance of power to balance of threat theory? What implications does such a move have for the nature of structural theory?

- In the text it is suggested that Waltz' error with respect to abstracting from interactions arises from confusing "third image" or systemic theory with structural theory. Why might Waltz make such a move? What do you think of it?

- What are the costs and benefits of the sort of broader, systemic theory illustrated in the text by Snyder's work on "process variables"? What would you imagine Waltz' reaction would be? Which approach do you prefer? Why?

- What are the costs and benefits of including "structural modifiers" such as technology and norms in realist theory? What kinds of technologies or norms are sufficiently systemic to be included, and what kinds need to be abstracted from even in Snyder's theory?

- In designing theories there usually is a trade-off between theoretical simplicity and the richness or range of explanations. What are the strengths and weaknesses of each strategy? To which are you more inclined? What does this imply about the structuralist project of maximum abstraction?

- In the particular case of norms and technology, is the additional explanatory power worth the increase in the number of variables and the complexity of the theory? Is your answer the same for both norms and technology? Are the implications of these two types of explanatory variables really comparable? In particular, would including norms not have a much greater impact on the character of realist theory than including technology?

Suggestions for further reading

Waltz' extremely abstract conception of balance of power is laid out on pp. 117–128 of *Theory of International Politics*. As with his disscussion of anarchy, this is the essential starting point for further reading. In direct opposition is Edward Gulick's *Europe's Classsical Balance of Power* (1967) which treats balance of power as a set of rule-governed, historically based social institutions. Martin Wight's essay "The Balance of Power International Order" (1973) presents a similar reading, and his *Systems of States* (1977) explores some of the variety of ways (of which balance of power is only one) in which states have ordered their relations. Luard (1992) adopts a similar perspective.

Seabury (1965) provides a good short collection of classic writings by theorists and practitioners. Along similar lines, see Wright (1975). Sheehan (1996) is a useful recent effort to link historical and theoretical issues connected with the balance of power. Dehio (1963) is a classic historical account of the evolution of the modern European states system.

Ernst Haas, "Balance of Power: Prescription, Concept or Propaganda?" (1953) examines the multiple, and often confused, senses in which the term is used by both theorists and practitioners. For a very different approach to the problem of multiple and indeterminate meanings, see Niou, Ordeshook, and Rose (1989), which provides a game-theoretic formalization of balance of power theory.

On the relative stability of bipolar and mulipolar orders, the classic arguments are still those of Waltz (1964) and Karl Deutsch and J. David Singer (1964). Waltz' argument was updated slightly in *Theory of International Politics*, pp. 161–163, 170–176. Rosecrance (1996) adopts something of an intermediate view. Dale Copeland's "Neorealism and the Myth of Bipolar Stability" (1996) is a creative recent effort to challenge Waltz' argument in favor of bipolarity by introducing the element of changes in relative positions over time.

I also want to draw special attention to two works highlighted in the last section of this chapter. The essays by Barry Buzan, Charles Jones, and Richard Little published collectively as **The Logic of Anarchy** (1993) outline a structural approach to international theory that rejects Waltz' narrow and thin vision of structure. The essay by Buzan in particular is a classic. A shorter piece by Buzan, Jones, and Little (1994) on the idea of the international system is also useful. Glenn Snyder's *Alliance Politics* (1997) is a challenging theoretical work that puts in practice such an expanded conception of structure and system in the case of alliances. A separately published version of the first chapter, **"Process Variables in Neorealist Theory"** (Snyder 1997) outlines a program for a much richer and more interesting style of neorealist theory.

5   Institutions and international society

Over the past decade, international theory in the United States has often been presented as locked in a struggle between realism and liberal institutionalism.[1] Such an understanding, as I suggested at the end of chapter 2, is largely misguided. Realism and institutionalism – or any other theory or approach – are not potential substitutes for one another. They are "competing" approaches only in the sense that they focus on different forces and thus may provide "better" or "worse" – or at least different – insights in particular cases.

Realist critiques of international institutions, however, do raise two important questions. How much of an impact can international institutions have in principle? And what effects do they in fact have in contemporary international relations? Or, to pose the problem from the opposite direction, can structural realism get by with ignoring (abstracting from) international institutions? I will argue that it cannot.

As is common in the discipline, I use "institutions" in the widest possible sense to refer to regularized patterns of interaction based on formal or informal rules and understandings. Institutions thus include, but go well beyond, bureaucratic organizations (a much narrower sense of the term).[2] They include social practices such as kinship, kingship, property, promises, alliances, sovereignty, and international law. Institutions provide a web of relationships through which social interaction is shaped and channeled.

Norms, understood as guiding rules or principles, are a part of most institutions. Norms establish rules, roles, and meanings that shape, constrain, enable, and even constitute states and other international

---

[1] For a good overview of this debate, see Baldwin (1993) and Powell (1994). The leading proponents of an institutional approach are Robert Keohane (1989: ch. 1; 1984) and Oran Young (1994). A good brief overview of the institutionalist agenda can be found in Burley (1993: 220–226). Steven Weber (1997) provides a useful introduction to some of the central elements of the approach applied to the question of change. On the new institutionalism more generally, see Robertson (1993).

[2] For a good discussion of this difference, and the analytical importance of identifying it, see Young (1989: ch. 2).

actors.[3] Although the phrase "norms and institutions" may be redundant, I will often use it in order to emphasize the regulative and other normative dimensions of international institutions.

The effects of international institutions

In a well-known, provocative essay, "The False Promise of International Institutions," John Mearsheimer develops a strong and uncompromising argument that "institutions have minimal influence on state behavior" (1994/95: 7). "Institutions cannot get states to stop behaving as short-term power maximizers" (1995: 82). Institutions, according to this familiar realist argument, can usually be ignored because they rarely exert a significant influence on the interests or interactions of states in anarchy. I will call this "the no effects thesis."

The no effects thesis

Mearsheimer's particular concern is security relations. Therefore, he looks for institutional effects on "stability," which he defines as "absence of wars and major crises" (1994/95: 6 n. 8). Can international institutions reduce the number, frequency, danger, or intensity of violent conflicts between states or nonviolent conflicts that might lead to war? This is indeed a reasonable test of the effects of international institutions. And if institutions have an effect on security relations, where realists expect institutions to be particularly insignificant, the no effects thesis can be treated as decisively refuted.

Mearsheimer, however, also poses a quite unreasonable test, reformulating the issue as "whether institutions cause peace" (1994/95: 15). And he defines "peace" in such a way that this test becomes absurd. "Genuine peace, or a world where states do not compete for power, is not likely" (1994/95: 9). "Peace, if one defines that concept as a state of tranquility or mutual concord, is not likely to break out in this world" (Mearsheimer 1994/95: 12).

Many hierarchical political orders also lack tranquility and mutual concord. This does not imply that domestic political institutions have no effects. Likewise, the absence of "genuine peace" tells us nothing about

---

[3] For an interesting effort to incorporate norms within realism, see Goertz and Diehl (1994). Norms, however, are usually associated instead with liberal and social constructivist perspectives. For a sampling of recent work in this burgeoning area of inquiry, see Katzenstein (1996), Klotz (1995), Checkel (1997), Kratochwil (1989), and Finnemore (1996). For an overview of some of the issues raised in the study of international norms, see Raymond (1997).

the effects of international institutions on stability and security relations. Security competition, even war, can persist in a world in which institutions have extensive and important effects on international stability.

To have an effect is to produce some change or result; as the *Oxford English Dictionary* puts it, to have an "operative influence." In a somewhat stronger sense of the term, we often speak of an actor being effective only if the result produced was intended (or at least desirable even if unintended). "Genuine peace," however, requires not merely that international institutions be effective but that they completely transform the character of international relations. This is an absurd stipulation – as is underscored by the fact that by this criterion balance of power politics has no effect on international peace or stability.

Confusing cause and effect

Mearsheimer also deceptively reformulates the issue when he argues that institutions "are based on the self-interested calculations of the great powers" (1994/95: 7). He seems to assume that showing that power or self-interest underlies an institution establishes that it has no effects. This, however, confuses causes and effects.

Suppose that I enter into a contract for purely self-interested reasons. If when I am required to perform my obligations I would have acted in the same way in the absence of the contract, we may be justified in saying that it has had no effect on my behavior.[4] But if I would have done something else in the absence of the contract, it has undeniably had an effect. The effects of an institution cannot be read directly from its source.

Nonetheless, Mearsheimer argues that liberal institutionalism

is predicated on the belief that cheating is the main inhibitor of international cooperation, and that institutions provide the key to overcoming that problem. The aim is to create rules that constrain states, but not to challenge the fundamental realist claims that states are self-interested actors (Mearsheimer 1994/95: 14).

Even if true this is irrelevant to the no effects thesis. Mearsheimer has shifted from the realist premises of anarchy, conflict, and the struggle for survival to the premise of rationality, stated here in the form of a claim that states pursue their self-interest. But as we saw in chapter 2, rationality is a theoretical premise shared by many non-realists.

Realists and liberal institutionalists do both assume that states pursue their self-interest; that is, that they are instrumentally rational. But they

---

[4] Even this is not entirely clear if, for example, the contractual obligation has altered my conception of self-interest.

have very different *substantive* conceptions of rational self-interest. Mearsheimer views states as "short-term power maximizers." Liberals, however, see "rational" states as those that pursue long-run utility. They thus derive an account of international institutions that *is* incompatible with the no effects thesis. By providing insurance against cheating, institutions may alter state behavior by allowing cooperation that otherwise would not have been possible. They do "challenge the fundamental realist claims that states are self-interested actors" in Mearsheimer's sense of that term (short-run power maximization).

Consider also Mearsheimer's claim that "to the extent that alliances cause peace, they do so by deterrence, which is straightforward realist behavior" (1995: 83). Even granting realists a patent on deterrence, it does not follow that alliances have no effects. Even if similar results might have been achieved by separate action, there still may be good reasons for saying that the alliance has had effects. For example, if institutionalized cooperation increases the probability of successfully deterring an adversary it can be said to have had an effect in producing "the same" outcome. So long as the process is significantly altered the institution can be said to have had effects.

"NATO was basically a manifestation of the bipolar distribution of power in Europe during the Cold War, and it was that balance of power, not NATO *per se*, that provided the key to maintaining stability on the continent" (Mearsheimer 1994/95: 14). Perhaps. But bipolarity *per se* did not cause European stability either. By contributing to maintaining stability, NATO had effects.

Consider the US-led war against Iraq in 1991. Even allowing that US interests were completely egoistic – oil, regional security, and international stability – institutional and normative factors were essential to the ability of the United States to realize those objectives. Without United Nations authorization, many Americans, as well as many "allies" in Europe and the Middle East, would have been less willing to participate. And without the principle of territorial integrity, narrower economic and security interests might not have been sufficient to mobilize such widespread national and international support.

With less or more reluctant support from at least some leading allies it would at least have been much harder and more costly for the United States to launch the war. Once launched, it might have proceeded differently in the absence of such widespread international support (or at least acquiescence). And even if fought to a similar conclusion, its meanings and results might have been different. To say that international norms and institutions had no effect is neither accurate nor illuminating.

A similar evasion is evident in Mearsheimer's claim that "concerts essentially reflect the balance of power, and are thus largely consistent with realism" (1994/95: 35). That does not mean that concerts have no effects on the behavior of states. If states are able to achieve results through institutionalized collaboration that they could not have achieved through uninstitutionalized balancing, the concert will have had an effect.

Even granting that "balance of power is the independent variable . . . institutions are merely an intervening variable" (Mearsheimer 1994/95: 13), "intervening variables" can have important effects. And they are not dependent variables. Their effects are independent of the "independent variable"; that is, they are independent variables in their own right, although modeled as less significant than the identified "independent variable." Furthermore, if an institution comes to serve functions different from or in addition to those for which it was initially created, as seems to be the case with NATO, such "independent" effects may be considerable.[5]

A large part of Mearsheimer's argument against international institutions boils down to such non sequiturs addressing the causes of, motives underlying, or objectives sought by international institutions, rather than their effects. And he never addresses the obvious *realist* refutation of the no effects thesis: why would rational, self-interested states go to the bother and expense of international institutions if they produce no effects?

Security institutions and the perils of anarchy

"Cooperation among states has its limits, mainly because it is constrained by the dominating logic of security competition, which no amount of cooperation can eliminate" (1994/95: 9). On its face, this too seems irrelevant to the no effects thesis: cooperation may remain limited while institutions have independent effects. But if the difficulty of cooperation prevents institutions from being formed, there will be no institutions to have any effects. Mearsheimer advances this narrow version of the no effects thesis when he argues that liberal institutionalism "is of little relevance in situations where states' interests are fundamentally conflictual and neither side thinks it has much to gain from cooperation" (1994/95: 15).

To use the currently popular phrase, "Duhhhhh!" If states don't want to cooperate, of course they won't form cooperative institutions. Any

---

[5] This point is familiar in the literatures on hegemonic stability and neo-functionalism. See, for example, Keohane (1984) and Nye (1971).

interest in this claim arises from the implicit suggestion that states in the security realm usually do not want to cooperate because of the dangers of anarchy. If security institutions are almost never established because of the perils of anarchy, then institutions cannot have security effects.

But just how dangerous is anarchy? Mearsheimer appeals to the "'special peril of defection' in the military realm, because the nature of military weaponry allows for rapid shifts in the balance of power" (1994/95: 13). In fact, however, not all weaponry allows rapid shifts in the balance of power. For example, when defense has a substantial advantage, the defender can relatively easily counter a potentially aggressive military build-up. Even when defense is at a disadvantage, monitoring may provide sufficient warning to allow states to prevent cheaters from tipping the balance of power.

Mearsheimer also claims that in security relations "there is the constant threat that betrayal will result in devastating military defeat" (1994/95: 19). Canada, however, cooperates militarily with the United States without any such fear. Institutionalized patterns of cooperation and trust have developed to the point that neither side seriously fears betrayal. We can even point to "security communities," areas in which states confidently expect that disputes will not be settled by the threat or use of force (Adler and Barnett 1998). Nordic military cooperation, for example, takes place largely without thought of betrayal. And for all the "fear" of Germany among its neighbors, none seriously considers the possibility of attack.

How can Mearsheimer overlook such obvious evidence? I think we must go back to his confusion of "effects" and "peace." "Realist" security competition continues outside of security communities, and operates even within most alliances. Cooperation does not produce peace, in the sense of eliminating conflict. But in his (otherwise not unreasonable) zeal to force us to confront the reality of conflict, Mearsheimer obscures the reality and effects of cooperation. Like Waltz, he is so beguiled by the fact of international anarchy that he fails to appreciate, or even take note of, the presence of elements of hierarchical, institutionalized cooperation.

The shift away from the effects of institutions to issues such as peace and cooperation is also reflective of what we are coming to see as a characteristic realist strategy of over-generalization from, even wild exaggeration of, an important insight. Anarchy does pose significant problems for cooperation. This does indeed illuminate important dimensions of international relations. As Gilpin puts it, "the realist position is that cooperation is difficult, especially in areas affecting national security, and is much more difficult than liberals believe" (1996: 4 n. 4). But a blanket attack on institutions simply does not follow from the difficulty of cooperation and the persistence of competition.

The realist disinclination to take cooperation seriously is especially dangerous because effective security cooperation is not restricted to allies. For example, the US-Soviet/Russian strategic arms control regime has altered the behavior of both states, allowing them partially to overcome the pursuit of short-term power maximization in favor of long-term self-interest conceived in largely defensive terms. The rules that define cheating and the monitoring mechanisms that facilitate compliance have functioned as effective institutions.

In noting this example, however, Mearsheimer again confuses cause and effect. "Rivals as well as allies cooperate. After all, deals can be struck that roughly reflect the distribution of power and satisfy concerns about cheating. The various arms control agreements signed by the superpowers during the Cold War illustrate this point" (1994/95: 13). That realists can account for the formation of a particular institution – it reflects the distribution of capabilities – actually counts against, not for, the no effects thesis in both its narrow and broad versions.[6]

Consider also the international nonproliferation regime. Monitoring by the International Atomic Energy Agency (IAEA), formal and informal cooperation by nuclear suppliers, and the persuasive force of international nonproliferation norms have substantially altered the security policies of nuclear and non-nuclear states alike. It has encouraged and enabled some to forgo the short-term power maximizing strategy of acquiring nuclear weapons. It has helped to constrain others, such as Brazil, that otherwise would have been more likely to proliferate. Even states such as Pakistan that have acquired nuclear arms have been forced to modify their nuclear pursuit and have borne additional costs as a result of it.[7]

Balance of power – not in Waltz' abstract sense, but as a complex pattern of institutionalized, rule-governed interactions – is also a social institution. Europe's "classical" nineteenth-century balance of power, as

---

[6] I also take Mearsheimer's passing reference to "non-realist institutions" and "realist institutions" (1994/95: 8 n. 17) as an implicit recognition that some institutions – "realist" ones – do have effects.

[7] Peacekeeping – both in its classic "thin blue line" form of interposing neutral troops between adversaries and in broader, multidimensional post-Cold War operations that also involve significant elements of "peace making" and "peace building" – provides another example of effective institutionalized security cooperation. For an analytical overview of such operations by both the UN and regional organizations through the early 1980s, see Haas (1983; 1986). Thakur and Thayer (1995) cover the conceptual changes in the post-Cold War era and provide useful case studies. See also Roberts (1996), Lorenz (1999), and Rupesinghe (1999).

Edward Gulick (1967: ch. 1) notes, rested on a certain degree of cultural order. To function, it required a certain degree of cultural homogeneity (a point to which we will return), a highly developed practice of interstate diplomacy, and a general normative commitment to the preservation of the system of relationships. Furthermore, balancing took place in particular rule-governed ways. For example, the institution of reciprocal compensations provided that gains by one power would be compensated by gains for other directly interested powers. Thus after Russia defeated Turkey in 1878 and forced the Turks to recognize the independence of Serbia and Romania (thus increasing Russian influence in the Balkans), Britain and Austria successfully insisted that they receive, respectively, Cyprus and administrative control over Bosnia and Herzegovina, not because they had played a major role in the war – they had not – but to restore balance in the Balkans and the Eastern Mediterranean. Without a well-established practice of reciprocal compensations, the outcome probably would have been different, and the process certainly would have been.[8]

We can also note that war itself is an institution that regulates and limits violence (compare Bull 1977: ch. 8). For all the violence of modern warfare, international relations simply is not a Hobbesian war of all against all. One kind of institutionalized group actor – the state – has claimed for itself an exclusive (national and international) right to use force.[9] Furthermore, states have agreed on rules for the use of force against one another, embodied in the laws of war. This helps to explain the concern over international terrorists, who, for the great amount of attention they receive, harm a surprisingly small number of people. They pose a double threat to this institutionalized system for regulating the use of force: not only are they non-state actors but also they often target their violence directly against civilians.

In security affairs, as in other domains of international life, it is an empirical not a theoretical question whether institutionalized cooperation will be achieved or will alter state behavior. And it is a simple matter to multiply such illustrations of security institutions having important effects.

---

[8] In a similar vein Wendt (1992) shows that "self-help," rather than being an inescapable consequence of anarchic orders, is a particular set of institutions for dealing with some of the problems posed by anarchy.

[9] This is not a natural or inevitable feature of anarchic orders. For example, mercenaries, as Machiavelli laments (P12, DI.43[2], DII.20), were the standard means of fighting in early Renaissance Italy. And as fine old Errol Flynn movies such as *The Sea Hawk* and *Captain Blood* remind us, privateers and pirates were a regular feature of early modern international relations. See also Thomson (1984).

Sovereignty, self-determination, aggression, and survival

Knowing that international institutions *may* have an effect, however, does not take us very far. The more important issue is *how much* of an effect they in fact have. This section offers an extended illustration of the central place of norms and practices dealing with sovereignty, self-determination, and aggression, and their impact on the key realist variable of survival.

Sovereignty and social recognition

As we have noted in previous chapters, sovereignty, and even the state, are not timeless features of international politics. Machiavelli, at the turn of the sixteenth century, is usually seen as the first major political theorist to make central use of the idea of the state (*lo stato*), understood as an institution fundamentally separable from both the ruler and the political community.[10] Jean Bodin's *Six Books of the Commonwealth* (1576) was the first work to give central place to the idea of sovereignty. And even Bodin's own translation from French to Latin replaces the novel French term *souveraineté* with the Latin *majestas*, a related but different idea (Onuf 1998: 132).

Sovereignty is conventionally defined as supreme juridical authority.[11] To be sovereign is to be subject to no higher (earthly) authority. There is no appeal, other than to force or divine intervention, above the sovereign.

Today we take sovereignty for granted. As Jens Bartelson puts it, sovereignty is "essentially uncontested as the foundation of modern political discourse" (1995: 14). In this sense of supreme rule over the entire community, however, most societies, in most parts of the world, throughout most of history, have not known the practice. Even in the West sovereignty is largely a modern phenomenon.

Medieval Europe was organized instead around a complex web of cross-cutting obligations. Authority was bifurcated into secular and religious domains, with individual princes, both religious and secular, sometimes subordinate and sometimes superior to one another. A particular lord often simultaneously owed certain duties to and held other rights against another lord. Customary restrictions and prescriptive rights further circumscribed the authority of princes, prelates, and magistrates.

---

[10] See Mansfield (1996: ch. 12). Compare Rubinstein (1971).

[11] Hinsley (1986) is the standard historical survey of the concept. James (1986) is an excellent, if somewhat dry, analytical overview. More recently, the concept has been treated to a variety of penetrating social constructivist interpretations. See, for example, Bierstecker and Weber (1996), Weber (1995), Walker (1991), and Ashley and Walker (1990).

There simply was no point of supreme authority (on earth) in most of the political communities of the medieval world. In fact, even the idea of separate and separable political communities was not clearly established, the relationships between Christendom and its constituent communities being a matter of considerable theoretical and practical controversy for several centuries.

Sovereignty is a complex and contingent institution with both internal (domestic) and external (international) dimensions. Internally, sovereignty is supreme authority. But when supreme authorities interact with one another, each is equal to the other. Domestically sovereignty expresses itself as hierarchy. Internationally it appears as anarchy. But sovereign anarchy embeds states within a system of mutual recognition.

Sovereign equality in contemporary international society has not been interpreted as a Hobbesian right of everyone to everything. Rather, the mutual recognition of sovereigns provides an authoritative global allocation of exclusive jurisdictions. Sovereignty thus functions much like a system of property rights in an economic market – another institution so familiar that we often forget it is a social institution.

The significance of mutual sovereign recognition can be vividly illustrated by the famous mission of Lord George Macartney to China in 1793.[12] China was a powerful, independent cultural and political unit that saw itself as The Middle Kingdom, the cultural and political point of contact between earth and heaven. And the Emperor, in the dominant Qing dynasty self-understanding, ruled by a mandate from heaven. Relations between the Emperor of Heaven and representatives of "western barbarian" (European) kings thus was, from the Chinese point of view, properly a matter of tributary submission, symbolized by a series of ritual genuflections and prostrations before the Emperor (the kowtow).

To Macartney, however, Hongli, the Qianlong emperor, was just another sovereign, neither superior nor inferior to King George III. Ritual prostration was a sign of subordination that he simply could not accept. Recognition, for Macartney, had to be mutual and equal. For the Emperor, it had to be unequal.[13]

Over the course of the next century, Britain and other Western powers, through a combination of force and international law, imposed their

---

[12] For a learned but immensely readable account of the Macartney mission, see Peyrefitte (1992).

[13] Hevia (1995) discusses issues of ritual involved in the Macartney mission, stressing the very different systems of meaning wrapped up in the encounter. The implication of this line of analysis is that the practice of diplomacy, as we understand it, simply did not exist in early Qing China. On the "invention" of diplomacy, see Mattingly (1955) and, from a very different perspective, Der Derian (1987). Reus-Smit (1997) raises similar issues in his comparison of ancient Greek and modern international relations.

understandings on a resistant China. And the demands of the Western powers were not merely ceremonial. They included a particular understanding of free trade, extending even to trade in addictive drugs – Britain fought China to prevent it from prohibiting the import of opium – and special legal, commercial, and religious rights for Westerners that were denied to Chinese subjects of the Emperor. China was even required to accept Western military garrisons on its territory.[14] Only when China finally agreed on eurocentric, Western-dominated international society's terms of participation was it admitted to full and equal membership in international society. The Chinese, with considerable justice, refer to this as the Era of the Unequal Treaties.

The variability of sovereignty

China illustrates the role of sovereignty in shaping the identity of international actors (states), as well as the importance of particular sovereignty practices in structuring relations between "units." The substance of Western demands on China also underscores the variability of the substance of sovereign rights. Both kinds of variability are no less important today.

At least since the 1970s, analysts have touted the decline of sovereignty in the face of interdependence, or as we are more likely to say today, globalization. In response, realists usually stress the continuing centrality of sovereign states. Both sides, I want to suggest, are right yet often misguided in their formulations.

Many functions that previously were monopolistically regulated by states are indeed slipping out of their control. But many of these functions were obtained only relatively recently. For example, national control over the money supply, which is being systematically undermined by global currency markets (and by regional institutions in Europe), simply was not an attribute of sovereign states during the heyday of the gold standard a century ago. Control over borders is another attribute of sovereignty that today seems increasingly precarious. But passports, the ultimate symbol of closed borders, did not even exist two hundred years ago. It never crossed anyone's mind that the capacity to exclude migration was central to sovereignty.

The "essential" attributes of sovereignty have always been fluid. Today we commonly define a state, following Max Weber, as that institution that has a monopoly on the legitimate use of force. But until the nineteenth

---

[14] Standard historical overviews can be found in Keeton (1928) and Willoughby (1927). Teng and Fairbank (1963) provide the major documentary evidence. Hertslet (1908) is the standard compendium of treaties.

century, mercenaries were a regular feature of international relations (Thomson 1994). In the sixteenth century, they were the principal means by which European states fought one other. States, in other words, leased rather than owned military force. They simply did not have monopolistic control.

Even the subjects of sovereignty have varied. Today we see sovereignty as held by states or peoples and tied to a fixed territory. In early modern Europe, however, kings held personal or dynastic sovereignty and passed on territory by birth and marriage. Thus early in the seventeenth century, England got a Scottish king, James VI (who become James I of England), when he inherited dominion over his southern neighbor. At the end of that same century, when James II's Catholicism became too much for many of his subjects to bear, they subjected themselves to a Protestant Dutch prince who had married into James' lineage.

The personal nature of sovereignty gave both national and international politics a particular character. And the dynastic disposal of territory had profound consequences for the nature of international relations. For example, marriage was a matter of high statecraft and wars were fought over disputed successions, which were no more a pretext than were territorial disputes in the nineteenth and twentieth centuries. The War of the Spanish Succession, for example, whatever other interests were involved, could not have been the war it was without a succession to dispute.

Current discussions of the demise of sovereignty tend to see it as something that one either has or does not have. Well into the twentieth century, however, the society of states recognized an extensive range of "imperfect" sovereignties. Positive international law recognized members of confederations (e.g. the American confederation of 1781–1789 and the German confederation of 1815–1866), vassal states under the suzerainty of another (e.g. Romania [1829–1878] and Egypt [1840–1914] under Turkey), protectorates (e.g. the Ionian Islands [1815–1863], Morocco [1906–1911], and Egypt [1914–1924]), administered provinces (e.g. Bosnia and Herzegovina, which were controlled by but not incorporated into Austria-Hungary from 1878 until 1908), self-governing British dominions (Canada, Australia, New Zealand, and South Africa, which until 1919 had no recognized international legal personality), colonies, League of Nations Mandates, neutralized states (e.g. Switzerland after 1815 and Luxemburg after 1867), belligerent communities and parties to a civil war (e.g. the American Confederacy), free cities (e.g. Krakow after the Congress of Vienna and Danzig between the world wars), native North American and African "tribes" (which were typically seen as only semi-sovereign), personal unions (e.g. between Britain and Hanover from 1714 until 1837), and various relations that Charles Fenwick (1924: 92) aptly described as "abnormal" (e.g. the extensive treaty rights of the United States in Cuba and Panama).[15]

In China the Western powers enjoyed an extensive series of special extraterritorial treaty rights that restricted, but did not extinguish, Chinese sovereignty. Japan and Siam operated under similar extraterritorial disabilities for shorter periods (Gong 1984: chs. 6, 7). An analogous regime of "capitulations" governed Western relations with the Ottoman empire.[16] We should also note that European diplomatic practice until well into the nineteenth century did not treat sovereigns as simply all formally equal, but instead recognized a complex array of status gradations (Wheaton 1936 [1866]: sect. 152–160). Even today, the special status of great powers remains codified in the veto power of the permanent members of the United Nations Security Council.

In the late twentieth century, semi-sovereign entities such as Puerto Rico and Andorra are minor exceptions. Once, however, they were perfectly ordinary, regular features of international relations. The doctrine of sovereign equality has evolved in such a way that we see sovereignty, survival, and independence as largely equivalent notions – which they simply were not a century ago. And recent discussions of an international protectorate for Kosovo, which are being aired seriously as I am completing revisions of this book, suggest that semi-sovereignty may be reacquiring some contemporary relevance.

States are indeed much more homogeneous today than they were in the eighteenth and nineteenth centuries. But that is not, as Waltz would have it (1979: 76, 93–97), the result of anarchy. The homogenization of the formal rights and duties of states under the doctrine of sovereign equality is the result of complex normative and institutional processes in the society of states. This becomes especially clear when we consider the parallel development of the doctrine of self-determination.

Self-determination and non-intervention

A hundred years ago, most Westerners considered it not merely acceptable but right that they exercised imperial control over almost all of Africa

[15] The importance of such distinctions is reflected in the extensive space devoted to them in nineteenth- and early twentieth-century legal manuals. See, for example, Wheaton (1936 [1866]: sect. 33–59), Fenwick (1924: 87–102), Hyde (1992: sect. 14–29), and Hall (1924: 23–35).

[16] Thayer (1923) provides a useful brief introduction. For much more extensive accounts, see Pélissié du Rausas (1910) and Susa (1933). For comparable discussions of the Dutch Indies and Africa, see Alexandrowicz (1967; 1973). British relations with the various rulers of the Indian subcontinent, both during and after the rule of the British East India Company, likewise fail to fit a simple model of "sovereign" and "not sovereign."

and most of South and Southeast Asia. But beginning in India and Indonesia in 1947, decolonization radically reshaped the map of the world, especially in a great burst in the two decades following Ghana's independence in 1957. In 1957 there were 78 member states of the United Nations. By 1967, that number had grown to 123, an increase of 60 percent. By 1981 the number had doubled to 156. In 1945, over 750 million people lived in non-self-governing territories. By 1990, despite the huge growth of global population, less than two million people resided in just eighteen remaining non-self-governing territories (Baehr and Gordenker 1992: 118).

These fundamental changes in the actors in international politics had little to do with changes in the distribution of capabilities. Belize, Botswana, Bahrain, and Brunei did not force independence on Britain, nor did they skillfully manipulate changes in global or regional balances of power to get another great power to take up their cause. In fact, many of the states created over the past forty years lack the capacity to provide even minimal self-defense.

The principal "power" resource of many of these states is their international recognition. These "quasi-states," to use Robert Jackson's (1990) needlessly inflammatory label, owe their existence largely to changes in the international society of states associated with the spread of the doctrine of national self-determination. The resulting changes in relations between people, territory, and government have been largely separate from changes in the distribution of capabilities.[17]

Consider the related issue of intervention.[18] It is often said that the logical corollary of sovereignty is non-intervention, that A's right to sovereignty places an obligation of non-intervention on B. This is in some important sense true. But the shape and scope of impermissible intervention, and thus the rights of sovereigns, have changed dramatically.

A century ago, extraterritorial rights for Western nationals and firms in China, in the Ottoman Empire, and in other "semi-civilized" countries[19] were seen as not merely consistent with but an outgrowth of the idea of sovereign equality. The special rights of Westerners were justified by minimum international standards of behavior that sovereign states might

---

[17] I do not want to suggest that decolonization was contrary to the interests of the United States or the Soviet Union or of the leading colonial powers. But that was as much a matter of changes in their conceptions of interest as of material or technological changes. And those changed interests often were at best only loosely connected with the distribution of power between metropolitan and colonial political units.

[18] The best general introduction to the subject is Bull (1984).

[19] A distinction was often drawn between "savages," who were a legitimate subject of direct colonization, and "semi-civilized" or "barbarian" peoples, who were seen to have impaired or legitimately restricted sovereign rights. See Gong (1984: 55–58).

choose to deny to their own nationals but could not legitimately deny to nationals of other states, over whom they did not have supreme jurisdiction. Likewise, military intervention by great powers in the affairs of small powers – for matters including offenses to national honor, collecting debts, protecting Christians and missionaries, assuring "free" trade and investment, or altering or maintaining political alignments – was a well-accepted part of international relations. Thus Edward Gulick lists intervention as one of the eight principal means of balance of power politics in its nineteenth-century European heyday (1967: 62–65).

In the "good old days" – when men were men and white men ruled the world – it often did appear that the strong did what they could, and the weak suffered what they must. Even then that was an exaggeration. Today it is not even a good first approximation.

The weak certainly still suffer. But what the strong can do has changed dramatically. If a country threatens to default on its debt, it is inconceivable that Western naval vessels would lob a few shells or fire missiles at the local capital. In a very real sense, it cannot happen. If the United States is unhappy with a Central American "banana republic," it no longer has the option of sending in the Marines to restore "order."

Change has occurred not in the relative balance of military resources between great powers, or between weak and powerful states, but in norms and practices relating to sovereignty and intervention, under the influence of changing ideas of national self-determination and the meaning of sovereign equality. As a result, there are many things that powerful states once could do that today in a real and important sense they cannot.

Aggression and survival

Such normative and institutional changes have even altered the role of force in international relations. In the nineteenth century, sovereign states had an absolute right of war. Each state was at liberty to fight whenever it chose, for whatever reason it deemed adequate. As a leading legal manual put it, in starkly Hobbesian terms, every state has

a right to resort to force, as the only means of redress for injuries inflicted upon it by others, in the same manner as individuals would be entitled to that remedy were they not subject to the laws of civil society. Each State is also entitled to judge for itself, what are the nature and extent of the injuries which will justify such a means of redress (Wheaton 1936 [1866]: § 290).

And this doctrine was clearly enshrined in practice. Thus Gulick lists war as another principal means of balance of power politics (1967: 89–91).

Compare Article 2(4) of the United Nations Charter, the leading contemporary statement of basic norms on the use of force: "All Members
shall refrain in their international relations from the threat or use of force
against the territorial integrity or political independence of any state." We
have already seen examples of the practical effects of this prohibition of
the use of force against the political independence of other states. The
prohibition of the use of force for territorial aggrandizement has become
even more deeply entrenched in contemporary international relations.

Through World War I force often (re)shaped international boundaries.
States regularly died and were born in war. As the breakup of Austria-
Hungary after World War I illustrates, even a great power could count on
survival only so long as it remained great. Throughout modern Western
history, lesser powers were constantly at risk of absorption or partition.

This simply is no longer the case. The last forcible territorial acquisi-
tion of significance was China's incorporation of Tibet in 1951. Israeli
control over the Occupied Territories has been recognized by no state,
and is not claimed by Israel to be permanent. The forcible partition of
Cyprus is recognized by no one other than Turkey.[20] Indonesia's incorporation of tiny East Timor in 1975 was never accepted by most countries.
And Iraq's invasion of Kuwait was not merely repulsed by Kuwait's allies
but condemned even by most states otherwise sympathetic to Iraq.

The rights to territorial integrity and political independence enjoyed by
most states today have surprisingly little to do with military resources or
the international distribution of capabilities.[21] They rest instead on the
more or less effective outlawing of aggressive war and on changing international norms of sovereignty, self-determination, and non-intervention.
Dozens of states could follow the example of Costa Rica and abolish their
army with no discernible impact on their security or prospects for survival.

Over the past half-century, military might and control over territory
have been substantially decoupled – and not just in "quasi-states." Even
many states with substantial military resources owe their territorial integrity less to their deterrent or defensive capabilities than to a system-wide
recognition of the principle of territorial integrity. Force has not been
eliminated from international relations. Consider, for example, the

---

[20] It must be noted, though, that Eritrea and Tigre did obtain international recognition
after a long and extremely violent struggle for independence from Ethiopia.

[21] For some states, military capabilities and the system-wide distribution of power are a
major part of the explanation for their survival. But even for large states, as we saw in
chapter 4, the character of nuclear weapons is an important part of the explanation even
in the standard structural realist story. And the impact of international norms may not be
entirely negligible. Certainly they are important parts of the story in the countries of the
former Yugoslavia and the smaller former republics of the Soviet Union.

victims of Iraqi aggression in Kuwait and of American bombing and embargo in Iraq; ethnic cleansing in Bosnia and Croatia; and the sufferings of Chechens, Russians, Armenians, Azeris, Ossetians, and many others in the Caucasus. But the use of force for territorial aggrandizement has been largely banished. Perhaps most strikingly, no great power has used military force for territorial gain in half a century.

As a result, survival is rarely at stake in contemporary international relations. Where once it was perfectly ordinary for states to die, today it is extraordinary.[22] In fact, the post-Cold War international community has often intervened to prevent, or at least attempt to deny the reality of, death. In failing and failed states such as Somalia, Bosnia, Liberia, and the Congo, regional and international powers and institutions have undertaken substantial, costly efforts to enforce the survival of these states, rather than absorb or partition them, as often would have happened in previous centuries.

Today most states do not pursue increases in wealth and power in order to increase their probability of surviving – which is already close to one hundred percent. What is at stake is not living, but living better (or worse). Even struggles with more powerful neighbors to increase autonomy rarely aim to increase the chances of survival. Greater autonomy is typically sought instead for its intrinsic value or in order to live better as a result of an improved bargaining position.

International anarchy persists. An active fear for survival, however, makes up a remarkably small part of the motivation of most states. Some states – for example, Israel – do have a real fear for their survival that is, at least in part, well grounded. But they are the relatively rare exceptions. A century ago they would have been the rule. Even most larger powers today maintain military forces not to assure their survival but to protect an array of "lesser" interests. Although theorists and policy makers still appeal to survival, the actual interests at stake usually have a tenuous, if not ludicrous, connection to survival in any serious sense of that term.

When survival is regularly at stake and potentially threatened from all directions, Hobbes' war of all against all may seem a good model of international relations. That simply is not the case in most of the world today – but not because of any change in "structure," as Waltz defines it. The dramatic decline in the salience of survival is due to changes in international norms and institutions, as well as changes in military and non-military technologies, the interests and values of leading powers, and a variety of

---

[22] When they do, as in the case of the Soviet Union or Yugoslavia, it is largely for internal reasons. And even then, strenuous efforts have been made to partition on the basis of existing boundaries, and to resist efforts to change those boundaries by force (most notably in Bosnia).

other "non-structural" forces that must be incorporated in any plausible account of contemporary international politics.

In chapter 2 we saw that the characteristic motives of even "realist" states extend far beyond survival. Here we have seen that changes in norms and institutions can decisively alter the very character of the "threats" against which states balance. The extent to which states seek survival is in part a function of the institutional structure within which they interact. A theory of international politics thus needs to know not only something about the character of states but also about the character of the norms, institutions, and relationships within which they interact.

An overriding concern with survival makes sense for certain kinds of actors in certain kinds of anarchic environments. It is not an inescapable consequence of anarchy. In particular, it is not an important feature of contemporary international relations in most of the world.

A realist rebuttal

One can readily imagine realists responding that the effects I have attributed to norms and institutions are in fact due to "deeper" material forces. "Realists believe that state behavior is largely shaped by the *material structure* of the international system" (Mearsheimer 1995: 91). If norms and institutions are simply "reflections of the distribution of power in the world" (Mearsheimer 1994/95: 7) then their effects, realists might argue, are not really "independent."

This argument, however, continues to confuse cause and effect. Consider a domestic analogy. Even if we grant that the power of the state provides the basis for a system of legal rules and institutions, the resultant legal system may – and in many states does – limit the exercise of state power. Just because A causes B does not mean that B can have no effects in the world. Even if A is initially the sole cause of B, B may still have "independent" effects, even on A. Whether in fact it does is an empirical, not a theoretical, question.

Realists must show that the same results could have been achieved, at comparable cost, without reliance on the norms or institutions in question. On the face of it, however, this is unlikely. Why would powerful states bother with norms and institutions, which enmesh them in constraining rules and procedures, if they could achieve the same results independently?

Even rational egoists often desire and make use of international institutions. For example, the Prisoners' Dilemma arises largely because of the absence of effective institutions to monitor and enforce compliance with agreements. If an agreement to cooperate could be effectively policed, there would be no dilemma at all. A different sort of collective action problem arises when actors are unable to agree on which particular co-operative solution to adopt, because they cannot resolve their disputes over the distribution of benefits and costs. Institutionalized decision making procedures may provide a way to achieve cooperation that would otherwise be impossible.

Institutions also reduce "transaction costs," the investment of time and resources in achieving a desired outcome. If rules can be agreed upon to cover situations of a particular sort in the future, one need not negotiate over every case. By providing order and predictability, norms and institutions allow states to behave differently, even if all this means is that they are able to pursue a wider range of interests in a greater variety of circumstances.

Rather than an empirical argument against institutions, Mearsheimer's realism instead reflects a philosophical predisposition to deny the reality of norms and institutions. Adherents of this philosophy may choose not to consider norms and institutions in their own work. But even then, their analyses must be tested against the experience of a world in which norms and institutions do exist. It is an empirical question whether their impact is sufficiently negligible that they can be ignored. And those who reject this reductionist, materialist philosophy still have good reason to explore the potential role of international norms and institutions.

A slightly different, but equally ineffective, version of this realist rebuttal is suggested by Waltz' claim that "rules, institutions, and patterns of cooperation, when they develop in self-help systems, are all limited in extent and modified from what they might otherwise be" (1986: 336). This confuses empirical and theoretical claims. Some rules may be of more limited extent in some self-help systems than in some hierarchical orders. But others may not.

Even if "in general" anarchic orders have fewer rules and lower levels of institutionalization than hierarchic orders, this tells us nothing about the nature or character of the rules and institutions of any particular order, either hierarchic or anarchic. The realist approach is roughly equivalent to saying that because most movies are commercial and formulaic, we can assume that all are. This may simplify the life of the film critic, but it is hardly a useful rule for the practice of the craft – let alone for those who rely on her analysis.

The reference to "what they might otherwise be" suggests that Waltz is operating with a model in which *real* institutions, rules, and cooperation arise only in hierarchic structures, with those in anarchic orders being somehow defective. But this is entirely unjustified. Rules may or may not function differently in anarchic and hierarchic societies. Moreover, the same rule or institution may function very differently in different societies, whether anarchic or hierarchic.

Consider also Waltz' claim, quoted in chapter 2, that there are qualitative differences between "politics conducted in a condition of settled rules and politics conducted in a condition of anarchy" (1979: 61). As the example of sovereignty indicates, contemporary international politics, despite the existence of anarchy, is conducted in an environment of settled rules. In fact, some dictatorial regimes may operate under less settled rules than, say, those within the European Union or those governing US–Canadian relations.

Institutions and the Prisoners' Dilemma

A very different illustration of the effects of institutions is provided by the Prisoners' Dilemma (PD), one of our six paradigms of realism. As we saw in chapter 1, PD models an anarchic environment in which both actors would be better off if they cooperated, but because of their fear of defection they rationally choose to compete.[23] The structural character of international institutions is strikingly illustrated by their capacity to ameliorate, and in some circumstances even overcome, this logic of competition.

Ameliorating the Dilemma

Robert Axelrod and Robert Keohane in a well-known article (1985) suggest a number of strategies for achieving cooperation when faced with a Prisoners' Dilemma. One of the most important is to "lengthen the shadow of the future." The temptation to defect arises in significant part because PD is a single-play game. If the actors see it as a step in an indefinite series of interactions, however, the value of the stream of cooperative benefits may induce them to risk cooperation.[24] Institutions, from informal agreements through international organizations with extensive enforcement powers, have considerable potential to lengthen the shadow of the future.

Issue linkage can also increase the benefits of cooperation (and thus reduce the incentives to defect). Instead of playing one game several times, two or more separate games may be linked. For example, in the

---

[23] See pp. 19–23.

[24] Technically it is necessary for the series of interactions to be indefinite. If one knows that, for example, round 100 of the game is to be the last, one will rationally defect then. But knowing that, it becomes rational to defect on round 99, and so forth in a regress that returns us to the logic of the single-play case.

negotiations leading to the 1982 Law of the Sea Convention broad consensus was reached on a package of issues, ranging from innocent passage through international straits to mining the deep seabed, that probably could not have been achieved in a series of separate negotiations. The temptation to defect on one issue was overcome by the need to acquire cooperation on another issue in the package deal.

A similar logic is reflected in the emphasis Axelrod and Keohane give to reciprocity. At a relatively narrow and technical level, Axelrod's work has shown the virtues, both theoretical and in simulations, of a reciprocating strategy of tit-for-tat (1984). More generally, states may have a broader interest in diffuse reciprocity, in which they cooperate not because of any immediate expectation of maximizing their gain (or minimizing their maximum possible loss) but because they expect to receive reciprocal cooperation in the future (Keohane 1986a). For example, diffuse reciprocity is likely among states interacting in Snyder's relations of amity. It is also more likely among participants in international regimes and intergovernmental organizations where there is a long-term, open-ended commitment to cooperate.

These strategies involve increasing the incentives to cooperate by increasing the stream of benefits. Conversely, one might try to reduce the risks of defection. Here too institutions can play a role.

The most obvious contribution would involve enforcement mechanisms for international agreements. Rarely, though, do states accept authoritative international adjudication of disputes. Somewhat more frequently, contemporary states accept dispute resolution mechanisms and even quasi-judicial settlement procedures, such as those of the World Trade Organization. Nonetheless, self-help remains the norm in international relations. An emphasis on coercive, judicial or quasi-judicial enforcement, therefore, suggests a relatively modest role for international institutions.

Much of the dilemma of PD arises, however, from uncertainty. (The related logic of the security dilemma even more clearly rests on uncertainty.) Institutions can remove some of that uncertainty by providing transparency. Many international agreements require and facilitate the exchange of reliable information. Some provide for international monitoring; for example, by the International Atomic Energy Agency (IAEA) to assure that nuclear materials are not diverted to military purposes.[25] Especially where early warning will allow potential victims to take counter-measures, institutionalized transparency can sometimes induce

---

[25] These mechanisms, and their importance in assuring compliance with international agreements, are discussed in Chayes and Chayes (1995: ch. 6–8).

states to take the risks of cooperation. The importance of good information is also enhanced when the games are open-ended or linked or when
actors are inclined to diffuse reciprocity.

Institutions and changing interests

The discussion so far has focused on changing the external environment
of actors and altering their perceptions of the intentions of those with
whom they interact. Institutions, however, may alter the preferences of
actors, and thus the basic structure of the game.

Consider a simple example. If "reward" (mutual cooperation) is preferred to "temptation" (defecting against a cooperative partner), PD is
transformed into Stag Hunt. The game then is represented, in the nota-
tion used in chapter 1, as R>T>P>S or CC>DC>DD>CD. The standard story is of a group of hunters after a stag. A rabbit runs by, tempting
one hunter to leave his position and thus risk letting the stag escape
through the resulting hole in the line of hunters. There is still a dilemma –
go after the smaller but more likely catch of the rabbit, or risk ending up
with nothing in order to increase the chance of the much more rewarding
catch of the stag – but it is less severe because each actor prefers reward
(mutual cooperation) over temptation.[26]

Snyder's discussion of alliances might suggest just such a transformation of interests. States originally ally because of a willingness to accept the
risk of cooperation (perhaps because of the greater risks of not cooperating
against a third power). Over time, however, as a result of a pattern of cooperative interactions, allies may come to prefer cooperating to defecting.
For example, even if NATO began as Waltzian balancing against a
common threat, a strong case can be made that today the members of the
alliance prefer mutual cooperation to temptation, in significant part
because of their history of institutionalized cooperation (Waever 1998).

The sovereignty example above also illustrates norms and institutions
inducing states to redefine their interests. Decolonization certainly did
reflect economic, technological, and political changes that reduced the
benefits to colonial powers of direct imperial rule (or reduced the costs of
granting independence). But changing norms of self-determination,
equality, and discrimination also led some powers to reconceptualize
their interest in colonial domination, independent of (or in interaction
with) such material changes (Jackson 1993).

Realists often treat interests as "exogenous"; that is, given or assumed

---

[26] For a classic discussion of cooperation under PD and Stag Hunt situations, see Jervis
(1978: 170–186).

independent of and prior to the interactions being analyzed, and thus outside the scope of the theory. Somewhat more subtly, structural realists treat interests as shaped by anarchy. Most characteristically, they argue that even states that otherwise would wish to pursue moral objectives are "forced" by anarchy to define their national interests if not in terms of power, at least in terms of more material interests. The internally generated preferences of states run up against the threats posed by anarchy, leading to a redefinition of the national interest.

In effect I have been arguing that international norms and institutions can no less effectively "shape and shove" states. This rarely happens on a system-wide basis (although the discussion of sovereignty above reminds us that "rarely" does not mean never). Regionally, however, it is not uncommon, especially in Europe. In many bilateral relations of amity as well, interests are transformed. Consider, for example, relations between the United States and Britain, Canada, and Mexico. And interests can also be transformed by institutions in particular issue areas, as we saw above in the case of nonproliferation.

When states truly do face a strong Prisoners' Dilemma, cooperation indeed faces serious structural hurdles. But not all of international relations is appropriately modeled as PD. And even where PD logic does operate, international norms and institutions may ameliorate the dilemma or even transform the game. In all of these cases, the failure of structural theories to account for international institutions can lead to profoundly wrong explanations and dangerous expectations.

The realist focus on anarchy provides valuable cautions against overestimating the ease of cooperation. PD reminds us that common interests often are not enough to bring about common action. But none of this amounts to an effective argument against placing international institutions at the heart of the study of international relations. That is an empirical question the answer to which is almost certain to change with time, place, issue, and the interests of analysts.

International institutions and international society

The discussions of sovereignty and PD have illustrated ways in which institutions can alter fundamental "realist" variables. In this final section I want to provide a more general overview of the functions of international norms and institutions,[27] concluding with a discussion of the idea of an international society of states.

---

[27] For a much more extensive theoretical discussion, undertaken from a fairly similar general position, see Kratochwil (1989).

The functions of international institutions

In discussing the Prisoners' Dilemma we have seen that institutions and norms both constrain undesirable behavior and enable desirable action. By providing both insurance against defection and additional incentives to cooperate they may enable states to realize benefits that could not otherwise be obtained. In other words, norms and institutions produce effects through both "negative" and "positive" means.

In slightly different language, we can say that norms and institutions both prohibit and authorize. Where fear of cheating predominates, prohibition is likely to be the focus of our attention. But even institutional solutions to cheating often involve authorizing preventive or punitive actions. And when a mechanism to reach agreement is required, the enabling function of institutions is central.

Authority in anarchic international relations is by definition horizontal, rather than vertical. But that does not make the authority any less real. International norms and institutions, no less than national political norms and institutions, are sources and expressions of authority.

For example, the spread of international human rights norms in recent decades has altered national and international conceptions of political legitimacy. Consider South Africa. Although the struggle against apartheid was primarily a national struggle, international pressure, mobilized almost exclusively on normative grounds, aided apartheid's opponents. And white rule was subtly undermined by a growing sense of the illegitimacy of racial domination, fostered in significant measure by international normative pressure.[28] Similar stories can be told about the collapse of communism in Central and Eastern Europe[29] and the decline of military dictatorship in Latin America in the 1980s.[30]

The language of authority and legitimacy also points to the importance of social roles. Institutions usually involve designated roles. Contracts, for example, in addition to specifying rules for exchanging what lawyers call "considerations," create right-holders and duty-bearers, occupants of particular social roles. The nonproliferation regime, beyond establishing rules on acquiring arms and handling nuclear materials, formalizes the roles of nuclear and non-nuclear states and vests the IAEA with special monitoring roles.

This reference to the IAEA and its monitors suggests a further function of international norms: they may *constitute*, rather than regulate, actors,

---

[28] For an extended version of such a reading, see Klotz (1995).

[29] See, for example, Gubin (1995), where the issue of Soviet compliance is explicitly explored in the context of competing realist and institutionalist explanations. More generally, see Thomas (forthcoming).   [30] On Argentina, see Brysk (1994).

practices, and meanings. Nonproliferation is not just the failure or refusal to acquire nuclear weapons. It is a complex set of social practices and meanings. Practicing nonproliferation means much more than merely not having nuclear weapons.

Institutions not only prescribe behavioral roles and constrain activity, they also constitute the identity of such agents and empower them to act on the basis of their institutional reality. Thus the creation of institutions . . . is not merely an act of rational choice. It is also an act of the construction of social reality that is grounded . . . on normative and epistemic agreements. Furthermore, it is the source and medium of practices that give meaning and direction to social choice and action (Adler 1998: 150).

Sovereignty even more clearly constitutes the actors of modern international institutions – sovereign states, not characterless "units" – and defines their basic (national and international) rights and duties. In a similar vein, the rules of international law constitute treaties, which by making possible the creation of international obligations respond to one of the most serious deficiencies of Hobbesian anarchy. Even in self-help orders there may be a huge difference between enforcing a treaty obligation and imposing one's preferences.

Constitutive international norms and institutions shape the very character of "units" and establish patterns of interaction that are no less important than the tendency of states to balance in anarchy. Enabling norms and institutions permit states to do things that they could not otherwise do. And regulative institutions of various sorts can substantially alter the interactions of even powerful states.

The international society of states

When international relations is highly institutionalized we may even be able to speak profitably of an international society. Not every international political system can be understood as a political society. For example, Persia may have been part of the political system of the ancient Greek world of the fifth century BC, but it was not part of Hellenic international society, which existed in at least a weak sense of that term.[31] The Ottoman Empire in the eighteenth century was on the edge of, a regular intervener in, but not part of, European international society. China in the nineteenth century was forcibly incorporated into the international political system, but was not part of European-dominated international

---

[31] Evidence for the existence of such a society of city-states can be found in shared religious festivals, such as the Olympic games, and in differing rules for treating Greeks and barbarians (including Persians). For an extended discussion of this example, see Wight (1977: ch. 3).

society. In the case of the contemporary world, however, it does make sense to talk about international society in a strong sense of that term.[32]

Here is not the place to address the question of whether there is, or is emerging, a global civil society[33] or a cosmopolitan world community. But even if we deny the contemporary reality of such an "international community" there is undoubtedly an international society of states. Despite anarchy, states interact not in a characterless void but within a complex web of constraining, enabling, and transforming norms and institutions. The extended discussion of sovereignty above amply illustrates both the reality of this society of states and the important difference for international relations that changes in the character of the basic norms and institutions of international society can make.[34]

The structural realist emphasis on anarchy, especially when it leads to exaggerated attacks on international institutions, obscures the fact that anarchy may be a form of social order. More precisely, many rather different forms of social order are anarchic. Knowing that international society is not hierarchic is for some purposes important. But Waltz' conception of structure allows us to say nothing about the kind of anarchic order that exists.

Where there is an international society in a strong sense of that term, as there undoubtedly is in the contemporary world, we will be unable to understand even most security relations between states without some knowledge of the system-wide norms and institutions of that particular international society, relevant international and regional regimes and

[32] The classic argument for this position is Bull (1977). For a good recent survey of the "English School," which has given the most attention to the idea of international society, see Dunne (1998) and, more briefly, Dunne (1995). For a useful overview of the process by which that society emerged out of a narrower European international society, see Bull and Watson (1984). Compare also Wight (1977). For a very different sort of approach to the issue of international social order, focusing on conflicts over ordering visions, see Skidmore (1997).

[33] By civil society we typically mean a domain of relations and associations outside the family and market but separate from the state. The concept has special relevance to efforts of resistance against oppression and in the discussion of social movements committed to change. Although civil society has traditionally been understood as national, cooperation by social movements – e.g. human rights, women's, and environmental movements – across national boundaries has led to some talk of a transnational civil society. A few analysts have argued that we can and should talk even more broadly of a truly global civil society. See, for example, Lipschutz (1996) and Turner (1998). For a less ambitious conception that sees such activities as part of transnational advocacy networks, see Keck and Sikkink (1998). On the related issue of civil society and multilateral organizations, see Knight (1999) and, more critically, Clark, Friedman, and Hochstetler (1998).

[34] Even Waltz at one point implicitly acknowledges this, when he notes that "to say that states are sovereign is to say that they are segments of a plural society" (1979: 95 n.). Typically, however, as we saw above, he treats sovereignty as if it were not a social relation.

organizations, and the relations and interactions (in Snyder's sense of those terms) of particular actors. Just as structure did not allow us to ignore all aspects of the character of states, it does not allow us to ignore the character of their interactions, which are significantly shaped by international norms and institutions.

Discussion questions

- What are the various ways in which the term "institutions" is typically used? What are the strengths and weaknesses of each usage? In particular, what are the special characteristics of understandings that see institutions as organizations and those that see institutions as rules?

- Are institutions just another language for functional differentiation? Does functional differentiation express itself in institutions? Are all institutions reflections of functional differentiation?

- What do you think of the distinction drawn in the text between the causes of institutions and their effects? Is the line as sharp as suggested there? In what ways might we want to say that the effects of an institution are inseparably linked to its causes?

- Are institutions (or other forms of cooperation) that are based entirely on self-interest really worthy of the name? What kind of self-interest underlies most social institutions? How is it related to the narrow, short-run, power-maximizing self-interest that Mearsheimer emphasizes?

- Let us grant that "intervening variables" such as institutions are simply independent variables that are modeled as less important than those factors labeled "independent variables." Is this not still an important distinction? Does it not at least partly justify the standard realist denigration of institutions?

- Consider the following realist rebuttal. Mearsheimer has taken the realist position to its logical extreme – if not over the edge. Of course, institutions have effects. They just do not often have very important effects. Is Mearsheimer's argument really just a straw man, no matter how prominent and respected its creator? How might institutionalists respond to this more modest, but also probably more powerful, attack on institutions?

- Mearsheimer may overstate the perils of anarchy. But does Donnelly not understate the constraints on institutions imposed by anarchy and the pursuit of survival? There are indeed a number of effective (security) institutions. But is the realist emphasis on constraints not in the end more enlightening than Donnelly's implicit optimism about the effects of institutions? Is the most important point not the realist one, namely, that even though security institutions operate effectively in a number of scattered (and occasionally even important) domains, the central fact about international relations remains the prevalence of anarchy and the dominance of fear?

- Balance of power can indeed be seen as a social institution. But cannot it also be profitably seen in Waltz' structural terms? Do we have here a case of one term, balance of power, used to label two rather different concepts, theories, or practices? If so, why should we accept the suggestion in the text that the institutional understanding is the better one?

- If war is an institution of order, what is the implicit understanding of the relation between war and violence? And however it is intended, is that not a perverse description of war?

- Is it true, as suggested in the text, that the main problem with Mearsheimer's argument is that he mistakes an empirical question for a theoretical one?

- Is sovereignty really essentially a matter of authority (and thus norms and institutions)? Can it not be thought of in more "realist" terms as simple independence in anarchy? What is gained and lost in each formulation?

- What is fixed in sovereignty and what is variable? How insightful is it to emphasize the variable? What impact does the actual degree of variability in sovereignty practices have for our assessment of (structural) realism?

- What is the relationship between the internal and the external dimensions of sovereignty? What implications does your answer have for the nature of international theory?

- Let us grant that sovereignty can be profitably seen as a complex set of institutional rules for regulating the interaction of states. Let us further grant that sovereignty is an institution characteristic of modern international relations (but not necessarily of all systems of anarchic relations). How much of a modification does this require in the structuralist project? How much of what structural realists attribute to "units" in anarchy really is about sovereign states, units of a particular kind interacting within a particular set of rules and roles?

- Following the argument of theoretical pluralism advanced at several points in the text, why should we not simply recognize multiple understandings of sovereignty that have different uses? What implications would such an approach have for our understanding of the nature of realism? Would Waltz or Mearsheimer be likely to be happy, or even comfortable, with such a conclusion?

- Non-intervention is clearly a norm of a particular international society, rather than a fact of all anarchical systems. How different are anarchic orders with and without the norm of non-intervention? How important is the implicit norm of non-intervention in realist accounts of "anarchic" politics?

- Is it really true that the change in the relationship between First World and Third World countries has little to do with changes in the balance of power? Might we not say instead that what has changed is the nature or forms of power? What happens to realist theories, however, if power differs in qualitative ways from time to time and case to case?

- Is the fact that few if any states have been eliminated as a result of international conflict sufficient to support the claim that survival is rarely at stake? What explanations other than the institutional ones pointed to in the text might account for the low death rate of states over the past half-century? Is the central issue really the frequency of risk? Even if death is rare, might it still not be an overriding fear?

- How do you assess Donnelly's claim that the realist denigration of institutions is more a matter of philosophical predisposition than empirical analysis? How is this related to issues of interest and importance that have been raised in earlier chapters?

- Even if institutions do regularly "shape and shove" states, is the difference between institutional and structural (in Waltz' sense of that term) shaping and shoving not important? Do realists not properly emphasize these differences, which institutionalists tend to minimize?

- How important is international society? Of course it exists – as do qualitative differences between states. But can we not, in the interest of theoretical economy and for the purposes of a rough first cut, usually ignore its impact? In other words, is not international society, like institutions in general, best treated as an intervening variable?

- Can institutions change interests? If in principle they can, do they in practice often have such transformative effects in international relations? These questions implicitly raise the issue of norms that are constitutive as well as regulative. How deep or powerful a challenge do constitutive norms pose to structural realism? In theory? With respect to contemporary international practice?

- Much of the argument in this chapter can be summarized in the claim that realists recognize only a regulative role for international norms and institutions, when they in fact also play central constitutive roles. And even among regulative norms and institutions, realists overemphasize constraining rules to the denigration of no less important enabling rules. How might realists respond? How would you evaluate these arguments?

- How helpful are these distinctions between regulative and constitutive norms and between constraining and enabling institutions? Are there other types of functions that we should include?

- Are realism and institutionalism best seen as different approaches with different applications rather than competitors for theoretical hegemony in the discipline? What are the strengths and weaknesses of each understanding?

Suggestions for further reading

The sharpest realist critique of international institutions is to be found in John Mearsheimer's "The False Promise of International Institutions" (1994/95). For a representative example of the post-World War II realist attack, see chapters 25–32 of Georg Schwarzenberger's *Power Politics* (1951), which end with a section titled "The Result: Power Politics in Disguise." In chapter 15, however, Schwarzenberger makes it clear that in principle there is no reason why international institutions might not be effective, even if in fact the disparity between profession and practice is what is most striking.

Not all realists, however, are committed to even that harsh a critique. Randall Schweller and David Priess' "Expanding the Institutions Debate" (1997), argues that core realist assumptions can be used directly to develop realist theories of the formation and functioning of international institutions. And as they point out, earlier realists, for all their attacks on the pretenses of international organizations as governing bodies, actually paid considerable attention to institutions. Consider, for example, the extended coverage of international organizations in Morgenthau's *Politics Among Nations*.

The institutionalist perspective, as we have already noted above, is the principal mainstream competitor to realism, at least in the United States. For a good review of the current state of the neorealist–neoliberal debate, see Baldwin (1993). Robert Keohane's "Neoliberal Institutionalism: A Perspective on World Politics" (1989: ch. 1), provides a good summary by a leading proponent of the approach. Oran Young's *Global Governance* (1994) begins with a major theoretical statement that is followed by an excellent application to international environmental issues. Another good example of the approach in action, again dealing with the environment, is the edited collection *Institutions for the Earth* (Haas, Keohane, and Levy 1993).

Sovereignty is a central institution of international society that in recent years has attracted the attention of a growing number of scholars, especially those with "social constructivist" orientations. Hinsley (1986) is the standard historical overview of the subject. James (1986) provides a good overview of major conceptual and analytical issues from a mainstream perspective. Robert Jackson's *Quasi-States* (1990) is a creative study of the central role of external recognition in contemporary sovereignty practices. Thomson (1994) and Spruyt (1994) explore the historical variability of sovereignty, focusing especially on the early modern era. Cynthia Weber's *Simulating Sovereignty* (1995) provides a useful introduction to post-structural and postmodern approaches. Bartelson (1995) is a brilliant application of Foucauldian analysis; it is tough reading, but immensely creative and insightful. *State Sovereignty as Social Construct* (Bierstecker and Weber 1996) provides a wide range of essays that emphasize the contingency and variability of sovereignty practices. The major realist rebuttal is Stephen Krasner's *Sovereignty: Organized Hypocrisy* (1999). The subtitle clearly indicates the approach, which is in many ways reminiscent of Schwarzenberger's.

The idea of international society – or, more precisely, the society of states – is particularly associated with Martin Wight, Hedley Bull, and the English School of international studies. Bull's *The Anarchical Society* (1977) is the leading statement of the perspective. Dunne (1998) provides a good history of the development of the school. Other major works are Butterfield and Wight (1966), Wight (1977), Wight (1992), Bull and Watson (1984), Mayall (1982), and Donelan (1978). Barry Buzan's "From International System to International Society: Structural Realism and Regime Theory Meet the English School" (1993) provides a good overview of points of convergence and divergence.

A growing number of analysts, however, use the term international society in a much less state-centric way. Some – e.g. Lipschutz (1996) and Turner (1998) – speak of global civil society, suggesting the emergence of something like a cosmopolitan world society. Others have revived and extended the idea of transnational actors, popular in the 1970s (e.g. Keohane and Nye 1972; 1977). *Bringing Transnational Relations Back In* (Risse-Kappen 1995) provides a good introduction to this approach. Margaret Keck and Kathryn Sikkink's *Activists Across Borders* (1998) is a superb application to transnational advocacy networks.

6   Morality and foreign policy

Although motivation, anarchy, structure, and international institutions have dominated recent academic discussions of realism, the exclusion of morality from foreign policy is a no less important feature of realism both in the popular understanding and in the work of many earlier realists. "Universal moral principles cannot be applied to the actions of states" (Morgenthau 1954: 9). "The process of government . . . is a practical exercise and not a moral one" (Kennan 1954: 48). "The search for power is not made for the achievement of moral values; moral values are used to facilitate the attainment of power" (Spykman 1942: 18). The problem of morality in international relations also flows naturally from the discussion of norms in the preceding chapter and relates directly to our earlier discussions of state motives and the national interest.

Human nature and international anarchy

Realists often appeal to "the limitations which the sordid and selfish aspects of human nature place on the conduct of diplomacy" (Thompson 1985: 20). "The ultimate sources of social conflicts and injustices are to be found in the ignorance and selfishness of men" (Niebuhr 1932: 23). "Man cannot achieve [justice,] for reasons that are inherent in his nature. The reasons are three: man is too ignorant, man is too selfish, and man is too poor" (Morgenthau 1970: 63). To act on moral concerns in the face of pervasive human evil, realists argue, would be foolish, even fatal.

But human nature is not *only* selfish and evil. Most realists allow that "men are motivated by other desires than the urge for power and that power is not the only aspect of international relations" (Spykman 1942: 7). They seek "an adequate view of human nature, which does justice to both the heights and depths of human life" (Niebuhr 1934: 113). "To do justice and to receive it is an elemental aspiration of man" (Morgenthau 1970: 61). Kenneth Thompson even contends that "man is at heart a moral being" and emphasizes "the insatiable quest of man for justice" (1966: 4, 75).

This more attractive side of human nature must create some potential for moral action in international relations – especially because the same human nature often allows moral concerns to be pursued, sometimes with considerable success, in personal relations and domestic politics. If morality in foreign policy is impossible, or at least unusually dangerous, it must be because anarchy causes or allows the potentialities of human nature to be expressed systematically differently in international society than in most national societies. "The cleavage between individual and international morality . . . corresponds to the difference between social relations in a community and those in a society bordering on anarchy" (Schwarzenberger 1951: 231). In the absence of international government "the law of the jungle still prevails" (Schuman 1941: 9).

But granting that "the nature of international society . . . makes a disparity between principle and practice inevitable" (Tucker 1968: 61) hardly requires that we give in to this disparity, let alone maximize it, by pursuing an amoral foreign policy. Consider two passages from Nicholas Spykman.

International society is . . . a society without central authority to preserve law and order, and without an official agency to protect its members in the enjoyment of their rights. The result is that individual states must make the preservation and improvement of the power position a primary objective of their foreign policy (1942: 7).

In international society all forms of coercion are permissible, including wars of destruction. This means that the struggle for power is identical with the struggle for survival, and the improvement of the relative power position becomes the primary objective of the internal and the external policy of states. All else is secondary (1942: 18).

The modest claim that the pursuit of power must be *a* primary objective of any state leaves considerable room for morality in foreign policy. But in the intervening pages nothing is advanced to justify the outrageous claim that power and security must be *the* principal aim of *both* the internal and external policy of *any* state.

In much the same vein, Ranke argues that "the position of a state in the world depends on the degree of independence it has attained. It is obliged, therefore, to organize all its internal resources for the purpose of self-preservation" (1973: 117–118). Even setting aside the confusion of independence and self-preservation, this passage fatally conflates assuring survival and organizing *all* internal resources for that purpose.

Such exaggerated extensions of fundamentally sound insights are common in realist discussions of morality. For example, Robert Art and Kenneth Waltz claim that "states in anarchy cannot afford to be moral.

The possibility of moral behavior rests upon the existence of an effective government that can deter and punish illegal actions" (1983: 6). This is obviously false – and not just because they confuse law and morality. Just as individuals may behave morally in the absence of government enforcement of moral rules, so moral behavior is possible in international relations. The costs of such behavior do tend to be greater in an anarchic system of self-help enforcement. Nonetheless, states often can and do act at least partly out of moral concerns or interests.[1]

There may be good policy reasons *in particular cases* to pursue an amoral, or even immoral, policy. Neither human nature nor international anarchy, however, requires that amoral foreign policy be the norm, let alone the universal rule. Even if "all politics is a struggle for power" (Schuman 1941: 261), (international) politics is not and ought not to be solely, or even primarily, a struggle for power.

The autonomy of politics and *raison d'état*

Beyond appeals to anarchy and egoism, many realists argue that morality is inappropriate in foreign policy because international politics is a distinct realm of human endeavor with its own standards and rules.

The autonomy of politics

Morgenthau was "especially concerned with the restoration of politics as an autonomous sphere of thought and action" (1962a: 3), with providing a "realist defense of the autonomy of the political sphere against its subversion by other modes of thought" (1954: 12). George Kennan similarly argues that the "primary obligation" of any government "is to the *interests* of the national society it represents" (1985/86: 206). As a result of this overriding obligation, "the same moral concepts are no longer relevant to it" (Kennan 1954: 48).

Why, though, is only *international* politics covered by such a claim? Morgenthau speaks of "the autonomy of politics" in general, not simply international politics. But such a view is obviously untenable. In domestic politics – and in personal relations as well – we may excuse immoral behavior, all things considered, but we would never accept a claim that moral concepts are irrelevant to national politics. Anarchy may increase the number of cases in which competing concerns pre-empt or override

[1] For a general argument to this conclusion, with considerable evidence from the foreign aid practices of the United States, see Lumsdaine (1993). US-led international interventions in Somalia and the former Yugoslavia (both Bosnia and Kosovo) provide clear examples of *partly* humanitarian uses of force over the past decade.

moral evaluations. It does not make morality categorically inappropriate in international relations.

Consider also Kennan's argument that an overriding concern for survival and the national interest is a matter of "unavoidable necessit[y]" and therefore "subject to classification neither as 'good' or 'bad'" (1985/86: 206). But if the national interest is not in some important sense good, why should we accept it as a standard for judging international political behavior? Kennan's "necessity" is not a matter of physical compulsion or impossibility. (In that case, the standard moral maxim "ought implies can" may apply; we can have no obligation to pursue values other than the national interest if doing so truly is impossible.) Rather, it is a matter of political choice – and thus in principle a matter of ethical evaluation and appropriately considered as good or bad.

Morality and the national interest

Beneath Kennan's ostensibly neutral appeal to unavoidable necessity is an implicitly ethical notion of the national interest – which many other realists make explicit. For example, Robert Tucker argues that "the statesman has as his highest moral imperative the preservation of the state entrusted to his care" (Osgood and Tucker 1967: 304 n. 71). Morgenthau even speaks of "the moral dignity of the national interest" (1951: 33–39).[2]

Such views are often associated with the *raison d'état* (reason of state) tradition (Meinecke 1957 [1924]; d'Entreves 1967: ch. 5), which holds that "the State is in itself an ethical force and a high moral good" (Treitschke 1916: 106). "Moralists must . . . recognize that the State is not to be judged by the standards which apply to individuals, but by those which are set for it by its own nature and ultimate aims" (Treitschke 1916: 99). In its stronger forms, states are seen as "individualities . . . spiritual substances" (Ranke 1973: 119; compare Meinecke 1957 [1924]: 1). In its extreme form, the state is seen as the source and necessary condition for the realization of all other values.

These are *ethical* arguments for an "amoral" foreign policy. They adopt the substantive moral position that "our" interests ought to count more than the interests of others (which "ordinary" morality enjoins us to consider as equal to our own). Such arguments express a radically communitarian political ethic.

Here is not the place to debate the relative virtues of communitarian

---

[2] As Tucker points out in his review of Morgenthau's book, however, it is a "mystery as to how the national interest can have a 'moral dignity' if international politics is simply a struggle of power against power" (1952: 221).

and universalistic/individualistic moral theories. It is important, however, to emphasize the contentious nature of the communitarian appeal to a moralized national interest. Even if we accept a communitarian ethic, we can ask why "our" interests should be treated as an ultimate law when the group is a state, but not when it is a smaller (or larger) group. Even if we agree that "power politics may be defined as a system of international relations in which groups consider themselves to be ultimate ends" (Schwarzenberger 1951: 13), why are classes, trade unions, multinational corporations, religious communities, or bowling leagues not equally (or instead) a law unto themselves?

The strongest argument is that the state reflects the limits of strong moral community in the contemporary world.[3] As Tucker argues, "the great majority persists in drawing a sharp distinction between the welfare of those who share their particular collective and the welfare of humanity" (1977: 139–140). To the extent that the nation or state is the practical terminal unit of moral (or at least political) community in contemporary international society, it is not implausible for realists to argue that political leaders ought to give systematic ethical preference to their own citizens and their interests.

Such a categorical ethical distinction between "us" and "them" certainly is morally contentious. It is, however, deeply rooted in the structure of an international political system of sovereign states. Realists thus have a plausible case for holding that the national interest is an important – although not necessarily decisive – ground for judging international political action in a world of sovereign states. Far less follows from the premise that international politics ought to be about the pursuit of the national interest, however, than realists usually suggest.

Consider Herbert Butterfield's appeal to the special office of the statesman.

If an individual consents to make self-sacrifice – even to face martyrdom before a foreign invader – it is not clear that he has a socially recognizable right to offer the same sacrifice on behalf of all his fellow-citizens, or to impose such self-abnegation on the rest of his society (1953: 11).

We can allow that a statesman may be guilty of grievous political misconduct if, in the pursuit of some moral goal, she were to sacrifice the

---

[3] This, however, is an historical fact, not a matter of logic. For example, Christendom in medieval Europe was in many ways a stronger and more meaningful political community than Burgundy, Normandy, or Gascony – let alone France. And the "national interest" of smaller political units within Christendom was that of princes, not peoples or territorial entities. Thus Robert Gilpin talks more broadly of "conflict groups" (1996: 7), of which states are simply the leading contemporary example.

sovereignty or independence of the country, let alone the lives of its citizens. The same, however, is true of the pursuit of alliances or economic objectives. Yet realists would (rightly) never think of excluding alliances or material gain from foreign policy because they may be pursued with excessive zeal. A valuable caution against moralistic excesses is once more inflated into an unsound general rule of statecraft. Many moral objectives can be pursued at a cost far less than national survival, sometimes even at little or no cost to the national interest defined in terms of power.

Furthermore, even if we grant that states "act as they must, in view of their interests as they see them" (Morgenthau 1962a: 278), there is no reason why states cannot, if they wish, define their national interests (in part) in moral terms. If citizens of a country value alleviating suffering in other countries, they are free to define their national interest to include, for example, providing clean water or preventing torture overseas. The characteristic realist argument against morality does not arise from the inescapable necessities of the national interest. Rather, it imposes a contentious substantive vision of what ought to be valued in foreign policy.

Realist conceptions of morality

Realists do not even have a clear, agreed-upon conception of the nature of the morality they reject. Some hold that moral values are relative. For example, E. H. Carr claims that "supposedly absolute and universal principles [are] not principles at all, but the unconscious reflexions of national policy based on a particular interpretation of national interest at a particular time" (1946: 87). But if ethical principles really are just unconscious reflections of the national interest, there is no reason at all not to pursue them in foreign policy. Reducing values to interests eliminates the very conceptual basis for excluding morality.

With somewhat more agnosticism, Kennan cautions us not to "assume that our moral values . . . necessarily have validity for people everywhere." "Our own national interest is all that we are really capable of knowing and understanding" (Kennan 1954: 47, 103). But this sort of ethical relativism does not logically imply that moral values ought not to be pursued in foreign policy. As our values, they may demand that we act upon them. In fact, such a relativism is fully compatible with the most ruthless imperialism and disregard for others. If Kennan is correct that "instead of setting ourselves up as judges over the morality of others, we would have done better to search for a stable balance of power" (1984: 159) it is because of the character or consequences of these two strategies. It does not follow from the relativity of values.[4]

Other realists believe that there are objective universal moral standards. For example, Morgenthau argues that "there is one moral code . . . [which] is something objective that is to be discovered" (1979: 10).[5] The problem, he contends, is that states cannot (should not) act on them in international relations.

"Unselfish (i.e., good) action intended or performed can never be completely good (i.e., completely unselfish); for it can never completely transcend the limitations of selfishness to which it owes its existence" (Morgenthau 1946: 192). But even Kant acknowledged the extreme rarity of acts undertaken entirely out of respect for the moral law, completely without admixture of other motives (1981: 20). Allowing that morality cannot be perfectly implemented does not imply that some degree of moral achievement is impossible, let alone that we should abstain from trying to do the right thing. The corruption of selfishness is an equally pervasive problem in private life, yet no realist would advance that as a reason for excluding morality in personal relations.

The shared opposition of realists to "moralism" – that is, their shared belief that the moral values appropriate to individual relations cannot be applied to the activities of states – gives the disparate realist views on morality and foreign policy a certain superficial coherence. But particular realist arguments against the pursuit of moral concerns in international relations are at best exaggerated. Taken together, they add up to an incoherent mess. And on closer examination, it turns out that even many emblematic realists reject amoralism.

Thucydides on justice and foreign policy

The Melian Dialogue[6] provides perhaps the best-known, and certainly one of the strongest, statements of realist amoralism. I will argue, however, that not only Thucydides, but even Machiavelli, rejects this view. "Standard" realist arguments for an amoral foreign policy thus prove not to be so standard after all.

In Thucydides' *History*, justice is appealed to by both weak and strong

---

[4] Joel Rosenthal develops a very different reading of Kennan, arguing that "far from draining the moral content from politics, Kennan's realism was all about how to make the moral factors count" (1991: xvi). I do not find this reading persuasive, but it does seem to me worth taking seriously. For a more recent article that might be interpreted more along Rosenthal's lines, see Kennan (1995).

[5] Compare Morgenthau (1962c: 43), where he criticizes Carr for an account of morality that rejects the possibility of a transcendental perspective.   [6] See pp. 23–24.

(e.g. II.72.1, 74.3; III.39.6, 40.4, 63.1, 67.3)[7] and arguments of justice figure in the majority of the political speeches.[8] Although often merely a "pleasing introduction to the concrete and effective factor" of power (Calder 1955: 179), justice sometimes plays an important, independent role.

The fate of Melos, sacrificed by Athens to fear and interest, parallels that of Plataea almost a dozen years earlier, after their pleas of justice were rejected by the Spartans (III.53–68). And Thucydides recounts Sparta's destruction of Plataea immediately after the Athenians narrowly avoid inflicting a similar fate on rebellious Mytilene.

An outraged Athenian assembly voted to slay the entire adult male population of Mytilene. But "the morrow brought repentance with it and reflection on the horrid cruelty of a decree which condemned a whole city to the fate merited only by the guilty" (III.36.4). When the assembly reverses its decision (III.49–50), Thucydides says nothing that would lead us to think that the original decision was anything other than the savagery the Athenian people on reflection realized it to be.

In a passage with strong echoes of *Antigone* (lines 450–459), Pericles earlier noted the Athenian respect for "those laws . . . which, though unwritten, bring upon the transgressor a disgrace which all men recognize" (II.37.3 [Smith]). Their reaction to the initial decision to kill all the Mytilenians points to similar minimum standards of international behavior. The temptation to brutality is strong – overwhelming by the time of the siege of Melos. But here the Athenians do finally respect the demands of justice. And the juxtaposed fates of Mytilene and Plataea underscore Sparta's injustice and inhumanity. A massacre of the innocent cannot be justified even by considerations of power and interest.

Following Sparta's destruction of Plataea, Thucydides discusses *stasis* (revolution, factional violence, civil war) in Corcyra, where the victorious democrats devoted themselves to "butchering those of their fellow-citizens whom they regarded as their enemies . . . There was no length to which violence did not go; sons were killed by their fathers, and suppliants dragged from the altar or slain upon it" (III.81.4–5). Later revolutionaries

---

[7] All otherwise unidentified references are to Thucydides' *History* by book, chapter, and, where appropriate, section. Translations are from the revised Crawley translation (Thucydides 1982), except for those identified as "[Smith]," which are by C. F. Smith in the Loeb edition (Thucydides 1919–1923).

[8] There are over 150 occurrences of *dikaios*, *dike* and words built on the same root, about half of which have a moral sense of "just" or "justice." (Most others refer to arbitration or legal proceedings, or have a sense of "proper" or "fitting" that is at best quasi-moral.) Various forms of *adikaios* ("unjust") occur approximately 150 times, usually with a moral sense. There are also about two dozen occurrences of *epieikeia* (equity, fairness) or *eikotos* (fairly, reasonably) used in a moral sense. See Essen (1964 [1887]).

in other cities "carried to a still greater excess the refinement of their inventions ... and the atrocity of their reprisals" (III.82.3). "Thus every form of iniquity took root" throughout Greece (III.83.1).

Words had to change their ordinary meanings and to take those which were now given to them. Reckless audacity came to be considered the courage of a loyal ally; prudent hesitation, specious cowardice; moderation was held to be a cloak for unmanliness; ability to see all sides of a question, inaptness to act on any. Frantic violence became the attribute of manliness; ... to forestall an intending criminal, or to suggest the idea of a crime where it was wanting, was equally commended (III.82.4–6).

Here we see Thucydides' outrage, based on the ordinary meaning of moral terms. Words actually retained their meanings, but exchanged their referents (Wilson 1982). The (really) good came to be considered bad, and vice versa. "The cause of all these evils was the lust for power arising from greed [pleonexia] and ambition" (III.82.8). The link with justice is the common Greek definition of justice as giving to each his own, and thus refraining from pleonexia, from taking that which is rightly another's.[9]

Mytilene, Plataea, and Corcyra are linked by the "realistic" use of savage, self-interested violence, which Thucydides describes in explicitly critical moral terms. Both externally at Plataea and internally at Corcyra this abhorrent politics of passionate violence arises from setting aside the restraints of justice. So too at Melos, Thucydides sees culpable moral failure.

In fact, Thucydides' catalogue of the repugnant consequences of stasis bears a striking resemblance to standard realist policy prescriptions. Stasis reduces politics to self-interest defined in terms of power. The leaders of factions, "recoiling from no means in their struggles for ascendancy ... and invoking ... the authority of the strong arm" (III.82.8), are much like the Athenians at Melos. "The fair proposals of an adversary were met with jealous precautions by the stronger" (III.82.7), as at Plataea and Melos. "Oaths of reconciliation ... held good only so long as no other weapon was at hand" (III.82.7), or, as the Athenians put it at Melos, justice is at issue only among equals in power. At Melos, words even change their meanings: the Athenians argue that both they and the Spartans "consider what is agreeable to be honorable and what is expedient just" (V.105.3 [Smith]).

Amoral power politics, far from being Thucydides' ideal, reduces man to barbarism. Two of Thucydides' three uses of omos, literally, "raw,"

---

[9] See, for example, Plato, Republic 359c, Aristotle, Nichomachean Ethics V.1–2, Rhetoric 1366b9–11.

"bloody," and thus metaphorically "savage," are in reference to the initial Athenian decision to kill all the Mytilenians (III.36.3) and the excesses of the Corcyraean revolutionaries (III.82.1). The third refers to the Eurytanians, who allegedly ate raw flesh (III.94.5).

It simply is not true that "what the Melians have tried to do is impossible in Thucydides' world. They have injected values and ideals into a sphere of interaction where they do not belong" (Saxonhouse 1978: 479–480). Much of the Dialogue's impact rests on not only the possibility but the appropriateness of the Melians introducing arguments of justice; the choice of the Athenians to dismiss them; and the consequences of this choice. Justice is rarely triumphant in Thucydides' *History*. It is, however, regularly present, relevant, and even important.

Effectual truth, political consequences, and the public good

Machiavelli is a more problematic case, if only because he typically introduces ethical considerations indirectly, sometimes even embedded in "machiavellian" doctrines.

Effectual truth

It has appeared to me more fitting to go directly to the effectual truth of the thing than to the imagination of it . . . a man who wants to make a profession of good in all regards must come to ruin among so many who are not good. Hence it is necessary to a prince, if he wants to maintain himself, to learn to be able not to be good, and to use this and not use it according to necessity (P15[1]).[10]

Although most initial readings focus on the need to do evil, this passage is extremely complex and subtle. The need to learn to do evil clearly suggests that the prince should be good. He must be able to use evil means, not be or become an evil man. Here, as throughout his work, Machiavelli accepts and implicitly endorses conventional moral understandings.

Good and evil are not mere labels attached to things in accord with a speaker's interests or desires. For example, Machiavelli contrasts the praise due to founders of cities and religions, triumphant generals, and those who excel at any art, with the opprobrium rightly earned by "the profane, the violent, the ignorant, the worthless, the idle, the coward. Nor will there ever be anyone, be he foolish or wise, wicked or good, who, if

---

[10] Citations of Machiavelli are incorporated into the text as follows. P = *The Prince*, by chapter and paragraph in the Mansfield translation (Machiavelli 1985). D = *The Discourses [on the First Ten Books of Livy]*, by book, chapter, and paragraph in Crick's revised Walker translation (Machiavelli 1970).

called upon to choose between these two classes of men, will not praise the one that calls for praise and blame the one that calls for blame" (DI.10[1]; compare P19[6–14]).

Furthermore, Machiavelli counsels a reluctant resort to evil. A prince must "not depart from good, when possible" (P18[5]). "To use fraud in any action is detestable," although when necessary it may be "praiseworthy and glorious" (DIII.40[1]). The moral standard is no less important than the political exception.

A new prince could never be as good as Marcus Aurelius (P17[1], P19[6]). "One must always offend those over whom he becomes a new prince" (P3[1]). But Machiavelli condemns the unchecked brutality of a Severus. "He should take from Severus those parts which are necessary to found his state and from Marcus those which are fitting and glorious to conserve a state that is already established and firm" (P19[4]). Evil means are to be used only when truly necessary, not when merely convenient, let alone arbitrarily, out of whim or habit, or for pleasure.

Consequentialism

Moral theorists typically distinguish between deontological theories, which rest on fixed, objective standards of right (e.g. Kant's categorical imperative), and consequentialist theories (e.g. utilitarianism), which consider the right course of action that which produces the greatest good.[11] For deontologists, moral actions are undertaken out of duty, for moral ends, using (not im)moral means. Consequentialist arguments, which focus on results rather than means and intentions, are by this definition not moral arguments. They do, however, judge individual interests and desires by a higher standard. Such appeals to considerations above the interests of the actor link deontologists and consequentialists – including Machiavelli.

Consider another "machiavellian" doctrine. "Those [cruelties] can be called well used (if it is permissible to speak well of evil) that are done at a stroke, out of the necessity to secure oneself, and then are not persisted in but are turned to as much utility for the subjects as one can" (P8[4]). Note once more that Machiavelli accepts, even implicitly endorses, the conventional conception of evil. He (parenthetically) draws our attention to the problematic nature of even necessary uses of evil means. And the requirement of maximizing the benefits to the people introduces a clear ethical dimension into what Sheldon Wolin calls Machiavelli's "economy of violence" (1960: ch. 7).

---

[11] For useful discussions of this contrast, with applications to international relations, see Nardin and Mapel (1992: chs. 7, 8, and 14).

"Prudence consists in knowing how to recognize the qualities of inconveniences, and in picking the less bad as good" (P21[6]; compare DI.6[6]). Because "one always finds that, bound up with what is good, there is some evil" (DIII.37[1]), one should emulate the Romans, who "always took the lesser evil to be the better alternative" (DI.38[2]). Consequences, measured in terms of good and evil, must be the statesman's focus.

We can distinguish three ideal types of consequentialism: egoist, cosmopolitan, and nationalist. For the egoist, consequences to others count only if they affect his or her interests or happiness. The cosmopolitan calculates the impact on all who may be affected. The relevant community of consequences is, in principle, the entire world. The nationalist considers consequences (only) for those in his or her polity or society.

Many passages in Machiavelli suggest egoistic consequentialism, the relevant egoist being the prince seeking to acquire or maintain power. "Government consists in nothing else but so controlling subjects that they shall neither be able to, nor have cause to, do you harm" (DII.23[2]; compare P17[5], P15[2]). I will argue, however, that Machiavelli's consequentialism, as suggested by the passage on cruelty well used, ultimately is nationalist, aimed at realizing the common good.

The common good

The history of imperial Rome, according to Machiavelli, reveals the coincidence of justice, the common good, and the interests of the prince.

When good princes were ruling . . . [one finds] a prince securely reigning among subjects no less secure, a world replete with peace and justice . . . its prince glorious and respected by all, the people fond of him and secure under his rule . . . [A]t the times of the other [evil] emperors . . . [one finds Rome] distraught with wars, torn by seditions, brutal alike in peace and in war, princes frequently killed by assassins, civil wars and foreign wars constantly occurring . . . countless atrocities perpetrated (DI.10[7–8]).

The defense of the good emperors "lay in their habits, the goodwill of the people, and the affection of the senate." But not even their armies could save the bad emperors "from the enemies they had made by their bad habits and their evil life" (DI.10[6]; compare DI.2[9], DIII.5[1]).

A prince may acquire a state through force, fraud, or fortune. To maintain it securely "it is necessary to have the people friendly" (P9[4]; compare P6[6], P19[2]). But this is relatively easy, for in contrast to the elite, who "desire to command and oppress," the people want only not to be oppressed (P9[1]; compare DI.4[5]). To maintain his state, a prince need only look after the interests of the people. "For when men are well governed, they do not go about looking for further liberty" (DIII.5[3]).

Thus Machiavelli excoriates fortresses because, beyond their military shortcomings, the seeming security they provide "give[s] you more courage in ill-treating your subjects" (DII.24[2]). The Sforzas, because of their fortress, "thought they were safe and could oppress their citizens and subjects." In fact, however, this lost them the people's support and made Milan easy prey for invaders (DII.24[4]). "The best fortress there is is not to be hated by the people" (P20[9]). Likewise, Machiavelli considers disarming the people, rather than securing their goodwill, a "malpractice" that will lead to "irremediable ruin" (DII.30[4]).

Deontological moralists may scorn all this as good done for the wrong reason, the public good reduced to an instrument for the prince's private interests. The "private" interests of such a prince, however, are not merely compatible with, but help to realize, the public good.[12] And not all of Machiavelli's arguments for justice are instrumental.

Good government

In discussing the Roman historian Polybius' cycle of regimes – the allegedly cyclical pattern of change from monarchy to tyranny to aristocracy to oligarchy to democracy to anarchy and then back to monarchy – Machiavelli distinguishes the good and bad forms of the rule of one, the few, and the many by their pursuit of public or private purposes (DI.2[7–8, 11–12]). Furthermore, he explicitly argues that governments that seek the public good are "good in themselves" (although in their pure forms short-lived) in contrast to the "inherent malignity" of those that pursue private, class interests (DI.2[4, 14]).

During the "happy days" of the Roman republic, "a citizen would by his triumph bring riches to Rome, yet himself remain a poor man" (DIII.25[4]). Pope Julius is praised because "he did everything for the increase of the Church and not of some private individual" (P11[3]). And Manlius Torquatus' severity was justified because it was "in the public interest, and was in no way affected by private ambition" (DIII.22[8]).

When Machiavelli traces the consequences by which "effectual truth" becomes known, "appearance" typically involves the immediate interests of the few, and "reality" involves the long-run good of the many. For example, Cesare Borgia's "cruel" repressions pacified and unified Romagna (P7[4], P17[1]). Florence's "merciful" refusal to suppress

---

[12] A "machiavellian" reading might even suggest that Machiavelli is trying to trick princes, notorious for the concern for their own interests and position, into acting for the common good.

factions in Pistoia, by contrast, ultimately destroyed Pistoia and intensified factional strife in Florence (P17[1], P20[4], DIII.27). A few should be allowed – if necessary, made – to suffer for the sake of the many.

"A prince, therefore, so as to keep his subjects united and faithful, should not care about the infamy of cruelty, because with very few examples he will be more merciful than those who for the sake of too much mercy allow disorders to continue" (P17[1]). Likewise, the seemingly liberal prince must take from the many to give to the few. The seemingly mean prince, however, by refusing to lavish benefits on a few, will not need "to burden the people extraordinarily" (P16[1]). *That* is true liberality.

For all his appreciation of the necessities of power and order, Machiavelli, like Thucydides, insists on the relevance, even centrality, of considerations of justice, decency, and the common good.

Honor, glory, and *virtù*

When the safety of one's country wholly depends on the decision to be taken, no attention should be paid either to justice or injustice, to kindness or cruelty, or to its being praiseworthy or ignominious. On the contrary, every other consideration being set aside, that alternative should be wholeheartedly adopted which will save the life and preserve the freedom of one's country (DIII.41[2]; compare DIII.47).

The references here to justice and kindness suggest the familiar realist sacrifice of conventional moral values and personal moral purity to the necessities of the national interest. Praise and ignominy, however, suggest a sacrifice of honor and reputation. For Machiavelli these too are important *ethical* concerns.

As we saw in chapter 2,[13] Machiavelli regularly refers to honor, shame, glory, infamy, or reputation in contexts where most twentieth-century writers would have discussed only safety, gain, or justice. To cite just one additional example, in counseling the destruction of rebel cities, Machiavelli, in language very peculiar to our ears, argues that "honor consists here in being able, and knowing how, to castigate" such offenses, and that failure to do so leads to one being "deemed either an ignoramus or a coward" (DII.23.[3]). In chapter 2 we examined the implications of the emphasis on glory for realist accounts of individual interest and state motives. Here we will consider the ethical dimensions of the pursuit of glory.

---

[13] See pp. 66, 69.

Heroic virtù *and Christian virtue*

Honor and glory are for Machiavelli closely tied to *virtù,* "virtue." The Latin *virtus,* from which the Tuscan/Italian term is derived, has its root in *vir,* man. *Virtù* refers to those things especially characteristic of man, the qualities that make us human. To oversimplify, Machiavelli uses *virtù* to refer both to "Christian" moral virtues, the conventional universalistic values embodied in the Golden Rule, and to a set of more particularistic "classical" virtues centered on honor. Together they comprise Machiavelli's account of the most noble and distinctive human excellences, achievements, and aspirations.[14]

In the "Christian" sense of the term, "one cannot call it virtue to kill one's citizens, betray one's friends, to be without faith, without mercy, without religion" (P8[2]). But such actions may indeed evidence "classical" *virtù.* For example, Hannibal was able to control an extremely diverse army fighting far from home because "his inhuman cruelty . . . always made him venerable and terrible in the sight of his soldiers; and without it, his other virtues would not have sufficed to bring about this effect" (P17[5]; compare DIII.21). Severus, "a wicked man" (DI.10[6]) who was "very cruel and very rapacious[,] . . . [had] so much virtue that . . . although the people were overburdened by him, he was always able to rule prosperously" (P19[8]).

Part of the *virtù* of Hannibal and Severus lies in their great skill or ability. Although rare in contemporary English usage (except in the term virtuoso, taken from the Italian), the *Oxford English Dictionary* defines it as "superiority or excellence; unusual ability, merit, or distinction." Machiavelli often uses *virtù* in this sense. For example, Agathocles accompanied his base life of crime with "such virtue of spirit and body" that he became king of Syracuse and held power despite great adversity (P8[2]; compare (DIII.6[17]). To translate *virtù* in such passages, however, as "skill" or "ability"[15] obscures the ethical overtones of Machiavelli's language. *Virtù* refers only to those abilities that command praise and deserve emulation.

The *virtù* of Hannibal, Severus, and Agathocles also involves virility, strength, and valor. This sense too is currently uncommon yet well

---

[14] On the concept of *virtù,* see Price (1973), Wood (1967), Mansfield (1996: ch. 1), and Plamenatz (1972).

[15] See, for example, Machiavelli (1988a: 31, 103–104; 1965: 36; 1908: 67). One of the great attractions of the Mansfield translation (Machiavelli 1985), which I use here, is his consistent rendering of *virtù* as "virtue." This reflects Mansfield's broader effort to capture Machiavelli's actual usage, rather than a translator's view of the closest contemporary analog, how we might put a similar idea today, or "what he must have meant" (rather than what he actually said).

established in English: "physical strength, force, or energy;" "the possession or display of manly qualities; manly excellence, manliness, valour."[16] Part of Romulus' virtue, according to Machiavelli, was that he was "a fierce and warlike king" (DI.19[1]). The biblical David showed his virtue in battle with his neighbors (DI.19[2]). And Machiavelli criticizes Christianity because, by refusing to interpret religion "in terms of *virtù*," it has "made the world weak" (DII.2[7]).

> The old religion did not beatify men unless they were replete with worldly glory ... Our religion ... has assigned as man's highest good humility, abnegation, and contempt for mundane things ... And if our religion demands that in you there be strength, what it asks for is strength to suffer rather than strength to do bold things (DII.2[6]).

Agathocles, crime, and tyranny

Although strongly associated with political (and military) success – "the virtue of the builder is discernible in the fortune of what was built" (DI.1[6]) – Machiavelli places clear ethical qualifications on equating virtue and success. Consider his evaluation of Agathocles, one of the most successful ancient tyrants prior to Julius Caesar.

> Whoever might consider the actions and virtue of this man will see nothing or little that can be attributed to fortune . . . [I]f one considers the virtue of Agathocles in entering into and escaping from dangers, and the greatness of his spirit in enduring and overcoming adversities, one does not see why he has to be judged inferior to any most excellent captain. Nonetheless, his savage cruelty and inhumanity, together with his infinite crimes, do not allow him to be celebrated among the most excellent men (P8[2]).[17]

Agathocles, Machiavelli argues, was able "to acquire empire, but not glory" (P8[2]; compare DIII.40[1]). Such an observation, were it even to occur to a twentieth-century commentator, would carry little force. For Machiavelli, it is a powerful condemnation.

Agathocles is Machiavelli's sole explicit example of cruelty well used. His success thus must have benefited his people,[18] which therefore will have provided him "some remedy . . . with God and with men" (P8[6]). Nonetheless, Machiavelli goes out of his way to discredit Agathocles. "One cannot attribute to fortune or to virtue what he achieved without

---

[16] Thus *virtù* is often translated as "courage," "strength," or "vigor," again missing the ethical dimension of Machiavelli's usage. See, for example, Machiavelli (1965: 35), Machiavelli (1954: 72), Machiavelli (1950: 31), Machiavelli (1908: 69).

[17] On what does, in Machiavelli's view, make a man most excellent, see Macfarland (1999) (although I should note that I reject many of Macfarland's particular interpretations).

[18] See the passage from P8[4] quoted on p. 171.

either" (P8[2]). Agathocles had so much strength, skill, and success that his power could not plausibly be attributed to fortune. But his "infinite crimes" so exceeded even the most minimal standards of human decency that he cannot be considered among the most excellent men.

Unlike Romulus (who rose to power through fratricide and regicide), Agathocles "always kept to a life of crime" (P8[2]), even after consolidating his power. He took only from Severus' cruelty and cleverness, not at all from Marcus' humanity and philosophical wisdom. He thus exceeded the bounds of necessity, further undermining his otherwise great virtue. In sharp contrast to Romulus, who "deserves to be excused" because he acted "for the common good and not to satisfy his personal ambition" (DI.9[4]), Agathocles had no broader public purpose.

Machiavelli's discomfort with figures such as Agathocles results in a rupture in the very structure of *The Prince*. He begins by arguing that new principalities are acquired "either by fortune or by virtue" (P1). Agathocles, however, is discussed in a chapter on principalities obtained through crimes. And although Machiavelli classifies all states as republics or principalities (P1, DI.2[1]), in the *Discourses* he explicitly distinguishes tyrannies from both (DI.10, DI.25[5]).

Tyranny, Machiavelli argues, usually brings destruction and decline. But even "should fate decree the rise of an efficient tyrant, so energetic and so proficient in warfare that he enlarges his dominions, no advantage will accrue to the commonwealth, but only to himself" (DIII.2[3]). Agathocles seems to present such a case. Tyranny precludes adopting policies, laws, and institutions that build lasting strength in a city or foster civic virtue in its people. "He alone profits by his acquisitions, not his country" (DIII.2[3]).

Justice, *virtù* (in both senses), power, and the public good thus prove to be complexly but centrally related. Machiavelli simply does not prefer or recommend an amoral politics of power and interest.

Arete, honor, and glory

Virtù encompasses what to a twentieth-century reader appear to be two distinct ethical complexes. The parallel term in Thucydides, *arete* ("virtue"), is much more univocal, corresponding primarily with what I have called the classical sense of virtue, emphasizing its origins. This conception of virtue can be more descriptively labeled the ethics of honor and glory;[19] or, to pinpoint its origins more precisely, the heroic ethic that

---

[19] Strictly speaking, honor and glory are different concepts. In particular, most honorable behavior is not glorious; quite the contrary, it is a matter of everyday conformance to

received its classic formulation in Homer. The universalistic ethic of reciprocity, which in discussing Machiavelli I called "Christian" virtue, is in Thucydides' work associated instead with the language of *dike* and *epieikeia*, justice, fairness, and equity.[20]

The heroic ethic of glory

One who successfully demonstrates *arete* is worthy of, even entitled to, honor (*time*), praise (*epainos*), and reputation (*doxa*). Failure to live up to the demands of *arete* brings shame (*aischron*), a reduction in socially perceived worth. And honor, glory, and shame, as we saw in chapter 2, are in Thucydides' world considerations of the greatest possible weight.[21] To add just one more example, once the Syracusans and their allies have assured their safety, they focus not on material gain but on glory (VII.56.2–3, 59.2, 86.2–3).

As we saw in chapter 2, honor and glory are competitive, a matter of distinction, of excelling, demonstrating superiority. They are gained or lost through a largely zero-sum struggle. Great events thus are specially valued for the quantities of glory they make available. "Out of the greatest dangers communities and individuals acquire the greatest glory [*time*, honor]" (I.144.3). Thus, as we saw above, Thucydides claims that the destruction of the Athenian force on Sicily was "the greatest Hellenic achievement of any in this war, or, in my opinion, in Hellenic history; it was at once most glorious to the victors, and most calamitous to the conquered" (VII.87.5). Metaphors of height and of weight must be combined to capture the full sense of excellence and distinction in this heroic ethic.

Honor is central to the moral inversions at Corcyra, where, as we saw in chapter 2, the victorious democrats devoted themselves to "butchering those of their fellow-citizens whom they regarded as their enemies" (III.81.4) and even words changed their meanings (III.82.4). Although the actions of the revolutionaries certainly were unjust, Thucydides focuses instead on the heroic virtues of courage, loyalty, manliness, and the ties of blood, along with their corresponding vices (III.82.4–7). *Stasis*,

---

footnote 19 (*cont.*)
  social norms. And in principle at least, glory may sometimes be obtained through dishonorable means. Here I will restrict discussion to the domain of overlap between honor and glory, which is the focal point of the ethical system in question here. Although there may be subtle differences even here – for example, we are more likely to praise the glorious but to respect the honorable – for our purposes such differences can be set aside.

[20] See pp. 167–169.

[21] Adkins (1972) extensively explicates this system of values and traces it through the course of ancient Greek political thought.

he argues, brings out every form of *kakotropia* (depravity, iniquity) (III.83.1); that is, it reduces all men to the habits of the *kakos*, the mean, low, base (in contrast to the *arete* of the *agathos*, the good or well-born). And he closes by lamenting the prevalence of *phauloteroi*, base characters of mean intellect and no distinction (III.83.3). Although the revolutionaries were guilty of great injustices, Thucydides judges them according to the standards of *arete* and honor.

The previously quoted passage from the conclusion of Pericles' final speech also needs to be considered again here.

Realize that Athens has a mighty name among all mankind because she has never yielded to misfortunes, but more freely than any other city has lavished lives and labors upon war, and that she possesses today a power which is the greatest that ever existed down to our time. The memory of this greatness . . . will be left to posterity forever, how that we of all Hellenes held sway over the greatest number of Hellenes, in the greatest wars held out against our foes whether united or single, and inhabited a city that was the richest in all things and the greatest . . . To be hated and obnoxious for the moment has always been the lot of those who have aspired to rule over others; but he who, aiming at the highest ends, accepts the odium, is well advised. For hatred does not last long, but the splendor of the moment and the after-glory are left in everlasting remembrance (II.64.3–5 [Smith]).

For a late twentieth-century reader, such glory and remembrance have little or no ethical content. Quite the contrary, the reliance on empire and war would render these achievements morally defective for most readers today. But for Thucydides, war and empire are paths to "the highest ends," concrete expressions of the *arete*, virtue, and merit of the Athenians. However foreign the ethic may appear to us, these are ethical appeals that rest on widely and highly valued public standards of individual and social excellence.

Honor and shame in the Melian Dialogue

When we look carefully, we even find honor and shame at least as prominent as justice in the Melian Dialogue. The Melians contend that not to resist servitude would be *kakos* and *deilos*, ignoble, shameful, contemptible, cowardly (V.100). And although the Athenians call shame merely a fine-sounding phrase (V.111.3), they do not dismiss it out of hand, as they did the earlier Melian appeal to justice (V.89). Even these cynically realistic men of the world preface their concluding appeal to interest (V.111.5) with an argument that to yield to overwhelming power is not disgraceful (*aischron*), or at least it is less shameful than the alternative (V.111.3–4; compare V.101).

Honor, however, demands that one die fighting rather than submit. For example, Thucydides calls the surrender of the Spartans on Sphacteria the "greatest surprise" of the war (IV.40.1), because no one would have imagined that the Spartans, with their preeminent reputation for *arete*, would have surrendered. The Athenians forcefully and effectively lay out the Melian interest in capitulation. The Melians, however, are willing to die rather than live with the shame of submission.

This shame is simply the other side of the honor of leadership and the glory of empire. The empire (although not the excesses of Athenian behavior at Melos) embodies the highest values of the heroic ethic. But so does Melos' resistance. The conflict is one in which "the stakes played for are the highest, freedom or empire" (III.45.6). For both sides, these stakes are a matter of honor as well as interest.

The Melians begin with an appeal to justice. They understand their interest and come to grips with their fear. But in the end, the Melians die for honor.

Realpolitik and the fall of Athens

Beyond renouncing the realism of the Melian Dialogue, Thucydides presents it as a central cause of Athens' demise. Thucydides argues that Pericles, through a combination of rank, ability, and judgment (*gnome*), together with great personal integrity and patriotism (II.60.5, 65.8), raised Athenian greatness to its zenith (II.65.5) and brought Athens into the war with a defensive strategy that would have assured success (II.65.7, 10–13). After his death, however, the Athenians pursued a strategy that "was the very contrary" (II.65.7; compare II.65.10–11). Although Pericles was hardly an idealist, Athens' decline and defeat rested largely on the growing "realism" of its post-Periclean leaders and policies.

Cleon, passion, and prudence

Recall the Mytilenian debate, just two years after Pericles' death, when Cleon, "the most violent man at Athens" (III.36.6), proposes killing all the Mytilenians. Pericles had struggled against the passions of the Athenians (e.g. I.140.1, II.22.1, 59.3, 60.1–2, 64.1, 65.9). Cleon, however, gives in to them. He begins by criticizing deliberation because it blunts one's anger (*orge*, passion) (III.38.1) and concludes by calling on the Athenians to remember "how you felt when they made you suffer, and how you would have given anything to crush them" (III.40.7 [Smith]).

This is admittedly the antithesis of the rational calculation advocated by realists such as Morgenthau and Waltz. But passion was essential to the initial Melos-like decision to destroy all the Mytilenians. And the desire for vengeance, or any other emotional satisfaction, is no less an "interest" than the material interests to which realists appeal. In fact, desire would seem to be the root of all interest. The Mytilenian debate thus gives us an insight into the passionate roots and end of a politics of naked interest.

We move one step further down that path when, following the stunning Athenian victory at Pylos, the Spartans propose peace (IV.2–20). The Athenians, however, "grasped at something further. Foremost to encourage them in this policy was Cleon" (IV.21.2–3). In Cleon we see the combination of savagery, grasping desire, and personal self-interest that lead to Melos. Athens has won: its empire is intact and the Spartans are too discouraged to continue fighting. But the unchecked "realistic" pursuit of power and gain – "at a maximum, [states] drive for universal domination" (Waltz 1979: 118) – causes Cleon and the Athenians to lose all.

To renounce ethical restraint in foreign affairs, whatever the intention, is to give free rein to passion. Without ethical restraints, the pursuit of interest is not clarified and purified, as realists would have it, but degenerates into an uncontrollable grasping desire that in the end destroys even the desirer. It is unrealistic, in the ordinary sense of that term, to expect rational long-term self-interest to control desire.

It is certainly utopian to expect any great number of people to have the wit to perceive or the will to follow the dictates of enlightened self-interest on the basis of sheer reason alone. Rational self-interest divorced from ideal principles is as weak and erratic a guide for foreign policy as idealism undisciplined by reason (Osgood 1953: 446).

"Prudent self-interest," as no less a realist than Niebuhr argues, is "almost as rare as unselfishness" (1932: 45). As Diodotus, Cleon's opponent in the Mytilenian debate, puts it, hope, desire, and fortune "urge men on . . . to take risks even when their resources are inadequate" (III.45.6).

Nicias, Alcibiades, reason, and restraint

There is a cool and seemingly powerful realist logic to the Athenian arguments at Melos. But if we look beyond the narrow confines to which that logic artificially restricts our attention, we find a city that has become deranged. Melos was neutral, not a rebel member of the empire (as Mytilene had been). The Melians posed no threat to Athens. In fact, the proceeds of the conquest probably did not even pay for the direct costs of the siege. Nonetheless, the Athenians treat the Melians barbarously for refusing to bow to their desires. And immediately after the destruction of

Melos, Thucydides recounts the fatal Athenian decision to attack the wealthy and powerful Sicilian city of Syracuse.[22]

Nicias warns the Athenians that their recent good fortune has made them unreasonably contemptuous of the still considerable power of Sparta (VI.11.5–7). He cautions them to resist their "morbid craving [*duseros*] for what is out of reach" (VI.13.1). But once more they grasp for something further, playing out the logic of the attack on Melos in pursuit of a much greater prize – at a much greater risk. As Cornford puts it, "Athens, tempted by Fortune, deluded by Hope, and blinded by covetous Insolence" (1965 [1907]: 201) sets out on a wildly overambitious campaign that ultimately proves its downfall.

This darker side of the Athenian character had challenged even Pericles (II.59–65). Now it dominates completely. Although partly the result of the pressures of war, the Athenians have acquired not new passions but rather the habit of acting out of passion and desire. This deadly habit can be attributed largely to their leaders, who embody a perverse "realistic" combination of expansive greed and narrow self-interest.

Thucydides claims that the most important Athenian error in the Sicilian campaign was removing Alcibiades from command, because of the fears, anger, and envy of the people, and the factional plotting of lesser leaders (II.65.11, VI.15.3, 27–29, 53, 60–61). But Alcibiades too was acting out of personal rather than public interests, advocating war to win personal honor and to acquire booty to support his extravagant style of living (VI.12.2, 15.2).

When indicted on trumped-up charges (VI.29.3), Alcibiades flees to Sparta (VI. 53, 61, 74.1, 88), where he offers a stunning defense against the charge that he is a dishonorable traitor.

I hope that none of you will think any worse of me if after having hitherto passed as a lover of my country I now actively join its worst enemies in attacking it . . . love of country is what I do not feel when I am wronged, but what I felt when secure in my rights as a citizen (VI.92.2–4).[23]

This reduction of patriotism to an instrument in the pursuit of personal gain (compare VI.16.1–5) simply extends the logic laid out by the Athenian envoys at Melos into domestic politics – with similar consequences.

Immediately before Alcibiades' speech at Sparta, Euphemus, the Athenian envoy to Camarina, argues that "for tyrants and imperial cities nothing is unreasonable if expedient, no one a kinsman unless sure; but

---

[22] On the Sicilian expedition, see Avery (1973), Lateiner (1985), and Green (1970).

[23] Pusey (1940) provides a good discussion of Alcibiades' argument. On Alcibiades more generally, see Ellis (1989), Forde (1989), Cawkwell (1997: ch. 5), and Bloedow (1973).

friendship or enmity is everywhere an affair of time and circumstance" (VI.85.1; compare V.105.3). Words thus change their meaning in Athens as well[24] – and here too as a result of faction, which Thucydides argues was first introduced into Athens during preparations for the Sicilian expedition (II.65.11). This is crucial because even after the defeat at Syracuse, Athens succumbs only when torn apart by factional strife (II.65.12).

Athens finally falls only after the "realistic" pursuit of naked interest removes all restraint from domestic politics, in much the same way, and with the same deadly results, as it had earlier in foreign policy. In fact, the decline of domestic politics comes about in part through the corrosive effects of immorality in foreign policy. Passions first unleashed in imperial politics become ever more difficult to control at home. The lack of justice, morality, and political restraint abroad gradually destroy judgment, restraint, and moderation at home.

A democracy, as Cleon argues, is incapable of empire (III.37.1) – or at least the kind of empire he advocates.[25] But the problem is not the inconstancy of democratic decision making that Cleon laments. Democracy rests on a formal political equality among citizens, who are otherwise very unequal, and on respect for civil laws and justice.[26] Neither can survive a foreign policy that knows no law (other than power) and no limits (other than desire). Evil – especially the self-conscious, shameless evil of the Melian Dialogue – cannot be walled off in foreign policy. And once domestic politics in Athens resembles Corcyra more than the Funeral Oration, everything else is lost.

The empire had always contained an element of tyranny (I.124.3, II.63.2). Now, however, there is nothing else. In past ages, "wherever there were tyrants, their habit of providing simply for themselves, of looking solely to their personal comfort and family aggrandizement . . .

---

[24] A. E. Raubitschek notes that although Euphemus uses the same words as the Athenian envoys at the congress at Lacedaemon in justifying the empire – *eikotos* (reasonable) and *axioi* (worthy) – they have a completely different sense in the two cases. In fact, he reads the initial Athenian speech as "a true picture of Periclean Athens before the condition of war demoralized men, people, and policies," "an authentic statement of the glory of the Athenian Empire in the days of Pericles" (1973: 36, 46, 48).

[25] On the relation between democracy and empire, see Raaflaub (1994), who approaches the question historically and cites most of the relevant scholarly literature.

[26] A. W. Gomme suggests another way of looking at this tension. "One thing that is fascinating about the Athenians is their complete awareness of the weakness of their democracy . . . But they would not give it up, or reform it out of all recognition in the interests of efficiency . . . The Athenians deliberately risked security for the sake of their freedom and variety of life and thought which they prized so highly" (1962: 192–193). To the extent that this is true, Athens provides a striking example of the priority of internal "second image" concerns over Waltz' structural "third image" imperatives.

prevented anything great proceeding from them" (I.17).[27] Athens too, once it has truly become a tyrant city, no longer achieves anything of value. In fact, it loses not only its empire, but its freedom.[28]

Like the tyrant of Plato's *Republic* (573c–589e), the Athenians become slaves to their passions. They effectively abdicate political responsibility to the worst elements in human nature. Politics is thus reduced to a device to realize desire. And fear, honor, and interest alike become corrupted.[29]

Fear – which at the time of the Persian invasion produced clear thought and a common purpose – becomes wild desperation, leading to confusion and disunity. Athenian politics swings violently from radical democracy, to oligarchy, and then back to democracy. Honor disappears in all but name, as the Athenians admit at Melos (V.105.3). And where Pericles appealed to an enlightened, even noble, conception of interest, the self-interest of Alcibiades' generation is mean and ultimately self-destructive. Interest alone destroys even itself.

That none of this was intended is an irony worthy of Thucydides, for realism is in many ways a theory driven by the desire to avoid the unintended consequences of idealist moralism. Thucydides certainly does caution against moralism. But a much more prominent theme in the *History* is the pathological unintended consequences of radical realism.

Without ethical restraints, the strong not only do what they can but attempt what they cannot. Beyond the external problem of restraining others' pursuit of their interests at the cost of one's own, states face the internal problem of restraining their own interests and the means used in their pursuit. Realist amoralism is inadequate to this task of internal self-restraint.

The statesman, rather than abdicate to desire, must temper fear and interest with a sense of public purpose and a certain respect for justice and honor.[30] Thucydides advocates an expansive and moderate public conception of the national interest and stresses the need to exercise power within limits set by judgment, justice, honor, and an enlightened public

---

[27] Note the striking parallel with Machiavelli's account of tyranny (DIII.2[3]), quoted on p. 177.

[28] On Thucydides' treatment of tyranny – a charge against Athens first raised by the Corinthians at I.122.3 – see Connor (1977), Hunter (1973/74), Raaflaub (1979), and (Palmer 1982a). More broadly, see McGlew (1993).

[29] Compare Cogan (1981a: 139–163) who sees a progressive degeneration from Pericles' limited objectives, through an ideological phase (marked by the progression from Mytilene, to Plataea, to *stasis* in Corcyra), and finally, by the time of Euphemus' speech, a hyperactive, almost hysterical, grasping cruelty.

[30] Immerwahr goes so far as to suggest that there is an inescapable tragic ambiguity rooted in the Athenian love of power (1973: 28–31).

notion of interest.[31] Thucydides' *History* certainly illustrates the difficulties of this style of statesmanship. But to abandon these moderating tasks and all concern for *arete* and justice is to court the infamy of Melos, and the disaster that followed.

Realist amoralism?

On closer examination – especially with this reading of Thucydides in mind – the views of many twentieth-century realists on morality in foreign policy also prove far more complex than standard programmatic statements would suggest.

Realist concern for morality

Niebuhr, for example, argues that "the moral cynicism and defeatism which easily result from a clear-eyed view of the realities of international politics are even more harmful" than the "too simple idealism" of "pure moralists" (1944: 126; compare 1932: 233; 1934: 123). He sees a perennial tension between the children of darkness, "moral cynics, who know no law beyond their will and interest" and who are "wise though evil," and the children of light, "who believe that self-interest should be brought under the discipline of a higher law" and who are "virtuous" but "usually foolish" (1944: 14–15). Nonetheless, Niebuhr's work seeks to reconcile these perspectives, and produce a politics that includes elements of both wisdom and virtue.

This involves much more than just using the "values of justice, fairness, and tolerance . . . instrumentally as moral justification for the power quest" (Spykman 1942: 18). It goes well beyond Henry Kissinger's backhanded praise for the historical role of American values in US foreign policy because they "contributed to our unity, gave focus to our priorities, and sustained our confidence in ourselves," or his defense of an ongoing commitment to these values because otherwise "this nation . . . will lose its bearings in the world" and its interest will be thereby harmed (1977: 200, 204). Moral values, for Niebuhr as for Thucydides, are not mere luxuries that "must be discarded the moment their application brings weakness" (Spykman 1942: 18).

---

[31] "Pericles' imperialism . . . did not originate in lust for power, but derived from a deep love for Athens, and was subordinated to higher ideas in which power politics were to be merged into one with cultural superiority and brilliance. However idealised Thucydides' picture of Pericles and Periclean democracy may be, there was a fundamental difference between his policy . . . and that of his successors. Under Pericles' leadership Athenian *polypragmosyne* [incessant activity] was turned into the useful and inspiring activity of a people politically and spiritually alive" (Ehrenberg 1947: 48).

Georg Schwarzenberger likewise argues that "a presentation of the motivations of power politics in terms of self-interest, suspicion, fear and lust for power would be open to justified criticism if the necessary qualifications of this analysis were not made with equal emphasis" (1951: 158). And he admits that although relatively rare "within international society there is scope for action based on motives such as justice and respect for law" (1951: 158).

John Herz insists that his theory is "not meant as a defense of, or resignation to, the extremism of political realism often met in practice." "In international relations the mitigation, channeling, balancing, or control of power has prevailed perhaps more often than the inevitability of power politics would lead one to believe" (1976: 11, 97). In fact, Herz, who coined the term "security dilemma," advocates "'realist liberalism' – an attempt, while starting from the recognition of the 'realist' facts (security dilemma, etc.), to ameliorate and mitigate its consequences" (1976: 11). Realist is the adjective, not the noun.

E. H. Carr, the most important figure in postwar British realism, argues that "we cannot ultimately find a resting place in pure realism." "Political action must be based on a co-ordination of morality and power." "Sound political thought and sound political life will be found only where both [reality and utopia, power and morality] have their place" (1946: 10). Thus in the last chapter of *The Twenty Years' Crisis* Carr reminds us that "it is an unreal kind of realism which ignores the element of morality in any world order" (1946: 235).

Ethics versus the autonomy of politics

Even Morgenthau notes "the curious dialectic of ethics and politics, which prevents the latter, in spite of itself, from escaping the former's judgment and normative direction" (1946: 177). In clear contradiction to his arguments for the autonomy of politics, he claims that "in order to be worthy of our lasting sympathy, a nation must pursue its interests for the sake of a transcendent purpose that gives meaning to the day-to-day operations of its foreign policy" (1960: 8). "Nations recognize a moral obligation to refrain from the infliction of death and suffering under certain conditions despite the possibility of justifying such conduct in the light of . . . the national interest" (Morgenthau 1948: 177). Morgenthau even claims, quite incredibly, that "I have always maintained that the actions of states are subject to universal moral principles" (1962a: 106). In fact, however, one of the central propositions of *Politics Among Nations* is that "universal moral principles cannot be applied to the actions of states" (1954: 9).

Something has gone profoundly wrong. Morgenthau correctly notes that "a man who was nothing but 'political man' would be a beast, for he would be completely lacking in moral restraints" (1954: 12). But his demand, just one page earlier, that the statesman "subordinate these other standards to the political one" (1954: 11) requires precisely such a beastly foreign policy. He argues that "when law and morality are judged as nothing, [a theory of international politics] must assign them to their rightful place" (1962a: 47). Unfortunately, that place, according to Morgenthau, is entirely outside of politics: "no moral argument can be presented against a foreign policy which is based upon considerations of the national interest" (1952b: 6). "By making power its central concept, a theory of politics does not presume that none but power relations control action" (1962a: 47). But to insist that statesmen act solely on the basis of "interest defined in terms of power" (1954: 5) is to require that they act as if power does control political action.

Once more, a large part of the problem arises from inflating valuable cautions, in this case against the dangers of moralism, into law-like counsels that prematurely narrow the range of political choice. For all their appreciation of the force of realist arguments, Thucydides and Machiavelli, along with Carr, Niebuhr, and Herz, suggest an approach to international politics that is much more "realistic," in the ordinary sense of that term, because it refuses to be confined to the narrow and ultimately inhuman realm defined by so-called realist laws.

States *choose* whether or not to pursue moral goals or respect ethical constraints. Such choices are constrained by the prevalence of self-interested behavior, the absence of international government, and a considerable array of competing objectives. But to deny the reality and importance of moral choice is to impoverish both our understanding and the practice of international relations.

Thucydides and Machiavelli (and Carr and Herz) treat the evil in human nature, the dangers of anarchic international relations, and the necessities of power and interest as problems and a challenge. They insist on the importance of struggling against the tendency towards power politics, even if that struggle can never fully succeed. Power politics perhaps cannot be eliminated. Some of its most destructive consequences, however, can, and must, be mitigated.

Morgenthau, by contrast, takes evil, anarchy, and power politics as facts of nature, and the final theoretical word. "Morgenthau the theorist took his stand, basically, on the demonic side of the social drama and left it to others . . . to side overtly with the angels" (Liska 1977: 105). This abdication of moral choice and responsibility, however, is not merely unnecessary but dangerous, both to morality and to the national interest.

Morgenthau's problem arises from treating realism as a general theory of international politics that seeks "eternal truths of foreign policy" (1952b: 3), "the eternal laws by which man moves in the social world. There are, aside from the laws of mathematics, no other eternal laws besides these" (1946: 220). *None* of the insights of realism, however, even remotely resembles eternal laws.

More generally as well, the principal failings of realism arise from a tendency to overestimate the character and significance of its undoubtedly important insights, to confuse valuable cautions and dangerous tendencies with prescriptive laws of international politics. In fact, I want to suggest that Carr is very close to the mark in viewing realism as a fundamentally negative orientation that must be kept in dialectical tension with utopianism to produce an adequate international theory.

Discussion questions

- Are moral norms qualitatively different from other sorts of norms? What does your answer imply about the nature of the problem of morality in foreign policy? Is it simply a subset of the broader issue of the role of norms?

- What is gained and what is lost by seeing (international) politics as autonomous? Why do many realists see international, but not national, politics as autonomous? What is present or absent in international relations that makes the difference? Do you think that the differences are sufficient to justify this realist understanding?

- *Why* do realists think that morality should be subordinated to the national interest in international relations? The text suggests that there are several different "realist" answers. How (if at all) are these varying grounds of realist amoralism related to one another?

- Realists may exaggerate, but is there not a real difference between the national interest and the human interest? And is there not an important sense in which we do (rightly) expect the statesman to pursue the national interest and the moralist to speak for the human interest? Does this not suggest the need for at least a certain degree of autonomy for (international) politics?

- Again, realists may often exaggerate, but is not necessity typically a more powerful force in international than national politics? Are there not in fact more options in most national political systems than in the international system?

- Is it fair to suggest, as Donnelly does, that the standard realist attack on morality in foreign policy simply gives in to the difficulties of acting morally rather than resisting? There are also great problems in acting morally in personal relations and in local and national politics. Why should we struggle harder on behalf of morality at these levels than in international relations? Or, to put the question in a slightly different form, is there really as much space for resistance against unpleasant "realist" tendencies (in international relations) as Donnelly suggests?

- Suppose we were to agree that the "standard" realist argument seriously exaggerates an important insight. How would we then understand the nature of the realist contribution? How might we better go about keeping that insight central without being carried away by it?

- In the case of morality and foreign policy, are we seeing once again the common realist problem of over-generalizing? Have realists (once more) taken *a* law-like regularity and confused it with *the* laws of international politics?

- Let us grant for the sake of argument that Thucydides implicitly recognizes minimum moral standards of international behavior. Is it really so clear that he goes beyond the very minimal requirement of avoiding savage butchery of one's enemies? Can we not see his view as fundamentally realist, with only relatively modest hedges that require not so much morality as simply the avoidance of barbarism?

- Grant for the sake of argument that *stasis* (revolutionary violence) in Corcyra simply applies realist amoralism to national politics. How might we keep it from infiltrating this domain, where everyone agrees it does not belong? If it is impossible, or even just very difficult, to keep international amoralism out of national politics, what does this imply about the unintended consequences of a realist foreign policy? Even more troubling, what happens if a realist foreign policy really is necessary *and* it cannot be kept from corrosively infiltrating national politics?

- Consider Machiavelli's advice to use evil means when necessary. How do we know when they are necessary, rather than merely convenient? And once we use them when necessary, how can we avoid the temptation to use them when they are not?

- What do you make of the argument that Machiavelli's concern for justice is more than instrumental? Has Donnelly gone too far in his reading (perhaps by reading too much Thucydides into Machiavelli)?

- Grant the argument in the text that Machiavelli is a nationalist consequentialist. Is that really a plausible ethical doctrine? If we allow this, are we not forced to call just about *any* doctrine that is not reducible to egoistic selfishness "ethical"?

- In discussing Machiavelli, Donnelly implies that intentions really do not matter, that those who avoid tyranny out of self-interest are no less entitled to praise than those who avoid it because it is bad. Do intentions really have so little ethical weight? Is there not some power to the deontological claim that why one does something is of moral significance? Does it make a difference to your answer whether we are talking about morality or about politics?

- In the text, not much is done with the distinction between ethics and morality. How might they be seen as much more different than Donnelly presents them? Think in particular about the idea of professional ethics. By pursuing such a distinction, can we reconstruct the realist argument (along *raison d'état* lines) as an argument that the professional ethics of the statesman regularly demands immorality in foreign policy?

- Donnelly treats *virtù* and *arete* as ethical values. Are they really of a character roughly comparable to justice and the "Christian" virtues? Might they be seen instead as something more like interests?

- How do you respond to the argument that the fall of Athens can be attributed in significant measure to its increasingly realist pursuit of a foreign policy of interest alone? Without ethical restraints, the strong not only do what they can but attempt what they cannot. Is this really the lesson of Thucydides?

- Is the link between passion and interest really as direct and unambiguous as is suggested in the text? What about reason and interest? On what grounds might reason select among interests? Are those grounds legitimately available to realists? Can realists (consistently) test interest by appeals to reason but not allow comparable appeals to morality?

- If many realists actually leave considerable space for the pursuit of morality in foreign policy, how did the common caricature emerge? Why does it persist?

- If many realists do leave considerable space for morality, should we simply eliminate amoralism from our list of characteristic realist doctrines? Is this not what contemporary structural realists have implicitly done?

- Once again it is suggested in the text that the root of the error of realists lies in exaggerating the substance of an important insight and then turning it into an alleged law of international politics. Does this argument seem right to you? Why or why not?

Suggestions for further reading

As I noted in the essay on chapter 1, two short pieces by George Kennan – "Morality and Foreign Policy" (1985/86) and "On American Principles" (1995) – provide excellent brief statements of a strong but sophisticated realist rejection of the pursuit of moral objectives in foreign policy in most circumstances. The most radical position, as we have noted several times, is that of Thucydides' Athenian envoys to Melos at the close of Book V of the *History*. If my argument is correct, though, such categorical rejections of morality in foreign policy simply cannot be sustained. Therefore, some suggestions on readings in the general area of ethics and international affairs are in order.

The essential starting point is Michael Walzer's *Just and Unjust Wars* (1977). Walzer begins with a powerful critique of realism, as expressed not only in the Melian Dialogue but also in General Sherman's notorious self-justificatory claim that "war is hell."[32] To the contrary, Walzer argues, war is an organized social practice, and thus subject to social, political, and moral evaluation. He then proceeds through a brilliant series of case studies of issues ranging from humanitarian intervention to nuclear deterrence that are as lively and accessible as they are carefully argued and thought-provoking. This is, in my view, not merely the best book on international ethics, but one of the best books in the entire field of international studies, written in the past quarter-century.

---

[32] This claim was made in the context of his barbaric destruction of a large swathe of the American South during the Civil War, with no concern for civilian casualties or rights.

Stanley Hoffmann's *Duties Beyond Borders: On the Limits and Possibilities of Ethical International Politics* (1981) is a classic statement by a leading international relations theorist from a perspective that is sympathetic to but ultimately rejects standard realist arguments. Beitz (1979) is an equally classic effort by a political theorist to address directly the possibility of ethical international relations. Its three parts criticize the Hobbesian vision of an international state of nature, address issues of state autonomy (sovereignty, intervention, and self-determination), and explore the possibilities for global distributive justice. Frances Harbour's *Thinking About International Ethics* (1999) provides a good introductory survey of the realist challenge and then offers eight case studies connected with US foreign policy. Mary Maxwell's *Morality Among Nations* (1990) is a quirky but often very interesting sociobiological cut at the issue.

There are a number of useful readers that address ethics and international affairs. One of the best, especially for those with a theoretical inclination, is Beitz *et al.* (1985). The essays, all drawn from *Philosophy and Public Affairs*, address the problem of moral skepticism in international relations, deterrence, the rules of war, the moral standing of the state, and international distributive justice. Joel Rosenthal, *Ethics and International Affairs: A Reader* (1995) provides a selection from the journal of the same name, an annual publication by the Carnegie Council on Ethics and International Affairs that is required reading for those interested in this emerging subfield of international studies.

Two recent collections from Britain are also worthy of note. *Human Rights in Global Politics* (Dunne and Wheeler 1999) offers a wide-ranging series of essays on this topic, which perhaps more than any other has pushed ethical concerns into the forefront of everyday foreign policy for a growing number of states over the past two decades. *Morality and International Relations: Concepts and Issues* (Wright 1996) covers a wide range of topics briefly yet thoughtfully.

Among the many other possible suggestions, I want to single out three. David Lumsdaine's *Moral Vision in International Politics* (1993) is particularly interesting for its empirical focus. Through a careful examination of post-World War II foreign aid policies and practices, he shows that state behavior in at least this one area of activity has indeed been significantly shaped – not entirely, but not trivially either – by genuine humanitarian concerns. Ken Booth's "Human Wrongs and International Relations" (1995) provides an eloquent, creative, and passionate argument for the importance of addressing human suffering as a central part of international studies. Smith (1992) provides a good survey of the resurgence of moral concerns in international studies.

What I have called the ethics of honor and glory is more typically discussed in terms of a distinction between guilt cultures (such as Christianity) and shame cultures (such as that of the Greeks). A good example of this distinction in the context of classical studies is Dodds (1951: ch. 2). From a broader anthropological perspective, see Peristiany (1966). Adkins (1972) provides a very accessible introduction to Greek moral and political values that comes largely out of such a perspective. Gagarin (1974), Havelock (1969), Creed (1973), Pearson (1957), and Dover (1974) provide relatively wide-ranging article-length examinations of justice and popular values in the ancient Greek world.

For broad considerations of Thucydides' treatment of moral values, Edmunds (1975) is particularly useful. See also Heath (1990), Hooker (1974), and Shorey (1893). Clifford Orwin's *The Humanity of Thucydides* (1994) is an excellent recent book-length study. Two articles by Stephen Forde (1992; 1995) compare Thucydides and Machiavelli, and challenge my reading of Machiavelli. Johnson (1993), Slomp (1990), and Schlatter (1945) provide useful comparisons of Thucydides and Hobbes.

Conclusion: The nature and contribution of realism

Realists such as E. H. Carr and John Herz – and, if my interpretation in the preceding chapter is correct, Thucydides and Machiavelli as well – see realism only as a starting point for or a single dimension of international theory. And they insist on keeping "realist" insights in dialectical tension with higher human aspirations and possibilities. As Carr puts it, "the impossibility of being a consistent and thorough-going realist is one of the most certain and most curious lessons of political science" (1946: 89). This brief Conclusion attempts to develop this reading of the nature and contribution of realism.

The negative, cautionary character of realism

The recurring patterns realists identify are not timeless laws of international relations. Realism identifies constraints, not unbreakable barriers. And other patterns and processes that are no less important to the study and practice of international relations are largely outside the scope of realism's comprehension. For example, granting Machiavelli's claim that men "will always give vent to the malignity that is in their minds when opportunity offers" (1970: Book I, ch. 3) no more suggests an amoral foreign policy than it implies that domestic law should treat the innocent and the guilty alike. As I have argued repeatedly, the need for caution must not be confused with the invariance or inevitability of that which demands caution.

Many postwar realists admit the reactive, negative character of their work. Georg Schwarzenberger, in the preface to the second edition of *Power Politics*, noted that in 1941 "it was necessary to be on guard against naive day-dreaming on international politics. Now it is imperative to be so against the other pernicious extreme: unrestrained cynicism" (1951: xv). Carr similarly noted that "*The Twenty Years' Crisis* was written with the deliberate aim of counteracting the glaring and dangerous defect of . . . the almost total neglect of the factor of power." Therefore, some passages "state their argument with a rather one-sided emphasis" (1946: vii, viii).

George Kennan, three decades after the initial publication of *American Foreign Policy*, admitted that "the problems of excessive legalism and moralism, as treated in the original lectures, are today, in large part, historical ones" (1984: vii). And the neorealist revival of the 1970s and 1980s was in significant part a reaction to approaches that stressed justice and change in international relations, such as dependency theory and the liberal internationalist emphasis on interdependence (Waltz 1970; 1979: chs. 2, 7).

Thus understood, realism's principal purpose is to warn against moralism, progressivism, and similar "optimistic" orientations. It emphasizes what is unlikely or difficult in international relations, rather than what is worth striving for. " 'Realism' denotes the disposition to take all factors in a social and political situation, which offer resistance to established norms, into account, particularly the factors of self-interest and power" (Niebuhr 1953: 119). It "depicts international affairs as a struggle for power among self-interested states and is generally pessimistic about the prospects for eliminating conflict and war" (Walt 1998: 31). This is an important part of international relations – but only one part.

This primarily negative and cautionary contribution of realism helps to explain its cyclical rise and fall. Realism may be "the necessary corrective to the exuberance of utopianism" (Carr 1946: 10). Once that correction has been made, though, its time as a fruitful dominant mode of thought has passed. In fact, postwar realism's very success in this negative, corrective task brought to the fore its shortcomings as a positive theory.

The laws of international politics to which some "realists" appealed in such a knowing way appeared on closer examination to rest on tautologies or shifting definitions of terms. The massive investigations of historical cases implied in their Delphic pronouncements about the experience of the past had not always, it seemed, actually been carried out . . . Indeed, not even the best of the "realist" writings could be said to have achieved a high standard of theoretical refinement: they were powerful polemical essays (Bull 1972: 39).[1]

A similar, though less severe, reaction against the thinness of structural realism's "indeterminate predictions" has characterized the 1990s.

Understood as an orientating set of insights – a philosophical orientation or research program[2] – realism is usually present in both academic and popular debates. Realism is a perennial tradition of argument – but only one such tradition – in international theory (compare Wight 1992: 1, 7, 15–24). Its prominence waxes and wanes in part as a result of changes in the broader social and political environment. Robert Rothstein's obser-

---

[1] Joel Rosenthal's *Righteous Realists* (1991) nicely captures this dimension of twentieth-century American realism.   [2] See pp. 75–77.

vation on the interwar marginalization of realism and its predominance during the Cold War has a more general application: "the different reactions which Realism engendered in the 1930s and 1940s are only partly, if at all, attributable to the superior insights of postwar Realists" (1972: 349; compare Ferguson and Mansbach 1988: 99).

The interaction of realist theories with their disciplinary and political contexts does not debunk realism and its insights – except in so far as it claims a timeless universal validity. It does, however, counsel care and even skepticism concerning realist law-like regularities. The substantial differences among, for example, Thucydides, Carr, Morgenthau, and Waltz suggest that the perennial truths some realists claim to offer are far more contextually specific than they would like to admit.

As is often the case, Morgenthau presents the most striking illustrations of the problem. Consider his fifth principle of political realism: "Political realism refuses to identify the moral aspirations of a particular nation with the moral laws that govern the universe" (1954: 10). Although Thucydides and Machiavelli probably would not have objected to such a claim, it never would have occurred to them as a fundamental principle. Like Morgenthau's first "fundamental rule" of diplomacy – "*Diplomacy must be divested of the crusading spirit*" (1948: 439) – it is a remarkably time-bound reaction against Wilsonian "idealism." These may have been valuable cautions for postwar American foreign policy. They certainly are not timeless political laws.

Realism is rooted in enduring insights into the constraints posed by human nature and international anarchy. Problems arise when they are allowed to squeeze out other no less important insights – which is especially likely when realism is treated as a general theory of international politics. Even among "realists" such as Thucydides, Machiavelli, Carr, and Herz we have seen the centrality of "non-realist" insights. Without that sense of balance – which is sorely lacking in leading figures such as Morgenthau, Waltz, and Mearsheimer – realism's insights are more likely to create than to solve theoretical and practical problems.

The realist research program

It would be unfair, however, to paint realism as a purely negative theory. Whatever the dangers of over-generalizing, the characteristic realist emphasis on egoism and anarchy does provide a promising basis for a research program that aims to develop partial, mid-level theories of international relations. Glenn Snyder's recent work on relationships, discussed in chapter 4, provides a good example of the kind of realist theory that I believe is worth pursuing. Snyder's work does not yield a general theory of international politics, or even a general realist theory of alliances. It does, however, provide considerable theoretical insight into the formation and management of alliances.

The task of theory thus understood is to specify clearly and precisely a particular theoretical logic, to elaborate in varying ways some of the potential consequences of the assumptions that make up the realist "hard core." It is an empirical question whether or not such logics have interesting applications to the world. But none can be expected to cover anything close to the entire field, or even a large subfield such as security relations.

This opens up considerable possibilities for constructive conversations, even collaborations, between realists and non-realists. Returning to the issue of international institutions, Randall Schweller and David Priess, rejecting Mearsheimer's blanket dismissal, have begun to develop realist theories of international institutions. Using the characteristic structural variable of polarity, they suggest that institutions in bipolar structures are likely to be informal and relatively closely tied to superpower interests, whereas in multipolar structures there is a tendency to greater formality and a special reliance on great-power support for the status quo (1997: 15–23). They also draw on the distinction between status quo and revisionist powers to further elaborate models of expected institutional dynamics.

These valuable insights are deeply rooted in the realist tradition. As such, they are perhaps less likely to be appreciated by those working within another tradition, such as liberal internationalism. But they are by no means an adequate general account of international institutions. Realist institutionalists have at least as much to learn from their liberal colleagues as vice versa.

This reading of realism suggests a pluralistic vision of the discipline of international studies. As I argued at the end of chapter 2, understanding realism as a philosophical orientation or research program requires us to abandon the gladiatorial vision of international relations theory. The issue is not whether realism (or liberal internationalism, or constructivism, or whatever) "is right" but when and where particular realist insights and theories can help us to understand and explain things that interest us.[3]

Realism understood as a research program is "a 'big tent,' with room for a number of different theories that make quite different predictions" (Elman 1996: 26). And international studies is an even bigger tent, with room for various other research programs as well. Different traditions or

---

[3] For a brief illustration of this point, in the case of competing interpretations of US–Latin American relations, see Hurrell (1996).

research programs do different things, rather than vie with one another to do the same thing.

Realism persists because it regularly offers insights into recurrent sources and patterns of conflict rooted in anarchy, competition, and diffidence. It tells us very little about cooperation, which many analysts find a no less important part of international relations. But this is not a failing – unless we happen to be interested in understanding cooperation. And even that failing is largely a function of our interests and purposes.

To offer a personal example, most of my own scholarly work has been in the field of international human rights. Realism here provides mostly negative insights into the difficulties of incorporating human rights concerns into foreign policy. It thus has not been of much help to me. Realists are entirely justified in saying that this is a function of my interests. But the usefulness of realism to them is just as much a matter of *their* interests, the parts of the world they have chosen to study. The usefulness of a particular theory or approach is largely a matter of what we choose to study or hope to find.

There is no objective standard of what is most important in the theory or practice of international relations. Let us grant that most international human rights initiatives fail to alter the behavior of their targets, for reasons that lie at the core of realist theories. That does not necessarily suggest that realism is a useful theory. For example, if we are interested in understanding when and how such initiatives succeed, realism is likely to be of little help.

We saw in chapter 2 that traditions and paradigms thrive when and because they tell us something important – but only some things – about our world. Realism, like other philosophies, traditions, or research programs, is an aid to understanding. It is a tool that works well for certain purposes, and not at all well for others. Our discipline clearly would be impoverished were it to be stripped of insights and understandings rooted in realism. But it is no less impoverished when realists assert, as many have in recent decades, an unjustified hegemony for their problems and visions.

The realist research program will continue to generate valuable theories. But the same is true of other research programs. The discipline needs non-realist theories no less than it needs realist ones. Rather than adversaries, let alone enemies, we need to see each other as concerned scholars with different interests, insights, and contributions.[4] Rather than *Theory*

---

[4] For a recent example of a realist expressing a similar understanding of the discipline, see Walt (1998).

of International Politics, we need *theories* of international politics, realist and non-realist alike, that together give us a chance to begin to come to terms with the multiple human purposes and complex practices and processes that make up world politics.

The influence of theoretical traditions

This book has treated "classic" realists, such as Thucydides, Machiavelli, and Hobbes, alongside and with the same respect as contemporary structuralists such as Waltz, Mearsheimer, and Snyder. Part of the reason for this is that Thucydides and Machiavelli, as we have seen in chapters 2 and 6, are at least as interesting and illuminating. But it also reflects my characterization of realism in chapter 1 as a tradition of analysis with a long and important history. I want to close with a few comments on this reading of the nature and character of realism.

Although twentieth-century realists do not rely on the authority of canonical texts, they typically do insist on their participation in a tradition.[5] Robert Gilpin, in an often cited essay, even speaks of "returning to the roots of the realist tradition" (1986: 308). The way these roots are conceived may influence the character of realist work.

A tradition helps to mold not only how we present what we see, but where we look, what we consider important, and in some cases what we see. Consider the careless claim by Art and Waltz (discussed in chapter 6)[6] that "states in anarchy cannot afford to be moral" (1983: 6). Such unreflective overstatements reveal deep tendencies of thought that can be shaped by how we read the great works in a tradition.

Traditions are transmitted by selective appropriation. Realists of every generation not only participate in an established tradition, but through their participation help to establish, retrospectively, the contours of that tradition. Thucydides, Machiavelli, Carr, Morgenthau, and Waltz are all exemplary realists. Yet, as we have seen, their differences are as striking as their similarities. And they lead us to think about and act in the world in different ways.

For example, Gilpin laments the fact that many people "abhor realism because it is believed to be an immoral doctrine at best and a license to kill, make war, and commit wanton acts of rapine at worst" (1986: 319). One important source of this belief is precisely the sort of reading of Thucydides and Machiavelli that I have tried to combat. If the Melian Dialogue is seen as a dangerous overstatement, rather than as the essence

---

[5] See, for example, Carr (1946: 63–67), Morgenthau (1954: 3–4), Waltz (1979: 117), and Gilpin (1986: 307).   [6] See pp. 162–163.

of realism, the character of at least some realist work may be altered. And realists and non-realists may interact differently.

One reason for such narrow and shallow understandings among contemporary students of international relations is the "exemplary" rather than "heuristic" use of the tradition,[7] by realists and non-realists alike. Students typically read carefully selected passages that demonstrate the realism of Thucydides or Machiavelli – when these texts are not simply ignored, or relegated to the trash heap euphemistically labeled "recommended readings." Studying excerpts with a predetermined contemporary relevance, however, reduces political theory to a source of illustration or confirmation, rather than a possible source of inspiration, insight, or discovery. A "great passages from great books" approach also keeps the reader from experiencing the distinctive character of their sustained theoretical reflection and confronting a different style of analysis. The result may even be serious distortion, as the case of Thucydides and the Melian Dialogue vividly illustrates.

We need a more open and inquisitive approach to classic texts. There is even the possibility of significant variation in *who* appropriates them. For example, my argument at the end of chapter 6 and the beginning of this Conclusion might be read as an effort to drive a wedge between heavily hedged "realists" such as Carr, Herz, and Thucydides and strong realists such as Morgenthau and Waltz. It might even be seen as an attempt to claim Thucydides back from the realists altogether. That such readings are no more contentious than those of the "mainstream" is illustrated by the fact that realist interpretations of Thucydides, although probably still predominant in international relations, are rare among contemporary classicists.

How we read realism may even have practical consequences. Kant, in *Perpetual Peace*, argues that realist amoralism does "not even deserve a hearing . . . since such a damaging theory may bring about the evil it prophesies" (Kant 1983: 133). This is very much in line with the reading of Thucydides at the end of chapter 6. To act as though there are no ethical restraints on the pursuit of interest may ultimately help bring into being such a beastly world.

In any case, how we understand realism – or any other tradition of analysis – may influence how we think and act today. This is especially true for those who self-consciously operate within that tradition. But if I am correct that realism is a perennial tradition in the study of international relations, even those who do not consider themselves realists cannot avoid engaging realism.

---

[7] I thank Eduardo Saxe for suggesting this language.

My own preference, clearly, is for a primarily critical engagement: carefully studying, and deeply appreciating, but ultimately rejecting, realism. Others, no less reasonably, may prefer a much more positive engagement. Any serious student of international relations, however, must grapple with the realist challenge of understanding the place of anarchy and egoism in international relations. Carr is certainly correct that sound theory and sound practice require a proper appreciation of both the strengths and the limitations of realism.

Discussion questions

- Is there as sharp and clear a distinction between the "negative" and "positive" insights of realism as Donnelly suggests? Consider the following alternative formulations. The (positive) insights of realism have a limited application. Many of the most important uses of realism's (positive) insights involve combating the prevalent tendency to excessive optimism. Are these formulations not at least as useful – and a lot more fair – than saying realism's contributions are largely negative? Does Donnelly not admit as much when he turns to considering the realist research program?

- Even granting the "negative" formulation of realism's contribution, that is still a substantial contribution. Can it be adequately appreciated if we treat realism as just one of many theories, approaches, traditions, or research programs? Are realism's insights not of such (theoretical and practical) importance that it deserves a special place even in a highly pluralistic discipline? Is some such special place not implied by Donnelly's claim that engaging realism is essential for the student of international politics?

- Granting all the arguments in the text about partial theories, is it not still important to ask which tradition or research program is (closer to) right than the others? And is realism not a lot closer to being right than the alternatives?

- What do you make of the argument in the text that how one understands theoretical traditions can have practical consequences? Can a realist accept such an argument?

- Having reached the end of the book, how (if at all) have your views about realism changed? What place do you see for realism in the discipline of international studies? Why?

Suggestions for further reading

The plea for a more pluralist discipline that is the heart of my conclusion is shared by a growing number of scholars of various persuasions. Those interested in taking stock of the current state of the discipline can begin with three fine edited collections: *International Theory: Positivism and Beyond* (Smith, Booth, and Zalewski 1996), *The Eighty Years' Crisis: International Relations 1919–1999* (Dunne, Cox, and Booth 1998), and *Exploration and*

Contestation in the Study of World Politics (Katzenstein, Keohane, and Krasner 1999). *Positivism and Beyond* is much more British, somewhat more interested in epistemology and methodology, and a bit more heterodox. *Exploration and Contestation* (which originally appeared as the Autumn 1998 issue of the journal *International Organization*) is more American and a bit less heterodox. Doyle and Ikenberry (1997), Burchill and Linklater (1996), Booth and Smith (1995), and Gill and Mittleman (1997) are also good recent collections looking at the state of the discipline.

For those particularly interested in postmodernism, Richard Devetak's chapter in Burchill and Linklater (1996) is unusually accessible and remains clearly focused on the significance of postmodernism for international studies. Peterson (1992) is also very accessible and links postmodernism with feminism. Rosenau (1990) is, in my experience, a bit harder for students to approach, but still relatively accessible, and especially good on the underlying epistemological and ontological issues.

Here in the concluding set of suggested readings it is also appropriate to note other books that provide a wide overview of realist theories, as well as some of the principal critical works that a reader of this volume might want to consult.

Michael Joseph Smith's *Realist Thought from Weber to Kissinger* (1986) is the essential starting point for anyone interested in the secondary literature on "classical" realist thought in the twentieth century. Thoughtful chapters on Weber, Carr, Niebuhr, Morgenthau, Kennan, and Kissinger are followed by an excellent overview and assessment. The perspective is critical but highly sympathetic.

Entirely different in focus, Stefan Guzzini's *Realism in International Relations and International Political Economy* makes an excellent (if not quite as accessible) companion to Smith. Part I focuses on the development of realism within the context of post-World War II American foreign policy up through the collapse of détente. Part II then considers Waltzian structuralism and realist thought in the field of political economy as a response to both policy and disciplinary crisis. The final two chapters offer a critique of the more epistemological turn of the 1980s and 1990s and an assessment of contemporary realism "at a crossroads." And all of this is situated within a broader account of the development of the field of international studies.

Friedrich Meinecke's *Machiavellism* (1957 [1924]) is a classic history of the development of the theory of political realism. Although most readers of this book are likely to find Meinecke's extended excursions into the history of political thought too arcane for their tastes, the first chapter is a brilliant analysis that belongs on any shortlist of recommended reading.

For other accounts of the place of realism in the development of the discipline, see Olson and Onuf (1985), Kahler (1997), Bull (1972), and Booth (1996). Palan and Blair (1993) offer an unusual twist, tracing realism back to certain strands of nineteenth-century German "idealist" thought. Schmidt (1998) provides an interesting disciplinary history that focuses on the centrality of the problems of anarchy and sovereignty. Schmidt emphasizes not only the close interconnection of realism and idealism during the formative decades, but also the link between national and international politics provided by the centrality of a theory of the state – a link that has been largely lost in contemporary structural realism. Lynch

(1999) powerfully challenges the foundational realist myth that "idealists" were in any important way responsible for World War II.

Finally, two idiosyncratic but most interesting accounts are worth mentioning. R. N. Berki's *On Political Realism* (1981) attempts to situate political realism within a broader philosophical framework, tackling issues such as necessity, freedom, and the tension with idealism in an original and often thought-provoking way. Roger Spegele's *Political Realism in International Theory* (1996) also takes off from dissatisfaction with the inadequately realist character of standard accounts of political realism. His solution is to incorporate elements of postmodern thought and ordinary language philosophy into a position he calls evaluative political realism. If such a project sounds even vaguely interesting, this book is well worth reading. A shorter version of the basic structure of the argument is available in Spegele (1987).

Among critical assessments, the standard starting point is Robert Keohane's *Neorealism and Its Critics* (ed. 1986). David Baldwin's collection *Neorealism and Neoliberalism* (1993) also offers an excellent overview of the debate identified by the title. Michael Doyle's *Ways of War and Peace: Realism, Liberalism, and Socialism* (1997) offers an excellent overview and assessment of these three approaches.

Jim George's textbook *Discourses of Global Politics* (1994) adopts an explicitly post-structuralist/postmodern perspective and gives considerable critical attention to realism. Andrew Linklater's *Beyond Realism and Marxism* (1990) effectively lays out the case for critical theory as an alternative perspective. Steve Smith's **"Positivism and Beyond"** (1996) is an excellent overview of the current state of epistemological debates in the discipline. Although it only touches on realism in passing, it is essential reading for those interested in beginning to come to terms with critics who reject realism as much on epistemological, ontological, or methodological as substantive grounds.

John Vasquez' *The Power of Power Politics* (1983) sharply criticizes the predominance of realist approaches in international studies. A fully revised and updated version (1998) extends the critique from Morgenthau's generation to Waltz' and beyond. For a provocative methodological critique of neorealism, see Vasquez (1997) and the replies it provoked in the December 1997 *American Political Science Review*. Although none of these works is to my taste, Vasquez approaches realism with considerable learning, energy, and passion, and is widely cited in the field.

Francis Beer and Robert Harriman's edited collection *Post-Realism: The Rhetorical Turn in International Relations* (1996) takes a very different tack. A series of essays explores the rhetoric of Kissinger, Kennan, Niebuhr, Carr, Wight, and Morgenthau. Another set contains essays that in varying ways deconstruct key realist concepts. And a third set extends rhetorical and deconstructive analysis to concrete policy contexts. The individual essays are disparate and of uneven quality, but the volume as a whole raises unusual and often penetrating criticisms and makes interesting linkages that often escape more mainstream critiques. I should also note, for those put off by any reference to "rhetoric," let alone "deconstruction," that the essays are generally quite readable.

Selected recommended readings

This list collects the readings highlighted in boldface in the bibliographic essays at the end of the individual chapters.

Axelrod, Robert and Robert O. Keohane. 1985. "Achieving Cooperation under Anarchy: Strategies and Institutions." *World Politics* 38 (October): 226–254.

Buzan, Barry, Charles A. Jones, and Richard Little. 1993. *The Logic of Anarchy: Neorealism to Structural Realism.* New York: Columbia University Press.

Cox, Robert W. 1986. "Social Forces, States and World Orders: Beyond International Relations Theory." In *Neorealism and Its Critics*, edited by Robert O. Keohane. New York: Columbia University Press.

Dunne, Tim, Michael Cox, and Ken Booth, eds. 1998. *The Eighty Years' Crisis: International Relations 1919–1999.* Cambridge: Cambridge University Press.

Hobbes, Thomas. 1986. *Leviathan,* edited by C. B. Macpherson. Harmondsworth: Penguin.

Katzenstein, Peter J., Robert O. Keohane, and Stephen D. Krasner, eds. 1999. *Exploration and Contestation in the Study of World Politics.* Cambridge, Mass.: MIT Press.

Keohane, Robert O. 1986. "Theory of World Politics: Structural Realism and Beyond." In *Neorealism and Its Critics*, edited by Robert O. Keohane. New York: Columbia University Press.

Machiavelli, Niccolò. 1970. *The Discourses,* translated by Leslie J. Walker. Harmondsworth: Penguin.

  1985. *The Prince,* translated by Harvey C. Mansfield. Chicago: University of Chicago Press.

Meinecke, Friedrich. 1957 [1924]. *Machiavellism: The Doctrine of Raison d'Etat and its Place in Modern History.* London: Routledge and Kegan Paul.

Milner, Helen. 1991. "The Assumption of Anarchy in International Relations Theory: A Critique." *Review of International Studies* 17: 67–85.

Morgenthau, Hans J. 1954. *Politics Among Nations: The Struggle for Power and Peace,* 2nd edn. New York: Alfred A. Knopf.

Niebuhr, Reinhold. 1932. *Moral Man and Immoral Society: A Study in Ethics and Politics.* New York: Charles Scribner's Sons.

Parry, Adam. 1972. "Thucydides' Historical Perspective." *Yale Classical Studies* 22: 47–61.

Ruggie, John Gerard. 1986. "Continuity and Transformation in the World Polity: Toward a Neorealist Synthesis." In *Neorealism and Its Critics*, edited by Robert O. Keohane. New York: Columbia University Press.

Smith, Michael Joseph. 1986. *Realist Thought from Weber to Kissinger.* Baton Rouge: Louisiana State University Press.

Smith, Steve. 1996. "Positivism and Beyond." In *International Theory: Positivism and Beyond,* edited by Steve Smith, Ken Booth, and Marisya Zalewski. Cambridge: Cambridge University Press.

Smith, Steve, Ken Booth, and Marisya Zalewski, eds. 1996. *International Theory: Positivism and Beyond.* Cambridge: Cambridge University Press.

Snyder, Glenn H. 1996. "Process Variables in Neorealist Theory." *Security Studies* 5 (Spring): 167–192.

Snyder, Glenn H. and Paul Diesing. 1977. *Conflict Among Nations: Bargaining, Decision Making, and System Structure in International Crises.* Princeton: Princeton University Press.

Thucydides. 1982. *The Peloponnesian War,* translated by Richard Crawley (revised by T. E. Wick). New York: Modern Library.

Tucker, Robert W. 1952. "Professor Morgenthau's Theory of Political 'Realism'." *American Political Science Review* 46 (March): 214–224.

Waltz, Kenneth N. 1979. *Theory of International Politics.* New York: Random House.

Walzer, Michael. 1977. *Just and Unjust Wars: A Moral Argument with Historical Illustrations.* New York: Basic Books.

Wendt, Alexander. 1987. "The Agent Structure Problem in International Relations Theory." *International Organization* 41 (Summer): 335–370.

1992. "Anarchy is What States Make of It: The Social Construction of Power Politics." *International Organization* 46 (Spring): 391–425.

Wight, Martin. 1978. *Power Politics.* Leicester: Leicester University Press.

References

Abrams, Elliott and Donald Kagan, eds. 1998. *Honor among Nations: Intangible Interests and Foreign Policy.* Washington, D.C.: Ethics and Public Policy Center.

Adkins, Arthur W. H. 1972. *Moral Values and Political Behaviour in Ancient Greece: From Homer to the End of the Fifth Century.* London: Chatto and Windus.

1976. "*Polupragmosune* and 'Minding One's Own Business': A Study in Greek Social and Political Values." *Classical Philology* 71 (October): 301–327.

Adler, Emanuel. 1998. "Seeds of Peaceful Change: The OSCE's Security Community-Building Model." In *Security Communities*, edited by Emanuel Adler and Michael Barnett. Cambridge: Cambridge University Press.

Adler, Emanuel and Michael Barnett, eds. 1998. *Security Communities.* Cambridge: Cambridge University Press.

Airaksinen, Timo and Martin A. Bertman, eds. 1989. *Hobbes: War Among Nations.* Aldershot: Avebury.

Alexandrowicz, Charles Henry. 1967. *An Introduction to the History of the Law of Nations in the East Indies.* Oxford: Clarendon Press.

1973. *The European–African Confrontation: A Study in Treaty Making.* Leiden: A. W. Sijthoff.

Alker, Hayward R. 1992. "The Humanistic Moment in International Studies: Reflections on Machiavelli and Las Casas." *International Studies Quarterly* 36 (December): 347–371.

1996. *Rediscoveries and Reformulations: Humanistic Methodologies for International Studies.* Cambridge: Cambridge University Press.

Andrewes, A. 1960. "The Melian Dialogue and Perikles' Last Speech." *Proceedings of the Cambridge Philological Society* 186 (n.s. 6): 1–10.

1962. "The Mytilene Debate: Thucydides 3.36–49." *Phoenix* 16 (Summer): 64–85.

Aron, Raymond. 1966. *Peace and War: A Theory of International Relations.* Garden City, N.Y.: Doubleday.

Aron, Raymond. 1971. "Max Weber and Power Politics." In *Max Weber and Sociology Today*, edited by Otto Stammer. New York: Harper Torchbooks.

Art, Robert J. and Kenneth N. Waltz. 1983. "Technology, Strategy, and the Uses of Force." In *The Use of Force*, edited by Robert J. Art and Kenneth N. Waltz. Lanham, Md.: University Press of America.

Ashley, Richard K. 1988. "Untying the Sovereign State: A Double Reading of the Anarchy Problematique." *Millennium* 17 (Summer): 227–262.

Ashley, Richard K. and R. J. B. Walker. 1990. "Reading Dissidence/Writing the Discipline: Crisis and the Question of Sovereignty in International Studies." *International Studies Quarterly* 34 (September): 367–416.

Avery, Harry C. 1973. "Themes in Thucydides' Account of the Sicilian Expedition." *Hermes* 10: 1–13.

Axelrod, Robert. 1981. "The Emergence of Cooperation Among Egoists." *American Political Science Review* 75: 306–318.

1984. *The Evolution of Cooperation.* New York: Basic Books.

Axelrod, Robert and Robert O. Keohane. 1985. "Achieving Cooperation under Anarchy: Strategies and Institutions." *World Politics* 38 (October): 226–254.

Baehr, Peter R. and Leon Gordenker. 1992. *The United Nations in the 1990s.* New York: St. Martin's Press.

Baldwin, David A., ed. 1993. *Neorealism and Neoliberalism: The Contemporary Debate.* New York: Columbia University Press.

Baron, Hans. 1961. "Machiavelli: The Republican Citizen and the Author of *The Prince*." *English Historical Review* 76: 217–253.

Bartelson, Jens. 1995. *A Genealogy of Sovereignty.* Cambridge: Cambridge University Press.

Beer, Francis A. and Robert Harriman, eds. 1996. *Post-Realism: The Rhetorical Turn in International Relations.* Ann Arbor: University of Michigan Press.

Beitz, Charles R. 1979. *Political Theory and International Relations.* Princeton: Princeton University Press.

Beitz, Charles R., Marshall Cohen, Thomas Scanlon, and A. John Simmons, eds. 1985. *International Ethics.* Princeton: Princeton University Press.

Berki, R. N. 1981. *On Political Realism.* London: J. M. Dent & Sons.

Bierstecker, Thomas J. and Cynthia Weber, eds. 1996. *State Sovereignty as Social Construct.* Cambridge: Cambridge University Press.

Black, Robert. 1990. "Machiavelli, Servant of the Florentine Republic." In *Machiavelli and Republicanism,* edited by Gisela Bock, Quentin Skinner, and Maurizio Viroli. Cambridge: Cambridge University Press.

Bloedow, Edmund. 1973. *Alcibiades Reexamined.* Wiesbaden: F. Steiner.

Bock, Gisela, Quentin Skinner, and Maurizio Viroli, eds. 1990. *Machiavelli and Republicanism.* New York: Cambridge University Press.

Booth, Ken. 1995. "Human Wrongs and International Relations." *International Affairs* 71: 103–126.

1996. "75 Years On: Rewriting the Subject's Past – Reinventing its Future." In *International Theory: Positivism and Beyond,* edited by Steve Smith, Ken Booth, and Marisya Zalewski. Cambridge: Cambridge University Press.

Booth, Ken and Steve Smith, eds. 1995. *International Relations Theory Today.* University Park: Pennsylvania State University Press.

Bosworth, A. B. 1993. "The Humanitarian Aspect of the Melian Dialogue." *Journal of Hellenic Studies* 113: 30–44.

Brooks, Stephen G. 1997. "Dueling Realisms." *International Organization* 51: 445–477.

Brown, Michael E., Sean M. Lynn-Jones, and Steven E. Miller. 1995. *The Perils of Anarchy: Contemporary Realism and International Security.* Cambridge, Mass.: MIT Press.

Brown, Robert Macafee, ed. 1986. *The Essential Reinhold Niebuhr: Selected Essays and Addresses*. New Haven: Yale University Press.

Bruckner, Gene A. 1983. *Renaissance Florence*. Berkeley: University of California Press.

Bruell, Christopher. 1974. "Thucydides' View of Athenian Imperialism." *American Political Science Review* 68 (March): 11–17.

Brysk, Alison. 1994. *The Politics of Human Rights in Argentina*. Stanford: Stanford University Press.

Bull, Hedley. 1969. "*The Twenty Years' Crisis* Thirty Years On." *International Journal* 24 (Fall): 625–638.

    1972. "The Theory of International Politics: 1919–1969." In *The Aberystwyth Papers: International Politics, 1919–1969*, edited by Brian Porter. London: Oxford University Press.

    1977. *The Anarchical Society: A Study of Order in World Politics*. New York: Columbia University Press.

Bull, Hedley, ed. 1984. *Intervention in World Politics*. Oxford: Clarendon Press.

Bull, Hedley and Adam Watson, eds. 1984. *The Expansion of International Society*. Oxford: Clarendon Press.

Burchill, Scott and Andrew Linklater, eds. 1996. *Theories of International Relations*. New York: St. Martin's Press.

Burke, Edmund. 1955 [1790]. *Reflections on the Revolution in France*. Indianapolis: Bobbs-Merrill.

Burley, Anne-Marie Slaughter. 1993. "International Law and International Relations Theory: A Dual Agenda." *American Journal of International Law* 87 (April): 205–239.

Butterfield, Herbert. 1949. *Christianity and History*. London: G. Bell and Sons.

    1953. *Christianity, Diplomacy, and War*. London: Epworth Press.

    1960. *International Conflict in the Twentieth Century: A Christian View*. New York: Harper.

Butterfield, Herbert and Martin Wight, eds. 1966. *Diplomatic Investigations: Essays in the Theory of International Politics*. Cambridge, Mass.: Harvard University Press.

Buzan, Barry. 1993. "From International System to International Society: Structural Realism and Regime Theory Meet the English School." *International Organization* 47 (Summer): 327–352.

    1995. "The Level of Analysis Problem in International Relations Reconsidered." In *International Relations Theory Today*, edited by Ken Booth and Steve Smith. University Park: Pennsylvania State University Press.

Buzan, Barry, Charles A. Jones, and Richard Little. 1993. *The Logic of Anarchy: Neorealism to Structural Realism*. New York: Columbia University Press.

    1994. "The Idea of 'International System': Theory Meets History." *International Political Science Review* 15 (July): 231–255.

Calder, William M. 1955. "The Corcyraean-Corinthian Speeches in Thucydides I." *Classical Journal* 50: 179–180.

Carr, Edward Hallett. 1946. *The Twenty Years' Crisis, 1919–1939: An Introduction to the Study of International Relations*, 2nd edn. New York: St. Martin's Press.

Cawkwell, George. 1997. *Thucydides and the Peloponnesian War*. London: Routledge.

Chabod, Federico. 1965. *Machiavelli and the Renaissance*. New York: Harper & Row.

Chayes, Abram and Antonia Handler Chayes. 1995. *The New Sovereignty: Compliance with International Regulatory Agreements*. Cambridge, Mass.: Harvard University Press.

Checkel, Jeffrey T. 1997. *Ideas and International Political Change: Soviet/ Russian Behavior and the End of the Cold War*. New Haven: Yale University Press.

Christensen, Thomas J. and Jack Snyder. 1990. "Chain Gangs and Passed Bucks: Predicting Alliance Patterns in Multipolarity." *International Organization* 44 (Spring): 137–168.

Clark, Ann Marie, Elisabeth J. Friedman, and Kathryn Hochstetler. 1998. "The Sovereign Limits of Global Civil Society: A Comparison of NGO Participation in UN World Conferences on the Environment, Human Rights, and Women." *World Politics* 51 (October): 1–35.

Clark, Ian. 1989. *The Hierarchy of States: Reform and Resistance in the International Order*. Cambridge: Cambridge University Press.

Claude, Inis L. 1962. *Power and International Relations*. New York: Random House.

Cogan, Marc. 1981a. *The Human Thing: The Speeches and Principles of Thucydides' History*. Chicago: University of Chicago Press.

    1981b. "Mytilene, Plataea, and Corcyra: Ideology and Politics in Thucydides, Book Three." *Phoenix* 35 (Spring): 1–21.

Connor, W. Robert. 1977. "Tyrannis Polis." In *Ancient and Modern: Essays in Honor of Gerald F. Else*, edited by John H. D'Arms and John W. Eadie. Ann Arbor: University of Michigan Center for the Coordination of Ancient and Modern Studies.

    1984. *Thucydides*. Princeton: Princeton University Press.

Copeland, Dale C. 1996. "Neorealism and the Myth of Bipolar Stability: Toward a New Dynamic Realist Theory of Major War." *Security Studies* 5 (Spring): 29–89.

Cornford, Francis Macdonald. 1965 [1907]. *Thucydides Mythistoricus*. London: Routledge & Kegan Paul.

Cox, Robert W. 1986. "Social Forces, States and World Orders: Beyond International Relations Theory." In *Neorealism and Its Critics*, edited by Robert O. Keohane. New York: Columbia University Press.

Coyle, Martin, ed. 1995. *Niccolo Machiavelli's "The Prince": New Interdisciplinary Essays*. Manchester: Manchester University Press.

Crane, Gregory. 1998. *Thucydides and the Ancient Simplicity: The Limits of Political Realism*. Berkeley: University of California Press.

Creed, J. L. 1973. "Moral Values in the Age of Thucydides." *Classical Quarterly* n.s. 23: 213–231.

Cusack, Thomas R. and Richard J. Stoll. 1990. *Exploring Realpolitik: Probing International Relations Theory with Computer Simulation*. Boulder: Lynne Rienner Publishers.

Davis, Harry R. and Robert C. Good, eds. 1960. *Reinhold Niebuhr on Politics: His Political Philosophy and Its Application to Our Age as Expressed in His Writings*. New York: Charles Scribner's Sons.

De Alvarez, Leo Paul S. 1999. *The Machiavellian Enterprise: A Commentary on "The Prince"*. DeKalb: Northern Illinois University Press.

Dehio, Ludwig. 1963. *The Precarious Balance: The Politics of Power in Europe 1494–1945*. London: Chatto & Windus.

d'Entreves, Alexander Passerin. 1967. *The Notion of the State: An Introduction to Political Theory*. Oxford: Clarendon Press.

Der Derian, James. 1987. *On Diplomacy: A Genealogy of Western Estrangement*. Oxford: Basil Blackwell.

Destler, David. 1989. "What's at Stake in the Agent Structure Debate?" *International Organization* 43 (Summer): 441–473.

Deudney, Daniel. 1996. "Authorities, Structures, and Geopolitics in Philadelphian Systems." In *State Sovereignty as Social Construct*, edited by Thomas J. Bierstecker and Cynthia Weber. Cambridge: Cambridge University Press.

Deutsch, Karl W. and J. David Singer. 1964. "Multipolar Power Systems and International Stability." *World Politics* 16 (April): 390–406.

Dodds, E. R. 1951. *The Greeks and the Irrational*. Berkeley: University of California Press.

Donelan, Michael, ed. 1978. *The Reason of States: A Study in International Political Theory*. London: George Allen & Unwin.

Dover, K. J. 1974. *Greek Popular Morality in the Time of Plato and Aristotle*. Berkeley: University of California Press.

Doyle, Michael W. 1990. "Thucydidean Realism." *Review of International Studies* 16: 223–237.

1991. "Thucydides: A Realist?" In *Hegemonic Rivalry: From Thucydides to the Nuclear Age*, edited by Richard Ned Lebow and Barry S. Strauss. Boulder: Westview Press.

1997. *Ways of War and Peace: Realism, Liberalism, and Socialism*. New York: Norton.

Doyle, Michael W. and G. John Ikenberry, eds. 1997. *New Thinking in International Relations Theory*. Boulder: Westview Press.

Dunne, Timothy. 1993. "Mythology or Methodology? Traditions in International Theory." *Review of International Studies* 19 (July): 305–318.

1995. "The Social Construction of International Society." *European Journal of International Relations* 1: 367–389.

1998. *Inventing International Society: A History of the English School*. New York: St. Martin's Press.

Dunne, Tim, Michael Cox, and Ken Booth, eds. 1998. *The Eighty Years' Crisis: International Relations 1919–1999*. Cambridge: Cambridge University Press.

Dunne, Tim and Nicholas J. Wheeler, eds. 1999. *Human Rights in Global Politics*. Cambridge: Cambridge University Press.

Edmunds, Lowell. 1975. "Thucydides' Ethics As Reflected in the Description of Stasis (3.82–83)." *Harvard Studies in Classical Philology* 79: 73–92.

Ehrenberg, Victor. 1947. "Polypragmosyne: A Study in Greek Politics." *Journal of Hellenic Studies* 68: 46–67.

Ellis, Walter M. 1989. *Alcibiades*. London: Routledge.

Elman, Colin. 1996. "Horses for Courses: Why *Not* Neorealist Theories of Foreign Policy?" *Security Studies* 6: 7–53.

Elman, Colin and Miriam Fendius Elman. 1997. "Lakatos and Neorealism: A Reply to Vasquez." *American Political Science Review* 91 (December): 923–926.

Essen, Martin Heinrich Nikolaus von. 1964 [1887]. *Index Thucydideus: Ex Bekkeri Editione Stereotypa.* Darmstadt: Wissenschaftliche Buchgesellschaft.

Euben, J. Peter. 1990. *The Tragedy of Political Theory: The Road Not Taken.* Princeton: Princeton University Press.

Fenwick, Charles G. 1924. *International Law.* New York: The Century Co.

Ferguson, Yale H. and Richard W. Mansbach. 1988. *The Elusive Quest: Theory and International Politics.* Columbia: University of South Carolina Press.

Finley, John H. Jr. 1963 [1942]. *Thucydides.* Ann Arbor: University of Michigan Press.

Finley, M. I. 1978. *The World of Odysseus*, rev. edn. New York: Viking Press.

Finnemore, Martha. 1996. *National Interests in International Society.* Ithaca: Cornell University Press.

Fleisher, Martin, ed. 1972. *Machiavelli and the Nature of Political Thought.* New York: Atheneum.

Fliess, Peter J. 1966. *Thucydides and the Poltiics of Bipolarity.* Baton Rouge: Louisiana State University Press.

Flower, H. 1992. "Thucydides and the Pylos Debate." *Historia* 41: 40–57.

Forde, Steven. 1989. *The Ambition to Rule: Alcibiades and the Politics of Imperialism in Thucydides.* Ithaca: Cornell University Press.

   1992. "Varieties of Realism: Thucydides and Machiavelli." *Journal of Politics* 54: 372–393.

   1995. "International Realism and the Science of Politics: Thucydides, Machiavelli, and Neorealism." *International Studies Quarterly* 39 (June): 141–160.

Fox, William T. R. 1985. "E. H. Carr and Political Realism: Vision and Revision." *Review of International Studies* 11 (January): 1–16.

Fox, William T. R. and Annette Baker Fox. 1961. "The Teaching of International Relations in the United States." *World Politics* 13 (April): 339–359.

Frankel, Benjamin. 1996. "Restating the Realist Case: An Introduction." *Security Studies* 5 (Spring): ix–xx.

Frankel, Benjamin, ed. 1996a. *Realism: Restatements and Renewal.* London: Frank Cass.

   1996b. *Roots of Realism.* London: Frank Cass.

Gagarin, Michael. 1974. "*Dike* in Archaic Greek Thought." *Classical Philology* 69 (July): 186–197.

Garnett, John C. 1984. *Commonsense and the Theory of International Politics.* London: Macmillan.

Garst, Daniel. 1989. "Thucydides and Neorealism." *International Studies Quarterly* 33: 3–28.

Gellman, Peter. 1988. "Hans J. Morgenthau and the Legacy of Political Realism." *Review of International Studies* 14 (October): 247–266.

George, Jim. 1994. *Discourses of Global Politics: A Critical (Re)Introduction to International Relations.* Boulder: Lynne Rienner Publishers.

Gerth, H. H. and C. Wright Mills, eds. 1946. *From Max Weber: Essays in Sociology*. New York: Oxford University Press.

Gilbert, Felix. 1939. "The Humanist Concept of the Prince and *The Prince* of Machiavelli." *Journal of Modern History* 11: 449–483.

1965. *Machiavelli and Guicciardini: Politics and History in Sixteenth-Century Florence*. Princeton: Princeton University Press.

Gill, Stephen and James H. Mittleman, eds. 1997. *Innovation and Transformation in International Studies*. Cambridge: Cambridge University Press.

Gilmore, Myron Piper, ed. 1972. *Studies on Machiavelli*. Florence: G. C. Sansoni.

Gilpin, Robert. 1975. *U.S. Power and the Multinational Corporation: The Political Economy of Direct Foreign Investment*. New York: Basic Books.

1981. *War and Change in World Politics*. Cambridge: Cambridge University Press.

1986. "The Richness of the Tradition of Political Realism." In *Realism and Its Critics*, edited by Robert O. Keohane. New York: Columbia University Press.

1988. "The Theory of Hegemonic War." *The Journal of Interdisciplinary History* 18 (Spring): 591–613.

1991. "Peloponnesian War and Cold War." In *Hegemonic Rivalry: From Thucydides to the Nuclear Age*, edited by Richard Ned Lebow and Barry S. Strauss. Boulder: Westview Press.

1996. "No One Loves a Political Realist." *Security Studies* 5 (Spring): 3–26.

Glaser, Charles L. and Chaim Kaufmann. 1998. "What is the Offense–Defense Balance and Can We Measure It?" *International Security* 22: 44–82.

Goertz, Gary and Paul F. Diehl. 1994. "International Norms and Power Politics." In *Reconstructing Realpolitik*, edited by Frank W. Wayman and Paul F. Diehl. Ann Arbor: University of Michigan Press.

Goldmann, Kjell. 1988. "The Concept of 'Realism' as a Source of Confusion." *Cooperation and Conflict* 23: 1–14.

Gomme, Arnold Wycombe. 1962. *More Essays on Greek History and Literature*. Oxford: Basil Blackwell.

Gong, Gerrit W. 1984. *The Standard of "Civilisation" in International Society*. Oxford: Clarendon Press.

Good, Robert C. 1960. "The National Interest and Political Realism: Niebuhr's 'Debate' with Morgenthau and Kennan." *Journal of Politics* 22 (November): 597–619.

Gowa, Joanne. 1986. "Anarchy, Egoism, and Third Images: The Evolution of Cooperation in International Relations." *International Organization* 40 (Winter): 167–186.

Grazia, Sebastian de. 1989. *Machiavelli in Hell*. Princeton: Princeton University Press.

Green, Peter. 1970. *Armada From Athens*. London: Hodder & Stoughton.

Grieco, Joseph M. 1988a. "Anarchy and the Limits of Cooperation: A Realist Critique of the Newest Liberal Institutionalism." *International Organization* 42 (Summer): 485–507.

1988b. "Realist Theory and the Problem of International Cooperation: Analysis with an Amended Prisoner's Dilemma Model." *Journal of Politics* 50: 600–624.

1990. *Cooperation among Nations: Europe, America, and Non-tariff Barriers to Trade.* Ithaca: Cornell University Press.

1997. "Realist International Theory and the Study of World Politics." In *New Thinking in International Relations Theory*, edited by Michael W. Doyle and G. John Ikenberry. Boulder: Westview Press.

Gubin, Sandra L. 1995. "Between Regimes and Realism – Transnational Agenda Setting: Soviet Compliance With CSCE Human Rights Norms." *Human Rights Quarterly* 17 (May): 278–302.

Gulick, Edward Vose. 1967. *Europe's Classical Balance of Power: A Case History of the Theory and Practice of One of the Great Concepts of European Statecraft.* New York: Norton.

Gunnell, John G. 1979. *Tradition and Interpretation.* Cambridge, Mass.: Winthrop Publishers.

Guzzini, Stefano. 1998. *Realism in International Relations and International Political Economy: The Continuing Story of a Death Foretold.* London: Routledge.

Haas, Ernst B. 1953. "The Balance of Power: Prescription, Concept or Propaganda?" *World Politics* 5 (July): 442–477.

1983. "Regime Decay: Conflict Management and International Organizations, 1945–1981." *International Organization* 37 (Spring): 189–256.

1986. *Why We Still Need the United Nations: Collective Management of International Conflict, 1945–1984.* Berkeley: Institute of International Studies.

Haas, Peter M., Robert O. Keohane, and Marc A. Levy, eds. 1993. *Institutions for the Earth: Sources of Effective International Environmental Protection.* Cambridge, Mass.: MIT Press.

Hall, William Edward. 1924. *A Treatise on International Law.* Oxford: Clarendon Press.

Hanson, Donald W. 1984. "Thomas Hobbes' 'Highway to Peace'." *International Organization* 38 (Spring): 329–354.

Harbour, Frances V. 1999. *Thinking About International Ethics.* Boulder: Westview Press.

Havelock, E. A. 1969. "*Dikaiosune*: An Essay in Greek Intellectual History." *Phoenix* 28 (Spring): 49–70.

Heath, M. 1990. "Justice in Thucydides Speeches." *Historia* 39: 385–400.

Hertslet, Godfrey E. P., ed. 1908. *Hertslet's China Treaties*, 3rd edn., 2 vols. London: His Majesty's Stationery Office.

Herz, John H. 1951. *Political Realism and Political Idealism.* Chicago: University of Chicago Press.

1976. *The Nation-State and the Crisis of World Politics: Essays on International Politics in the Twentieth Century.* New York: D. McKay.

Hevia, James Louis. 1995. *Cherishing Men from Afar: Qing Guest Ritual and the Macartney Embassy of 1793.* Durham, N.C.: Duke University Press.

Hinsley, F. H. 1986. *Sovereignty*, 2nd edn. Cambridge: Cambridge University Press.

Hirsch, Fred. 1976. *Social Limits to Growth.* Cambridge, Mass.: Harvard University Press.

Hixson, Walter L. 1989. *George F. Kennan: Cold War Iconoclast.* New York: Columbia University Press.

Hobbes, Thomas. 1986. *Leviathan*, edited by C. B. Macpherson. Harmondsworth: Penguin.

1996. *Leviathan,* edited by Richard Tuck. Cambridge: Cambridge University Press.

Hoffman, Stanley. 1973. "Choices." *Foreign Policy* 12 (Fall): 3–42.

1981. *Duties Beyond Borders: On the Limits and Possibilities of Ethical International Politics.* Syracuse: Syracuse University Press.

Holbrand, Carsten. 1970. *The Concert of Europe: A Study in German and British International Theory.* London: Longman.

Hollis, Martin. 1977. *Models of Man: Philosophical Thoughts on Social Action.* Cambridge: Cambridge University Press.

Hooker, J. T. 1974. "Charis and Arete in Thucydides." *Hermes* 102: 164–169.

Howe, P. 1994. "The Utopian Realism of E. H. Carr." *Review of International Studies* 20: 277–297.

Hsiung, James C. 1997. *Anarchy and Order: The Interplay of Politics and Law in International Relations.* Boulder: Lynne Rienner Publishers.

Hulliung, Mark. 1983. *Citizen Machiavelli.* Princeton: Princeton University Press.

Hunter, Virginia. 1973/74. "Athens *Tyrannis*: A New Approach to Thucydides." *Classical Journal* 69 (December–January): 120–126.

Hurrell, Andrew. 1996. "The United States and Latin America: Neorealism Re-examined." In *Explaining International Relations since 1945,* edited by Ngaire Woods. Oxford: Oxford University Press.

Hyde, Charles Cheney 1922. *International Law: Chiefly as Interpreted and Applied by the United States.* Boston: Little, Brown, and Company.

Immerwahr, Henry R. 1960. "*Ergon*: History as Monument in Herodotus and Thucydides." *American Journal of Philology* 81: 261–290.

1973. "Pathology of Power and the Speeches in Thucydides." In *The Speeches in Thucydides,* edited by Philip A. Stadter. Chapel Hill: University of North Carolina Press.

Jackson, Robert H. 1990. *Quasi-States: Sovereignty, International Relations and the Third World.* Cambridge: Cambridge University Press.

1993. "The Weight of Ideas in Decolonization: Normative Change in International Relations." In *Ideas and Foreign Policy: Beliefs, Institutions, and Political Change,* edited by Judith Goldstein and Robert O. Keohane. Ithaca: Cornell University Press.

James, Alan. 1986. *Sovereign Statehood: The Basis of International Society.* London: Allen & Unwin.

Jervis, Robert. 1978. "Cooperation under the Security Dilemma." *World Politics* 30 (January): 167–214.

1993. "International Primacy: Is the Game Worth the Candle?" *International Security* 17 (Spring): 52–67.

1994. "Hans Morgenthau, Realism, and the Study of International Politics." *Social Research* 61 (Winter): 853–877.

John, Ieuan, Moorehead Wright, and John Garnett. 1972. "International Politics at Aberystwyth 1919–1969." In *The Aberystwyth Papers. International Politics: 1919–1969,* edited by Brian Porter. London: Oxford University Press.

Johnson, Laurie M. 1993. *Thucydides, Hobbes, and the Interpretation of Realism.* DeKalb: Northern Illinois University Press.

Johnson-Bagby, Laurie. 1994. "The Use and Abuse of Thucydides." *International Organization* 48: 131–153.

Jones, Charles. 1996. "E. H. Carr: Ambivalent Realist." In *Post-Realism: The Rhetorical Turn in International Relations*, edited by Francis A. Beer and Robert Harriman. Ann Arbor: University of Michigan Press.

Jones, Daniel M. 1994. "Balancing and Bandwagoning in Militarized Interstate Disputes." In *Reconstructing Realpolitik*, edited by Frank W. Wayman and Paul F. Diehl. Ann Arbor: University of Michigan Press.

Kagan, Donald. 1969. *The Outbreak of the Peloponnesian War.* Ithaca: Cornell University Press.

   1974. *The Archidamian War.* Ithaca: Cornell University Press.

   1975. "The Speeches in Thucydides and the Mytilene Debate." *Yale Classical Studies* 24: 71–94.

   1981. *The Peace of Nicias and the Sicilian Expedition.* Ithaca: Cornell University Press.

   1987. *The Fall of the Athenian Empire.* Ithaca: Cornell University Press.

Kagan, Korina. 1997/98. "The Myth of the European Concert: The Realist–Institutionalist Debate and Great Power Behavior in the Eastern Question, 1821–1841." *Security Studies* 7: 1–57.

Kahler, Miles. 1997. "Inventing International Relations: International Relations Theory After 1945." In *New Thinking in International Relations Theory*, edited by Michael W. Doyle and G. John Ikenberry. Boulder: Westview Press.

Kant, Immanuel. 1981. *Grounding for the Metaphysics of Morals*, translated by James Ellington. Indianapolis: Hackett.

   1983. *Perpetual Peace and Other Essays*, translated by Ted Humphrey. Indianapolis: Hackett.

Katz, Jerrold J. 1998. *Realistic Rationalism.* Cambridge, Mass.: MIT Press.

Katzenstein, Peter, ed. 1996. *The Culture of National Security: Norms and Identity in International Politics.* Ithaca: Cornell University Press.

Katzenstein, Peter J., Robert O. Keohane, and Stephen D. Krasner, eds. 1999. *Exploration and Contestation in the Study of World Politics.* Cambridge, Mass.: MIT Press.

Kauppi, Mark V. 1995/96. "Thucydides: Character and Capabilities." *Security Studies* 5 (Winter): 142–168.

Kavka, Gregory S. 1986. *Hobbesian Moral and Political Theory.* Princeton: Princeton University Press.

Keck, Margaret E. and Kathryn Sikkink. 1998. *Activists Beyond Borders: Advocacy Networks in International Politics.* Ithaca: Cornell University Press.

Keeton, G. W. 1928. *The Development of Extraterritoriality in China.* London: Longmans, Green and Co.

Kegley, Charles W. and Robert W. Bretall, eds. 1956. *Reinhold Niebuhr: His Religious, Social, and Political Thought.* New York: Macmillan.

Kennan, George F. 1951. *American Diplomacy, 1900–1950.* New York: New American Library.

   1954. *Realities of American Foreign Policy.* Princeton: Princeton University Press.

   1967. *Memoirs, 1925–1950.* Boston: Little, Brown.

   1972. *Memoirs, 1950–1963.* Boston: Little, Brown.

   1977. *The Cloud of Danger: Current Realities of American Foreign Policy.* Boston: Little, Brown.

1984. *American Diplomacy*, 2nd edn. Chicago: University of Chicago Press.

1985/86. "Morality and Foreign Policy." *Foreign Affairs* 63 (Winter): 205–218.

1989. *Sketches From a Life*. New York: Pantheon Books.

1995. "On American Principles." *Foreign Affairs* 74 (March-April): 116–216.

Keohane, Robert O. 1984. *After Hegemony: Cooperation and Discord in the World Political Economy*. Princeton: Princeton University Press.

1986a. "Reciprocity in International Relations." *International Oganization* 40 (Winter): 1–27.

1986b. "Theory of World Politics: Structural Realism and Beyond." In *Neo-Realism and Its Critics*, edited by Robert O. Keohane. New York: Columbia University Press.

1989. *International Institutions and State Power: Essays in International Relations Theory*. Boulder: Westview Press.

Keohane, Robert O., ed. 1986. *Neorealism and Its Critics*. New York: Columbia University Press.

Keohane, Robert O. and Joseph S. Nye. 1977. *Power and Interdependence: World Politics in Transition*. Boston: Little, Brown.

1987. *"Power and Interdependence* Revisited." *International Organization* 42 (Autumn): 725–753.

Keohane, Robert O. and Joseph S. Nye, eds. 1972. *Transnational Relations and World Politics*. Cambridge, Mass.: Harvard University Press.

Kissinger, Henry. 1957. *A World Restored: Metternich, Castlereagh and the Problems of Peace, 1812–22*. Boston: Houghton Mifflin.

1977. *American Foreign Policy*. 3rd edn. New York: Norton.

1994. *Diplomacy*. New York: Simon and Schuster.

Klotz, Audie. 1995. *Norms in International Relations: The Struggle Against Apartheid*. Ithaca: Cornell University Press.

Knight, W. Andy. 1999. "Engineering Space in Global Governance: The Emergence of Civil Society in Evolving 'New' Multilateralism." In *Future Multilateralism: The Political and Social Framework*, edited by Michael G. Schecter. Tokyo: United Nations University Press.

Kocis, Robert. 1998. *Machiavelli Redeemed: Retrieving His Humanist Perspectives on Equality, Power, and Glory*. Bethlehem, Pa.: Lehigh University Press.

Koebner, Richard. 1961. *Empire*. Cambridge: Cambridge University Press.

Koebner, Richard and Helmut Dan Schmidt. 1965. *Imperialism: The Story and Significance of a Political Word, 1840–1960*. Cambridge: Cambridge University Press.

Krasner, Stephen D. 1978. *Defending the National Interest: Raw Materials Investments and U.S. Policy*. Princeton: Princeton University Press.

1999. *Sovereignty: Organized Hypocrisy*. Princeton: Princeton University Press.

Kratochwil, Friedrich. 1982. "On the Notion of 'Interest' in International Relations." *International Organization* 36 (Winter): 1–30.

1989. *Rules, Norms, and Decisions: On the Conditions of Practical and Legal Reasoning in International Relations and Domestic Affairs*. Cambridge: Cambridge University Press.

Kulp, Christopher B., ed. 1997. *Realism/Antirealism and Epistemology*. Lanham, Md.: Rowman & Littlefield.

Kydd, Andrew. 1997. "Sheep in Sheep's Clothing: Why Security Seekers Do Not Fight Each Other." *Security Studies* 7 (Autumn): 114–154.

Labs, Eric J. 1997. "Beyond Victory: Offensive Realism and the Expansion of War Aims." *Security Studies* 6: 1–49.

Lake, David A. 1996. "Anarchy, Hierarchy, and the Variety of International Relations." *International Organization* 50 (Winter): 1–33.

Lang, Mabel L. 1972. "Cleon as the Anti-Pericles." *Classical Philology* 57: 159–169.

Lateiner, Donald. 1985. "Nicias' Inadequate Encouragement (Thucydides 7.69.2)." *Classical Philology* 80 (July): 201–213.

Liebeschuetz, W. 1968. "The Structure and Function of the Melian Dialogue." *Journal of Hellenic Studies* 88: 73–77.

Linklater, Andrew. 1990. *Beyond Realism and Marxism: Critical Theory and International Relations.* Basingstoke: Macmillan.

Lipschutz, Ronnie D. 1996. *Global Civil Society and Global Environmental Governance: The Politics of Nature from Place to Planet.* Albany: State University of New York Press.

Liska, George. 1977. "Morgenthau vs. Machiavelli: Political Realism and Power Politics." In *Truth and Tragedy: A Tribute to Hans J. Morgenthau,* edited by Kenneth W. Thompson and Robert J. Myers. Washington D.C.: New Republic Book Company.

Long, David. 1996. *Towards a New Liberal Internationalism: The International Theory of J. A. Hobson.* Cambridge: Cambridge University Press.

Long, David and Peter Wilson, eds. 1995. *Thinkers of the Twenty Years' Crisis: Interwar Idealism Reassessed.* Oxford: Clarendon Press.

Loraux, Nicole. 1986. *The Invention of Athens: The Funeral Oration in the Classical City.* Cambridge, Mass.: Harvard University Press.

Lorenz, Joseph P. 1999. *Peace, Power, and the United Nations: A Security System for the Twenty-first Century.* Boulder: Westview Press.

Luard, Evan. 1992. *The Balance of Power: The System of International Relations, 1648–1815.* New York: St. Martin's Press.

Lumsdaine, David. 1993. *Moral Vision in International Politics: The Foreign Aid Regime, 1949–1989.* Princeton: Princeton University Press.

Lynch, Cecilia. 1999. *Beyond Appeasement: Reinterpreting Interwar Peace Movements in World Politics.* Ithaca: Cornell University Press.

Lynn-Jones, Sean M. 1995. "Offense–Defense Theory and Its Critics." *Security Studies* 4 (Summer): 660–691.

Macfarland, Joseph C. 1999. "Machiavelli's Imagination of Excellent Men: An Appraisal of the Lives of Cosimo de' Medici and Castruccio Castracani." *American Political Science Review* 93 (March): 133–146.

Machiavelli, Niccolò. 1908. *The Prince,* translated by W. K. Marriott. London: J. M. Dent.

    1950. *"The Prince" and "The Discourses."* New York: Random House (The Modern Library).

    1954. *The Prince,* translated by Hill Thompson. New York: The Heritage Press.

    1961. *The Letters of Machiavelli,* translated by Allan Gilbert. New York: Capricorn Books.

    1965. *Chief Works, and Others,* translated by Allan H. Gilbert, 3 vols. Durham, N.C.: Duke University Press.

1970. *The Discourses*, translated by Leslie J. Walker. Harmondsworth: Penguin.

1985. *The Prince*, translated by Harvey C. Mansfield. Chicago: University of Chicago Press.

1988a. *Florentine Histories*, translated by Lara F. Banfield and Harvey C. Mansfield Jr. Princeton: Princeton University Press.

1988b. *Machiavelli: The Prince*, edited by Quentin Skinner and Russell Price. Cambridge: Cambridge University Press.

1989. *The Prince*, translated by Leo Paul S. de Alvarez. Prospect Heights, Ill.: Waveland Press.

1996. *Discourses on Livy*, translated by Harvey C. Mansfield and Nathan Tarcov. Chicago: University of Chicago Press.

Macleod, C. W. 1974. "Form and Meaning in the Melian Dialogue." *Historia* 23: 385–400.

1979. "Thucydides on Faction (3.82–83)." *Proceedings of the Cambridge Philological Society* 205 (n.s. 25): 52–68.

Maghroori, Ray and Bennett Ramberg. 1982. *Globalism versus Realism: International Relations' Third Debate*. Boulder: Westview Press.

Mansfield, Harvey C. Jr. 1979. *Machiavelli's New Modes and Orders: A Study of the Discourses on Livy*. Ithaca: Cornell University Press.

1996. *Machiavelli's Virtue*. Chicago: University of Chicago Press.

Mastanduno, Michael. 1991. "Do Relative Gains Matter? America's Response to Japanese Industrial Policy." *International Security* 16: 73–113.

1997. "Preserving the Unipolar Moment: Realist Theories and U.S. Grand Strategy after the Cold War." *International Security* 21 (Spring): 49–88.

Masters, Roger D. 1996. *Machiavelli, Leonardo, and the Science of Power*. Notre Dame, Ind.: University of Notre Dame Press.

Matthews, John C. III. 1996. "Current Gains and Future Outcomes: When Cumulative Relative Gains Matter." *International Security* 21 (Summer): 112–146.

Mattingly, Garrett. 1955. *Renaissance Diplomacy*. Boston: Houghton Mifflin.

Maxwell, Mary. 1990. *Morality Among Nations: An Evolutionary View*. Albany: State University of New York Press.

Mayall, James, ed. 1982. *The Community of States: A Study in International Political Theory*. London: George Allen & Unwin.

Mayers, David. 1988. *George Kennan and the Dilemmas of US Foreign Policy*. New York: Oxford University Press.

McGlew, James F. 1993. *Tyranny and Political Culture in Ancient Greece*. Ithaca: Cornell University Press.

McIntire, C. T., ed. 1979. *Herbert Butterfield: Writings on Christianity and History*. New York: Oxford University Press.

Mearsheimer, John J. 1990. "Back to the Future: Instability in Europe After the Cold War." *International Security* 15 (Summer): 5–56.

1994/95. "The False Promise of International Institutions." *International Security* 19: 5–49.

1995. "A Realist Reply." *International Security* 20 (Summer): 82–93.

Meiggs, R. 1963. "The Crisis of Athenian Imperialism." *Harvard Studies in Classical Philology* 67: 1–36.

1972. *The Athenian Empire*. Oxford: Clarendon Press.

Meinecke, Friedrich. 1957 [1924]. *Machiavellism: The Doctrine of Raison d'Etat and its Place in Modern History.* London: Routledge and Kegan Paul.

Meyer, Donald B. 1988. *The Protestant Search for Political Realism, 1919–1941.* Middletown, Conn.: Wesleyan University Press.

Midgley, Mary. 1995. *Beast and Man: The Roots of Human Nature,* rev. edn. London: Routledge.

Milner, Helen. 1991. "The Assumption of Anarchy in International Relations Theory: A Critique." *Review of International Studies* 17: 67–85.

Miscamble, Wilson D. 1992. *George F. Kennan and the Making of American Foreign Policy, 1947–1950.* Princeton: Princeton University Press.

Morgenthau, Hans J. 1946. *Scientific Man Versus Power Politics.* Chicago: University of Chicago Press.

   1948. *Politics Among Nations: The Struggle for Power and Peace.* New York: Alfred A. Knopf.

   1951. *In Defense of the National Interest: A Critical Examination of American Foreign Policy.* New York: Alfred A. Knopf.

   1952a. "Another 'Great Debate:' The National Interest of the United States." *American Political Science Review* 46 (December): 961–988.

   1952b. "What is the National Interest of the United States?" *The Annals* 282 (July): 1–7.

   1954. *Politics Among Nations: The Struggle for Power and Peace,* 2nd edn. New York: Alfred A. Knopf.

   1960. *The Purpose of American Politics.* New York: Knopf.

   1962a. *Politics in the Twentieth Century,* vol. I: *The Decline of Democratic Politics.* Chicago: University of Chicago Press.

   1962b. *Politics in the Twentieth Century,* vol. II: *The Impasse of American Foreign Policy.* Chicago: University of Chicago Press.

   1962c. *Politics in the Twentieth Century,* vol. III: *The Restoration of American Politics.* Chicago: University of Chicago Press.

   1970. *Truth and Power: Essays of a Decade, 1960–70.* New York: Praeger.

   1979. *Human Rights and Foreign Policy.* New York: Council on Religion and International Affairs.

   1985. *Politics Among Nations: The Struggle for Power and Peace,* 6th edn. New York: Alfred A. Knopf.

Morrow, James D. 1994. *Game Theory for Political Scientists.* Princeton: Princeton University Press.

Murray, A. J. H. 1996. "The Moral Politics of Hans Morgenthau." *Review of Politics* 58 (Winter): 81–108.

Myerson, Roger B. 1991. *Game Theory: Analysis of Conflict.* Cambridge, Mass.: Harvard University Press.

Nardin, Terry and David R. Mapel, eds. 1992. *Traditions of International Ethics.* Cambridge: Cambridge University Press.

Nicholson, Michael. 1992. *Rationality and the Analysis of International Conflict.* Cambridge: Cambridge University Press.

Niebuhr, Reinhold. 1932. *Moral Man and Immoral Society: A Study in Ethics and Politics.* New York: Charles Scribner's Sons.

   1934. *Reflections on the End of an Era.* New York: Charles Scribner's Sons.

   1940. *Christianity and Power Politics.* New York: Charles Scribner's Sons.

1941. *The Nature and Destiny of Man: A Christian Interpretation,* vol. I: *Human Nature.* New York: Charles Scribner's Sons.

1943. *The Nature and Destiny of Man: A Christian Interpretation,* vol. II: *Human Destiny.* New York: Charles Scribner's Sons.

1944. *The Children of Light and the Children of Darkness: A Vindication of Democracy and a Critique of its Traditional Defence.* New York: Charles Scribner's Sons.

1953. *Christian Realism and Political Problems.* New York: Charles Scribner's Sons.

Niou, Emerson M. S., Peter C. Ordeshook, and Gregory F. Rose. 1989. *The Balance of Power: Stability in International Systems.* Cambridge: Cambridge University Press.

Nye, Joseph S. 1971. *Peace in Parts: Integration and Conflict in Regional Organization.* Boston: Little, Brown.

Offerman-Zuckerberg, Joan, ed. 1991. *Politics and Psychology: Contemporary Psychodynamic Perspectives.* New York: Plenum Press.

Olson, William and Nicholas Onuf. 1985. "The Growth of a Discipline: Reviewed." In *International Relations: British and American Perspectives,* edited by Steve Smith. Oxford: Basil Blackwell.

O'Neill, Barry. 1999. *Honor, Symbols, and War.* Ann Arbor: University of Michigan Press.

Onuf, Nicholas. 1998. *The Republican Legacy in International Thought.* Cambridge: Cambridge University Press.

Onuf, Nicholas and Frank F. Klink. 1989. "Anarchy, Authority, Rule." *International Studies Quarterly* 33 (June): 149–173.

Orwin, Clifford. 1984. "The Just and the Advantageous in Thucydides: The Case of the Mytilenian Debate." *American Political Science Review* 78 (June): 485–494.

1988. "Stasis and Plague: Thucydides on the Dissolution of Society." *Journal of Politics* 50 (November): 831–847.

1994. *The Humanity of Thucydides.* Princeton: Princeton University Press.

Osgood, Robert Endicott. 1953. *Ideals and Self-Interest in America's Foreign Relations: The Great Transformation of the Twentieth Century.* Chicago: University of Chicago Press.

Osgood, Robert E. and Robert W. Tucker. 1967. *Force, Order, and Justice.* Baltimore: Johns Hopkins University Press.

Oye, Kenneth A., ed. 1986. *Cooperation Under Anarchy.* Princeton: Princeton University Press.

Palan, Ronen P. and Brook M. Blair. 1993. "On the Idealist Origins of the Realist Theory of International Relations." *Review of International Studies* 19 (October): 385–399.

Palmer, Michael. 1982a. "Alcibiades and the Question of Tyranny in Thucydides." *Canadian Journal of Political Science* 15 (March): 103–124.

1982b. "Love of Glory and the Common Good." *American Political Science Review* 76 (December): 825–836.

Parekh, Bhikhu. 1997. "Is There a Human Nature?" In *Is There a Human Nature?,* edited by Leroy S. Rouner. Notre Dame, Ind.: University of Notre Dame Press.

Parel, Anthony, ed. 1972. *The Political Calculus: Essays on Machiavelli's Philosophy.* Toronto: University of Toronto Press.

Parkinson, F. 1977. *The Philosophy of International Relations: A Study in the History of Thought.* Beverly Hills: Sage Publications.

Parry, Adam. 1972. "Thucydides' Historical Perspective." *Yale Classical Studies* 22: 47–61.

Pearson, Lionel. 1957. "Popular Ethics in the World of Thucydides." *Classical Philology* 52 (October): 228–244.

Pélissié du Rausas, G. 1910. *Le Régime des capitulations dans l'Empire ottoman,* 2nd edn., 2 vols. Paris: Arthur Rousseau.

Pennock, J. Roland and John W. Chapman, eds. 1977. *Human Nature in Politics.* New York: New York University Press.

Peristiany, John G., ed. 1966. *Honour and Shame: The Values of Mediterranean Society.* Chicago: University of Chicago Press.

Peterson, V. Spike. 1992. "Transgressing Boundaries: Theories of Knowledge, Gender and International Relations." *Millennium* 21: 183–206.

Peyrefitte, Alain. 1992. *The Immobile Empire.* New York: Knopf.

Pitkin, Hanna Fenichel. 1984. *Fortune is a Woman: Gender and Politics in the Thought of Niccolò Machiavelli.* Berkeley: University of California Press.

Plamenatz, John. 1972. "In Search of Machiavellian *Virtu.*" In *The Political Calculus: Essays on Machiavelli's Philosophy,* edited by Anthony Parel. Toronto: University of Toronto Press.

Pocock, J. G. A. 1975. *The Machiavellian Moment: Florentine Political Thought and the Atlantic Republican Tradition.* Princeton: Princeton University Press.

Posen, Barry R. 1984. *The Sources of Military Doctrine: France, Britain, and Germany between the World Wars.* Ithaca: Cornell University Press.

Posen, Barry R. and Andrew L. Ross. 1996/97. "Competing Visions for U.S. Grand Strategy." *International Security* 21 (Winter): 5–53.

Powell, Robert. 1991. "Absolute and Relative Gains in International Relations Theory." *American Political Science Review* 85 (December): 1303–1320.

    1993a. "Guns, Butter, and Anarchy." *American Political Science Review* 87 (March): 115–132.

    1993b. "Response." *American Political Science Review* 87 (September): 735–737.

    1994. "Anarchy in International Relations Theory: The Neorealist–Neoliberal Debate." *International Organization* 48 (Spring): 313–344.

Pozzi, Dora C. 1983. "Thucydides ii.35–46: A Text of Power Ideology." *Classical Journal* 78 (February–March): 221–231.

Price, Russell. 1973. "The Senses of *Virtu* in Machiavelli." *European Studies Review* 3: 315–345.

Pusey, N. M. 1940. "Alcibiades and *to philopoli.*" *Harvard Studies in Classical Philology* 51: 215–231.

Quester, George H. 1977. *Offense and Defense in the International System.* New York: John Wiley & Sons.

Raaflaub, K. 1979. "Polis Tyrannos." In *Arktouros: Hellenic Studies Presented to Bernard M. W. Knox on the Occasion of his 65th Birthday,* edited by G. W. Bowersock, Walter Burkert, and Michael C. J. Putnam. New York: Walter de Gruyter.

1994. "Democracy, Power, and Imperialism in Fifth-Century Athens." In *Athenian Political Thought and the Reconstruction of American Democracy*, edited by J. Peter Euben, John R. Wallach, and Josiah Ober. Ithaca: Cornell University Press.

Rahe, Paul A. 1995/96. "Thucydides' Critique of *Realpolitik*." *Security Studies* 5 (Winter): 105–141.

Ranke, Leopold von. 1973. *The Theory and Practice of History*. Indianapolis: Bobbs-Merrill.

Raubitschek, A. E. 1973. "The Speech of the Athenians at Sparta." In *The Speeches in Thucydides*, edited by Philip A. Stadter. Chapel Hill: University of North Carolina Press.

Rawlings, Hunter R. III. 1981. *The Structure of Thucydides' History*. Princeton: Princeton University Press.

Raymond, Gregory A. 1997. "Problems and Prospects in the Study of International Norms." *International Studies Quarterly* 41 (November): 205–245.

Reus-Smit, Christian. 1997. "The Constitutional Structure of International Society and the Nature of Fundamental Institutions." *International Organization* 51 (Autumn): 555–589.

Risse-Kappen, Thomas, ed. 1995. *Bringing Transnational Relations Back In: Non-State Actors, Domestic Structures, and International Institutions*. Cambridge: Cambridge University Press.

Roberts, Adam. 1996. "The United Nations: Variants of Collective Security." In *Explaining International Relations Since 1945*, edited by Ngaire Woods. Oxford: Oxford University Press.

Robertson, David Brian. 1993. "The Return to History and the New Institutionalism in American Political Science." *Social Science History* 17 (Spring): 1–36.

Romilly, Jacqueline de. 1963 [1947]. *Thucydides and Athenian Imperialism*. Oxford: Basil Blackwell.

1966. "Thucydides and the Cities of the Athenian Empire." *Bulletin of the Institute of Classical Studies* 13: 1–12.

Rosecrance, Richard N. 1966. "Bipolarity, Multipolarity, and the Future." *Journal of Conflict Resolution* 10 (September): 314–327.

Rosenau, James N. and Mary Durfee. 1995. *Thinking Theory Thoroughly: Coherent Approaches to an Incoherent World*. Boulder: Westview Press.

Rosenau, Pauline. 1990. "Once Again Into the Fray: International Relations Confronts the Humanities." *Millennium* 19: 83–110.

Rosenthal, Joel H. 1991. *Righteous Realists: Political Realism, Responsible Power, and American Culture in the Nuclear Age*. Baton Rouge: Louisiana State University Press.

Rosenthal, Joel H., ed. 1995. *Ethics and International Affairs: A Reader*. Washington, D.C.: Georgetown University Press.

Rothstein, Robert. 1972. "On the Costs of Realism." *Political Science Quarterly* 87 (September): 347–62.

Rubinstein, Nicolai. 1971. "Notes on the Word *stato* in Florence before Machiavelli." In *Florilegium Historiale: Essays Presented to Wallace K. Ferguson*, edited by William H. Stockdale. Toronto: University of Toronto Press.

Ruggie, John Gerard. 1986. "Continuity and Transformation in the World Polity: Toward a Neorealist Synthesis." In *Neorealism and Its Critics*, edited by Robert O. Keohane. New York: Columbia University Press.

Rupesinghe, Kumar. 1999. "From Civil War to Civil Peace: Multi-Track Solutions to Armed Conflict." In *Future Multilateralism: The Political and Social Framework*, edited by Michael G. Schecter. Tokyo: United Nations University Press.

Russell, Greg. 1990. *Hans J. Morgenthau and the Ethics of American Statecraft*. Baton Rouge: Louisiana State University Press.

Sagan, Scott D. and Kenneth N. Waltz. 1995. *The Spread of Nuclear Weapons: A Debate*. New York: W. W. Norton.

Saxonhouse, Arlene W. 1978. "Nature and Convention in Thucydides' *History*." *Polity* 10 (Summer): 461–87.

Schlatter, R. 1945. "Thomas Hobbes and Thucydides." *Journal of the History of Ideas* 6: 350–362.

Schmidt, Brian C. 1998. *The Political Discourse of Anarchy: A Disciplinary History of International Relations*. Albany: State University of New York Press.

Schroeder, Paul. 1994. "Historical Reality vs. Neo-realist Theory." *International Security* 19 (Summer): 108–148.

Schuman, Frederick Lewis. 1941. *International Politics: The Western State System in Transition*, 3rd edn. New York: McGraw-Hill.

Schwarzenberger, Georg. 1941. *Power Politics: An Introduction to the Study of International Relations and Post-war Planning*. London: J. Cape.

1951. *Power Politics: A Study of International Society*, 2nd edn. London: Stevens.

Schweller, Randall L. 1994. "Bandwagoning for Profit: Bringing the Revisionist State Back In." *International Security* 19 (Summer): 72–107.

1996. "Neorealism's Status-Quo Bias: What Security Dilemma?" *Security Studies* 5 (Spring): 90–121.

1997. "New Realist Research on Alliance: Refining, Not Refuting, Waltz's Balancing Proposition." *American Political Science Review* 91 (December): 927–930.

1998. *Deadly Imbalances: Tripolarity and Hitler's Strategy of World Conquest*. New York: Columbia University Press.

Schweller, Randall L. and David Priess. 1997. "A Tale of Two Realisms: Expanding the Institutions Debate." *Mershon International Studies Review* 41 (May): 1–32.

Seabury, Paul, ed. 1965. *Balance of Power*. San Francisco: Chandler Publishing Company.

Sheehan, Michael. 1996. *The Balance of Power: History and Theory*. London: Routledge.

Shorey, Paul. 1893. "On the Implicit Ethics and Psychology of Thucydides." *Transactions of the American Philological Association* 24: 66–88.

Singer, J. David. 1961. "The Level of Analysis Problem in International Relations." *World Politics* 14 (October): 77–92.

Skidmore, David, ed. 1997. *Contested Social Orders and International Politics*. Nashville, Tenn.: Vanderbilt University Press.

Slomp, G. 1990. "Hobbes, Thucydides, and the Three Greatest Things." *History of Political Thought* 11: 565–585.

Smith, Michael Joseph. 1986. *Realist Thought from Weber to Kissinger.* Baton Rouge: Louisiana State University Press.

Smith, Steve. 1992. "The Forty Years' Detour: The Resurgence of Normative Theory in International Relations." *Millennium* 21 (Winter): 489–506.

1996. "Positivism and Beyond." In *International Theory: Positivism and Beyond*, edited by Steve Smith, Ken Booth and Marisya Zalewski. Cambridge: Cambridge University Press.

Smith, Steve, Ken Booth, and Marisya Zalewski, eds. 1996. *International Theory: Positivism and Beyond.* Cambridge: Cambridge University Press.

Snidal, Duncan. 1985. "The Game *Theory* of International Politics." *World Politics* 38 (October): 25–57.

1991a. "International Cooperation Among Relative Gains Maximizers." *International Studies Quarterly* 35 (September): 387–402.

1991b. "Relative Gains and the Pattern of International Cooperation." *American Political Science Review* 85 (September): 701–726.

1993. "Response." *American Political Science Review* 87 (September): 738–742.

Snyder, Glenn H. 1996. "Process Variables in Neorealist Theory." *Security Studies* 5 (Spring): 167–192.

1997. *Alliance Politics.* Ithaca: Cornell University Press.

Snyder, Glenn H. and Paul Diesing. 1977. *Conflict Among Nations: Bargaining, Decision Making, and System Structure in International Crises.* Princeton: Princeton University Press.

Speer, James P. 1986. *World Polity. Conflict and War: History, Causes, Consequences, Cures.* Fort Bragg, N.C.: QED Press.

Spegele, Roger D. 1987. "Three Forms of Political Realism." *Political Studies* 35 (June): 189–210.

1996. *Political Realism in International Theory.* Cambridge: Cambridge University Press.

Spruyt, Hendrik. 1994. *The Sovereign State and its Competitors: An Analysis of Systems Change.* Princeton: Princeton University Press.

Spykman, Nicholas J. 1942. *America's Strategy in World Politics: The United States and the Balance of Power.* New York: Harcourt, Brace and Company.

Stadter, Philip A., ed. 1973. *The Speeches of Thucydides.* Chapel Hill: University of North Carolina Press.

Starr, Chester G. 1988. "Athens and Its Empire." *Classical Journal* 83: 114–123.

Ste.-Croix, G. E. M. 1954/55. "The Character of the Athenian Empire." *Historia* 3: 1–41.

Stein, Arthur A. 1990. *Why Nations Cooperate: Circumstance and Choice in International Relations.* Ithaca: Cornell University Press.

Stephanson, Anders. 1989. *Kennan and the Art of Foreign Policy.* Cambridge, Mass.: Harvard University Press.

Stevenson, Leslie. 1974. *Seven Theories of Human Nature.* Oxford: Clarendon Press.

Strassler, Robert B., ed. 1996. *The Landmark Thucydides: A Comprehensive Guide to the Peloponnesian War.* New York: The Free Press.

Strauss, Barry R. 1986. *Athens After the Peloponnesian War: Class, Faction and Policy, 403–386BC.* Ithaca: Cornell University Press.

1991. "Of Balances, Bandwagons, and Ancient Greeks." In *Hegemonic Rivalry:*

From Thucydides to the Nuclear Age, edited by Richard Ned Lebow and Barry S. Strauss. Boulder: Westview Press.

Strauss, Leo. 1959. *Thoughts on Machiavelli*. Glencoe, Ill.: Free Press.

Suganami, Hidemi. 1996. *On the Causes of War*. Oxford: Oxford University Press.

Sullivan, Vickie B. 1996. *Machiavelli's Three Romes: Religion, Human Liberty and Politics Reformed*. DeKalb: Northern Illinois University Press.

Susa, Nasim. 1933. *The Capitulatory Regime of Turkey: Its History, Origin, and Nature*. Baltimore: Johns Hopkins Press.

Tellis, Ashley. 1995/96. "Reconstructing Political Realism: The Long March to Scientific Theory." *Security Studies* 5 (Winter): 3–101.

Teng, Ssu-yu and John K. Fairbank, eds. 1963. *China's Response to the West: A Documentary Survey, 1839–1923*. New York: Atheneum.

Thakur, Ramesh and Carlyle A. Thayer, eds. 1995. *A Crisis of Expectations: UN Peacekeeping in the 1990s*. Boulder: Westview Press.

Thayer, Lucius Ellsworth. 1923. "The Capitulations of the Ottoman Empire and the Question of their Abrogation as it Affects the United States." *American Journal of International Law* 17 (April): 207–233.

Thomas, Daniel C. forthcoming. *The Helsinki Effect: International Human Rights Norms and the Demise of Communism*.

Thompson, Kenneth W. 1952. "The Study of International Politics: A Survey of Trends and Developments." *Review of Politics* 14 (October): 433–467.

1966. *The Moral Issue in Statecraft: Twentieth Century Approaches and Problems*. Baton Rouge: Louisiana State University Press.

1985. *Moralism and Morality in Politics and Diplomacy*. Lanham, Md.: University Press of America.

Thompson, Kenneth W. and Robert J. Meyers, eds. 1977. *Truth and Tragedy: A Tribute to Hans J. Morgenthau*. Washington, D.C.: New Republic Book Co.

Thomson, Janice E. 1994. *Mercenaries, Pirates, and Sovereigns: State-Building and Extraterritorial Violence in Early Modern Europe*. Princeton: Princeton University Press.

Thucydides. 1919–23. *Thucydides*. Cambridge, Mass.: Harvard University Press.

Thucydides. 1972. *History of the Peloponnesian War*, translated by Rex Warner. Harmondsworth: Penguin Books.

1982. *The Peloponnesian War*, translated by Richard Crawley (revised by T. E. Wick). New York: Modern Library.

1998. *The Peloponnesian War: A New Translation, Backgrounds, Interpretations*. New York: W. W. Norton.

Treitschke, Heinrich von. 1916. *Politics*, 2 vols. London: Constable.

Trigg, Roger. 1988. *Ideas of Human Nature: An Historical Introduction*. Oxford: Basil Blackwell.

Triska, Jan F., ed. 1986. *Dominant Powers and Subordinate States: The United States in Latin America and the Soviet Union in Eastern Europe*. Durham, N.C.: Duke University Press.

Tucker, Robert W. 1952. "Professor Morgenthau's Theory of Political 'Realism'." *American Political Science Review* 46 (March): 214–224.

1977. *The Inequality of Nations*. New York: Basic Books.

Turner, Scott. 1998. "Global Civil Society, Anarchy, and Governance:

Assessing an Emerging Paradigm." *Journal of Peace Research* 35 (January): 25–42.

Van Evera, Stephen. 1985. "Why Cooperation Failed in 1914." *World Politics* 38: 80–118.

1998. "Offense, Defense, and the Causes of War." *International Security* 22: 5–43.

1999. *Causes of War: Structures of Power and the Roots of International Conflict.* Ithaca: Cornell University Press.

Vasquez, John A. 1983. *The Power of Power Politics: A Critique.* New Brunswick, N.J.: Rutgers University Press.

1997. "The Realist Paradigm and Degenerative versus Progressive Research Programs: An Appraisal of Neotraditional Research on Waltz's Balancing Proposition." *American Political Science Review* 91 (December): 899–912.

1998. *The Power of Power Politics: From Classical Realism to Neotraditionalism.* Cambridge: Cambridge University Press.

Viroli, Maurizio. 1998. *Machiavelli.* Oxford: Oxford University Press.

Waever, Ole. 1998. "Insecurity, Security, and Asecurity in the West European Non-War Community." In *Security Communities*, edited by Emanuel Adler and Michael Barnett. Cambridge: Cambridge University Press.

Walker, R. B. J. 1991. "State Sovereignty and the Articulation of Political Space/Time." *Millennium* 20 (Winter): 445–461.

Walt, Stephen M. 1987. *The Origins of Alliances.* Ithaca: Cornell University Press.

1996. *Revolution and War.* Ithaca: Cornell University Press.

1998. "International Relations: One World, Many Theories." *Foreign Policy* 110: 29–46.

Waltz, Kenneth N. 1959. *Man, the State, and War: A Theoretical Analysis.* New York: Columbia University Press.

1964. "The Stability of a Bipolar World." *Daedalus* 93 (Summer): 881–909.

1970. "The Myth of National Interdependence." In *The International Corporation*, edited by Charles P. Kindleberger. Cambridge, Mass.: MIT Press.

1979. *Theory of International Politics.* New York: Random House.

1986. "Reflections on *Theory of International Politics*: A Response to My Critics." In *Neo-Realism and Its Critics*, edited by Robert O. Keohane. New York: Columbia University Press.

1990. "Nuclear Myths and Political Realities." *American Political Science Review* 84 (September): 731–745.

1991. "Realist Thought and Neo-Realist Theory." In *The Evolution of Theory in International Relations: Essays in Honor of William T. R. Fox*, edited by Robert L. Rothstein. Columbia: University of South Carolina Press.

1993. "The Emerging Structure of International Politics." *International Security* 18 (Fall): 44–79.

1996. "International Politics Is Not Foreign Policy." *Security Studies* 6: 54–57.

1997. "Evaluating Theories." *American Political Science Review* 91 (December): 913–917.

Walzer, Michael. 1977. *Just and Unjust Wars: A Moral Argument with Historical Illustrations.* New York: Basic Books.

Wasserman, Felix Martin. 1947. "The Melian Dialogue." *Transactions of the American Philological Association* 78: 18–36.

1954. "Thucydides and the Disintegration of the Polis." *Transactions of the American Philological Association* 85: 46–54.

1956. "Post-Periclean Democracy in Action: The Mytilenian Debate (Thuc. II 37–48)." *Transactions of the American Philological Association* 87: 27–41.

Wayman, Frank W. and Paul F. Diehl. 1994. "Realism Reconsidered: The Realpolitik Framework and its Basic Propositions." In *Reconstructing Realpolitik*, edited by Frank W. Wayman and Paul F. Diehl. Ann Arbor: University of Michigan Press.

Weber, Cynthia. 1995. *Simulating Sovereignty: Intervention, the State, and Symbolic Exchange.* Cambridge: Cambridge University Press.

Weber, Katja. 1997. "Hierarchy Amidst Anarchy: A Transaction Costs Approach to International Security Cooperation." *International Studies Quarterly* 41 (June): 321–340.

Weber, Steven. 1997. "Institutions and Change." In *New Thinking in International Relations Theory*, edited by Michael W. Doyle and G. John Ikenberry. Boulder: Westview Press.

Wendt, Alexander. 1987. "The Agent Structure Problem in International Relations Theory." *International Organization* 41 (Summer): 335–370.

1992. "Anarchy is What States Make of It: The Social Construction of Power Politics." *International Organization* 46 (Spring): 391–425.

Wendt, Alexander and Daniel Friedheim. 1995. "Hierarchy Under Anarchy: Informal Empire and the East German State." *International Organization* 49 (Autumn): 689–721.

Westlake, H. D. 1968. *Individuals in Thucydides.* Cambridge: Cambridge University Press.

Wet, B. X. de. 1963. "Periclean Imperial Policy and the Mytilenian Debate." *Acta Classica* 6: 106–124.

1969. "The So-Called Defensive Policy of Pericles." *Acta Classica* 12: 103–119.

Wheaton, Henry. 1936 [1866]. *Elements of International Law.* Oxford: Clarendon Press.

Wight, Martin. 1973. "The Balance of Power and International Order." In *The Bases of International Order: Essays in Honour of C. A. W. Manning*, edited by Alan James. London: Oxford University Press.

1977. *Systems of States.* Leicester: Leicester University Press.

1978. *Power Politics.* Leicester: Leicester University Press.

1992. *International Theory: The Three Traditions.* New York: Holmes & Meier (for the Royal Institute of International Affairs).

Willoughby, Westel W. 1927. *Foreign Rights and Interests in China*, rev. edn., 2 vols. Baltimore: Johns Hopkins Press.

Wilson, John. 1982. "'The Customary Meaning of Words Were Changed' – or Were They? A Note on Thucydides 3.82.4." *Classical Quarterly* n.s. 32: 18–20.

Winnington-Ingram, R. P. 1965. "*Ta Deonta Eipein*: Cleon and Diodotus." *Bulletin of the Institute of Classical Studies* 12: 70–82.

Wohlforth, William C. 1994/95. "Realism and the End of the Cold War." *International Security* 19 (Winter): 91–129.

Wolfers, Arnold. 1962. *Discord and Collaboration: Essays on International Politics.* Baltimore: Johns Hopkins Press.

Wolin, Sheldon S. 1960. *Politics and Vision: Continuity and Innovation in Western Political Thought.* Boston: Little, Brown.

Wood, Neal. 1967. "Machiavelli's Concept of *Virtu* Reconsidered." *Political Studies* 15: 159–172.

————. 1972. "Machiavelli's Humanism of Action." In *The Political Calculus: Essays on Machiavelli's Philosophy,* edited by Anthony Parel. Toronto: University of Toronto Press.

Woodhead, A. G. 1960. "Thucydides' Portrait of Cleon." *Mnemosyne* 13: 289–317.

————. 1970. *Thucydides on the Nature of Power.* Cambridge, Mass.: Harvard University Press.

Wright, Moorhead, ed. 1975. *The Theory and Practice of the Balance of Power, 1486–1914.* London: Dent.

————. 1996. *Morality and International Relations: Concepts and Issues.* Aldershot: Avebury.

Young, Oran R. 1989. *International Cooperation: Building Regimes for Natural Resources and the Environment.* Ithaca: Cornell University Press.

————. 1994. *International Governance: Protecting the Environment in a Stateless Society.* Ithaca: Cornell University Press.

Zakaria, Fareed. 1998. *From Wealth to Power: The Unusual Origins of America's World Role.* Princeton: Princeton University Press.

Index